Spree Killers

Practical Classifications for Law Enforcement and Criminology

Spree Killers

Practical Classifications for Law Enforcement and Criminology

by
Mark Safarik and Katherine Ramsland

CRC Press
Taylor & Francis Group
Boca Raton London New York

CRC Press is an imprint of the
Taylor & Francis Group, an **informa** business

CRC Press
Taylor & Francis Group
6000 Broken Sound Parkway NW, Suite 300
Boca Raton, FL 33487-2742

Printed on acid-free paper

International Standard Book Number-13: 978-0-367-37000-8 (Hardback)

Visit the Taylor & Francis Web site at
http://www.taylorandfrancis.com

and the CRC Press Web site at
http://www.crcpress.com

To my parents, Jerome and Hilda (passed) Safarik,
for their unconditional love and support for
everything I have done and tried in my life.

To my sons, Matthew and Justin, you are my ultimate joy.

Contents

List of Figures

List of Tables

Foreword

Once there was just one term used to describe someone who killed multiple victims – mass murderer. Then in the late 1970s, a new term became current, and we divided killers of multiple victims into two groups – mass murderers killed many people at one time and place, and serial killers killed many people at many different times and places. Study of multiple homicide cases led eventually to a further subdivision, and the term spree killer was coined to describe this group of killers who killed many people over a relatively short period of time in different places. Spree killings inhabit the gray area between mass murders and serial killings. Looked at one way, spree killings appear to be a subtype of serial murder. Looked at another way, spree killings share a lot of the characteristics of mass murder, especially when the geographical area is small, and the time period is short.

If one takes a Procrustean approach to the classification of multiple homicides, all spree killings can be shoehorned into either the category of mass murder or the serial killing category. With a little effort, one can easily eliminate the spree killing category by forcing spree killings into one of the other two categories, and that is what the FBI decided to do in its 2008 report *Serial Murder: Multi-Disciplinary Perspectives for Investigators*. The stated reasons were (1) the difficulty of separating spree killings from serial murders, and (2) "The designation does not provide any real benefit for use by law enforcement."

One of the dissenters on the panel which produced that report co-authored this book, which serves as a refutation of the theory that the designation "spree killer" is not useful to law enforcement. A serial killer acts from very different motives than a spree killer. Because the two types of killers work from different motives, the dynamics of their killings differ markedly. By studying the different dynamics of spree killings, the authors find factors which can and do provide "real benefit for use by law enforcement." Indeed, the authors demonstrate that if certain types of spree killings can be identified early enough in the spree, law enforcement can take steps to identify the killer and protect the lives of intended victims targeted by spree killers. Such measures are hardly possible with either serial killers or mass murderers.

Working from a database of almost 400 spree killings worldwide, the authors classify spree killings into several subtypes, identify the characteristics of the killings and the killers, and make suggestions for dealing with those types which are amenable to proactive intervention. They fully recognize the indistinct borders separating the various classifications, but they make a strong case for the proposition that indistinct borders do not invalidate either the need for recognizing spree killing as a class of multiple homicide or the usefulness of the concept for investigating and dealing with ongoing murder sprees.

Spree Killers: Practical Classifications for Law Enforcement and Criminology does a great service by calling attention to a little-recognized subtype of multiple homicide and making suggestions for proactive measures to deal with those types of spree killers whose motives and methods render them amenable to life-saving intervention. This book will not only give the careful reader an appreciation for the unique characteristics of spree killings; it should also serve as a catalyst for further study and encourage the formulation of protocols for anticipating and dealing with spree killings.

–George R. Dekle, Sr.
Lead prosecutor in the Orlando Ted Bundy murder trial
Author of The Last Murder: The Investigation, Prosecution, and Execution of Ted Bundy

Acknowledgments

From Mark Safarik:

I am no stranger to research and writing, having penned many articles and book chapters. The research for this book was complex, but through all the days and weekends identifying and writing up these cases, my wife Lisa has always been there to support and encourage me, and to listen to me describe a case in order to help me determine its best placement in the greater text. More importantly, through our decades of marriage, she has always been there for me. The unwavering support and encouragement she gives me have made an enormous difference in my life.

I also owe a debt of unending gratitude to my former mentor and partner Robert Ressler. As I was wrapping up my career with the Behavioral Analysis Unit, Bob asked me to join him as his partner in his business and to succeed him when he retired. I worked with Bob for seven years before he passed, at which point we lost a pioneer and giant in the field. His early, critical work in serial and mass murder paved the way for many who would succeed him – including me and Katherine. In fact, Bob's early work laid the foundation for our work now, as well as in our reevaluation of spree murder.

My friend and coauthor, Katherine Ramsland … Katherine and I were having dinner as I was preparing to lecture at DeSales University. We began discussing a recent multicide case and how the concept of spree could be useful to law enforcement. Out of that conversation grew the idea of writing an article – but when we dove into the material, we realized there was a plethora of cases and material to examine … enough for an entire text on the subject. That said, I could not have written this book without her. Katherine's publishing acumen and literary connections smoothed the way for us. Her organization, especially keeping us to a defined schedule, made this process a great deal easier.

My dear friend of 26 years Alan Jacobson, I value the support you have always given me and the countless edits you have done for all my publications. As a bestselling author, your attention to detail and research has given you this amazing way with words that has always helped me say more with less. I am honored you used me as a character in a couple of your books and highlighted my research in elder sexual homicide as part of the plot.

In the preparation of this book, Katherine and I thought it was very important to include as many international cases as possible to demonstrate that spree killers exist in every country and culture. I reached out to many of my international colleagues who were eager to assist in this project and provided investigative resources that we simply did not have access to. Because of their support for this endeavor, I would like to thank the following international colleagues whose collaboration was extremely helpful, especially my dear friends María Laura Quiñones, Bo Astrom, Jan Jarlbeck, Dr. Gérard Labuschagne, and Dr. Bernat-Nóel Tiffon. I would also like to thank Dr. Heng Choon Oliver Chan, Félix Ríos Abréu, Eduardo Bieber, Ilana Casoy, Hamasaki Kenichi, Paola Giannetakis, Carlo Schippers, Lee Rainbow, Thomas Mueller, and Dr. Odette Terol Levy.

Finally, I would like to thank Kaelee Rupell, our tireless intern with her expertise in Excel. She organized and charted our data, ran the numbers, created our charts, and graciously did anything we asked of her (and we asked for a lot). She deserves, and has, our appreciation and gratitude for helping this book come to fruition.

From Katherine Ramsland:

When we first started this project, we had little idea of how involved it would become, so I thank Mark Safarik, my coauthor, for his enthusiasm for it and his deep research. I especially appreciated his ability to see a broader picture than the end result the FBI symposium yielded.

Many people have contributed to my knowledge about multiple murder, but Marilyn Bardsley, who recently passed, made the most significant difference, so I thank her. I wrote about some of these killers for The Crime Library earlier in my career.

Lee Mellor gave us a hand with the Canadian spree killers, helping us to find stories that weren't readily available with searches.

Kaelee Rupell, our analytics assistant, always responded quickly to our needs for visuals and data.

Mark Listewnik, our editor, showed immediate support for this project before we formally proposed it, and encouraged us throughout.

My agent and longtime friend, John Silbersack, ensured professional handling and support for this and all of my books. I'm ever grateful.

Authors

Mark E. Safarik was a member of the Federal Bureau of Investigation's elite Behavioral Analysis Unit. He established himself as an internationally recognized expert in the analysis of violent criminal behavior. Safarik's law enforcement career spans over 30 years. He served 23 years with the FBI, the last 12, as a criminal profiler. He has lectured around the world, sharing his expertise in the analysis of homicide and complex crime scene behavior with over 20,000 personnel from police chiefs to violent crime investigators, prosecutors, medical examiners, and other professionals. He currently consults with law enforcement, attorneys, universities, writers, television producers, and foreign government entities. Safarik has a graduate degree from Boston University, Massachusetts, and is adjunct faculty at Boston College, Massachusetts. He has conducted internationally renowned research on the sexual assault and homicide of elder females and received the prestigious Jefferson Medal from the University of Virginia. He is a member of the highly respected Vidocq Society. He has published articles and book chapters on his research and work. He has appeared on numerous television programs to discuss his cases and analyses. He has three cold case television series both in the US and Europe. He has been a consultant for the television series *CSI: Las Vegas*, *Bones*, and *The Blacklist*.

Katherine Ramsland is a professor of forensic psychology and an assistant provost at DeSales University, Pennsylvania. She has published over 1,000 articles, stories, and reviews, and 65 books, including *The Psychology of Death Investigation, Forensic Investigation: Methods from Experts*, *Confession of a Serial Killer: The Untold Story of Dennis Rader, the BTK Killer*; *The Mind of a Murderer*; *The Forensic Science of CSI*; *Inside the Minds of Serial Killers*; and *The Forensic Psychology of Criminal Minds*. She presents workshops to law enforcement, psychologists, coroners, and attorneys, and has consulted for several television series, including *The Alienist*, *CSI*, and *Bones*. She writes a regular blog for *Psychology Today* and has appeared in more than 100 crime documentaries.

CHAPTER 1

Spree: A Muddled Concept

In Australia on April 28, 1996, Martin Bryant used a semiautomatic rifle to kill the two owners of Seascape guesthouse before he drove to the Port Arthur tourist area. He entered a crowded café. In about 15 seconds, the troubled 28-year-old fatally shot 20 people and wounded 15. He went out to the parking lot to shoot more. He got into his car, drove a short distance, shot again, stole a car, took a hostage, and returned to the guesthouse. From there, he shot people driving by and killed his hostage. Overnight, the police surrounded him. When the building eventually went up in flames, Bryant emerged and was arrested. Police found three bodies inside. Bryant's total number of victims was 35 dead and 23 hurt or wounded. He was not suicidal, but he was mentally ill, had a low IQ, and had suffered recent stresses. Some criminologists call him a mass murderer; others say he is a spree killer. He qualifies as both. Therein lies confusion.

Crime experts tend to place offenders in distinct categories to study their maturation, motives, and behavior. They develop criteria and make comparisons for analysis among categories. However, some cases fit more than one. In addition, not all experts agree on the criteria for these categories. As they publish their research, confusion develops. This only increases as categories get changed, dropped, or renamed.

Such is the case with a category of multicide known as "spree killing." Some lists include just two murders in two locations, but this overlaps the FBI's current definition of serial killer, so more distinguishing criteria are needed for qualifying as a spree. Some think that a spree killer requires at least four victims, making it overlap the criteria for mass murder. In addition, some killers are mass murderers or serial killers who then go on a spree, or spree killers who then become one of the other two. To further complicate matters, some crime experts use "rampage" killer, which combines mass and spree killers in a single category. Yet there is reason for keeping them distinct. In this book, we will sort through the discussions and standardize the definition while providing a database of more than 350 spree cases involving more than 400 killers from 43 different countries that we analyzed for categories, subcategories, and trends.

After 2005, the FBI stopped using the spree category, due to its lack of utility for law enforcement. We believe this reasoning was based on input that failed to fully examine spree incidents. We think it is worthwhile to consider reestablishing its use. To appreciate our position and to see why we also think it's important to further refine the spree concept, we must first understand what led to the FBI's decision.

TWISTS IN THE HISTORY OF A CONCEPT

Although it was once the case that any type of incident that involved a number of murders was called "multiple murder," "multicide," or "mass murder," eventually it became clear that distinctions were needed to sort out different types (Douglas, Burgess, Burgess, & Ressler, 1992). Multiple murders, or multicides, have traditionally been categorized as double (2), triple (3), mass (4 or more), serial, and spree. Mass and serial have been further divided into multiple subcategories. Nevertheless, over the years, the definitions have shifted.

Since the focus of this book is on the FBI's approach, we show how the Agency devised and revised the multicide concepts. Initially, classifications were based on psychological disorders, but in 1973, the National Advisory Commission mandated the development of criminal classification programs throughout the American justice system (Megargee & Bonn, 1979). Offender personality and behavior were considered important aspects of this effort, but the proffered tools from the psychiatric community (usually personality assessments) failed to focus on crime. When the FBI's Behavioral Science Unit formed during the 1970s, the agents developed the Crime Analysis and Criminal Personality Profiling Program.

Ressler and Shachtman (1992) describe the few criminological analyses available at the time. Among them were accounts by prison psychiatrist Marvin Ziporyn on mass murderer Richard Speck (Altman & Ziporyn, 1967) and by criminology professor James Melvin Reinhardt (1960) on the case of spree killer Charles Starkweather (detailed later in this book). Describing the "remorseless ego," Reinhardt offered a theoretical framework for understanding the type of offenders the agents would one day be tracking. In Santa Cruz, California, over the course of 2 years, psychiatrist Donald Lunde (1976) had the opportunity to examine a mass, a spree, and a serial killer up close: John Linley Frazier murdered five people at the Ohta home, Herbert Mullin murdered 13 people in 4 months, and Edmund Kemper picked up and killed six female hitchhikers, plus three relatives and an acquaintance. For psychiatric insight,

The Diagnostic and Statistical Manual for Mental Disorders (*DSM*), then in its revised third edition, defined an array of psychological conditions from anxiety to depression to psychosis. However, diagnosis required background in psychiatry, and this manual did not work well for forensic purposes.

Although serial murder has been observed for many centuries, the modern iteration of the term, serial killer, has been attributed to former FBI criminal profiler Robert Ressler, who utilized it to describe repeated killings over time by the same offender as serial in nature. Redefining this descriptor in the early 1980s ushered in an era of extensive research and publication by the FBI's Behavioral Science Unit (BSU) at the FBI Academy in Quantico, Virginia. These agents began to study repeat killers through cases they examined for attendees of the FBI National Academy and by traveling to prisons to interview the offenders regarding their crimes. The FBI defined the characteristics of serial murder as three or more victims occurring in three or more locations. These killings were considered separate events with a "cooling off" period between the events. The key aspect differentiating serial murder from other types of murder was the "cooling off" period or temporal separation between the killing events. Unfortunately, the concept of cooling off remained undefined. It could be brief, such as a few days or weeks, or it could last months, even years; it was a period of time that the offender would be inactive before he or she acted out again in another separate but distinct event from previous killings.

They defined mass killings, more commonly referred to as mass murder, as four or more victims killed at one location. The "cooling off" period did not apply because the murders had occurred as a single event. The presence or absence of a *cooling off* period differentiated serial murder from mass murder.

Researchers and law enforcement recognized that a category of murder existed between serial and mass that appeared to have characteristics of both: the spree killer. Prior to the FBI defining this category, the use of the term had not evolved to the point where it described a separate and distinct category of multicide. When Reinhardt studied Charles Starkweather at the end of 1959, he referred to the behavior as "chain-killing." The term, while appropriate, did not catch on. For several decades, "spree" was often used to describe aspects of serial and mass murder. Within the serial concept, it referred to the continuation of murders over time, and within the mass concept, it described the annihilation of multiple victims over a short period or in close locations.

In a review of literature that has specifically addressed the spree killer phenomenon (Casteldon, 2011; Cawthorne, 2009; Cimino, 2010; Crockett, 1991; Jensen, 2015; Mellor, 2013; Newton, 1992: Pantziarka, 2002; Parker, 2012), nearly every book has included both mass and serial murder cases in the category. Despite focusing on the specific topic of spree murder, many of these texts fail to provide a clear definition or to offer a way to look at different types of sprees. Rarely do they distinguish spree adequately from serial or mass. Only Newton addresses the various FBI categories of multicide.

However, this blending of concepts became – and still is – confusing, so the FBI tried again, this time delineating spree murder as separate and distinct from serial and mass murder. Spree murder was defined as two or more victims murdered in one event that takes place in two or more locations. Because it was considered one event with the murders linked together, there was no cooling off period. Thus, spree murder appeared to be a hybrid crime, sharing multiple locations with serial murder yet being a single event like a mass murder. This seemed to work until the FBI later changed its definition of serial murder (see discussion below).

The FBI's research helped to support the development during the early 1980s of the National Center for the Analysis of Violent Crime (NCAVC). Munn (1992) describes it as an agency that assisted law enforcement with multidisciplinary expertise in behavioral analysis and data processing for "unusual, bizarre, and/or repetitive violent crime" (p. 309). Staffed with psychologists, crime analysts, political scientists, sociologists, and police specialists, it focused on teaching, consulting, and research. Initially, it contained three units: the Behavioral Science Services Unit, the Special Operations and Research Unit, and the Investigative Support Unit. Agents underwent trainings in the Criminal Investigative Analysis Program (CIAP) and the Violent Criminal Apprehension Program (ViCAP). The support services were offered free to domestic and foreign agencies.

NCAVC behavioral analysts conduct detailed analyses of complex violent crimes from a review of the behavioral, forensic, and physical evidence in order to understand what happened during an incident; how the event(s) unfolded before, during, and after the crime; and why the offender engaged in these activities. The review evaluated many attributes from both a chronological and temporal perspective. The goal was to provide law enforcement agencies tasked with investigating complex crimes a better understanding of offender motivations and behaviors in order to assist with the investigative strategies. This analysis aimed to help identify the offender and resolve the case.

The agents analyzed crimes and crime scenes, and performed a comprehensive victimology. They looked at police reports, autopsy protocols, and victim information to develop critical characteristics (a profile) of the type of person who might have committed the crime or series of crimes in question. They also offered suggestions for investigation, apprehension, search warrants, and interviewing strategies when suspects were taken into custody. If a case went to court, the NCAVC personnel offered strategies for prosecution and jury selection. As Munn put it, “Data are collected and assessed, the situation is reconstructed, hypotheses are formulated, a profile is developed and tested, and the results are reported back” (p. 310). The effectiveness depended on the quality and quantity of data available.

When Supervisory Special Agent and profiler John Douglas et al. (1992) heard an offender brag that he could fake any mental illness described in the *DSM*, he came up with a plan to turn the informal concepts the agents used into formal categories, with a standardized numbering system. He joined with profiler Robert Ressler and Allen and Ann Burgess to develop *The Crime Classification Manual* (*CCM*), published in 1992. Other members of the Investigative Support Unit also contributed material.

“With *CCM*,” Douglas wrote, “we set about to organize and classify serious crimes by their behavioral characteristics and explain them in a way that a strictly psychological approach such as the *DSM* has never been able to do” (p. 347). Behavioral evidence provided the distinguishing factors, so that the investigative legal community could focus on those items most relevant to their work. To use the manual, an investigator had to know information about the victim, crime scene, and the nature of the relationship or exchange between the victim and the offender. They had to know the number of crime scenes involved, the type of environment, the number of offenders, the body disposition, potential evidence of staging, undoing, and depersonalization and items that might be missing (such as something removed from the victim(s) as either a souvenir or trophy). They would need to know the cause and manner of death and the evidence of sexual assault, if present and whether activity engaged in by the offender was related to his *modus operandi* (MO) or ritualized (need-driven) behavior.

The *CCM* defined the multicidal types. Mass murder was based on four or more victims in one location involving a single incident. The other categories were defined as:

> A spree murder involves killing at two or more locations with no emotional cooling off period between murders. The killings are all the result of a single event, which can be short or long duration. Serial murders involve three or more separate events, with an emotional cooling off period between homicides.
>
> (Douglas et al., 2013, p. 12)

No minimum number of victims was identified for a spree killing, but at this time, the minimum number for serial murder was three. (This would change.)

As an academic in criminal justice, Steve Egger (1998) called for a clearer definition of serial murder. He provided seven criteria, using a minimum of two incidents of murder as the basis, because he thought this number was sufficient for understanding these offenders. Sometimes they got caught after two but would have otherwise continued. Thus, they qualified. There was generally no prior relationship between the offender and the victims, Egger wrote, subsequent murders have no connection to the initial murder, each murder is in a different geographical location, the motive is not financial gain (it is for power or dominance), victims have a symbolic value for the killer, and victims are most typically vagrants, homeless, children, single woman, homosexuals, or prostitutes. Members of law enforcement and other academics agreed that there were problems with the FBI's concept, but diverged on requirements for a definition. Eggers' idea seemed too complex and too narrow. In addition, some cases failed to fit well into any category.

SERIAL SPREE

Around 10 p.m. on September 22, 1980, a 14-year-old African American boy, Glenn Dunn, was fatally shot while sitting in a car near a supermarket in Buffalo, New York. The next day, two black males, Harold Green and Emmanuel Thomas, were shot and killed. Green had been eating a cheeseburger while Thomas was walking across the street near his home. Neither had been engaged in a high-risk activity. A fourth fatal incident in nearby Niagara Falls involved the murder of Joseph McCoy, shot twice. The spree had lasted 36 hours and the victims had all been shot in the left side of the head. Witnesses had seen a dark-haired white man running from one scene with a bag large enough to hold a gun. Police found a dropped .22-caliber shell casing. Each victim had the same type of wound, and eventually all were linked. Reporters in Buffalo called this shooter the ".22-Caliber Killer." Three months passed without identifying him.

Then on December 22, another homicidal series began in Manhattan, with some differences. In 13 hours, a knife-wielding man attacked one Hispanic and five black males, killing four. News accounts dubbed him the "Midtown Slasher." A week later, a killer struck between December 29 and January 1, stabbing men in Buffalo and Rochester, New York. Some reporters dubbed him Buffalo Bill.

The .22-Caliber Task Force developed more than 2,000 possible suspects, but investigators were stymied until they got an unexpected break. A 25-year-old private at Fort Benning, Georgia, named Joseph G. Christopher was hospitalized after slashing a black soldier and cutting himself. He admitted to a psychiatric nurse that he'd killed some black people in Buffalo, following "orders," as any good soldier would. Evidence found among his effects linked him to both series.

Christopher was indicted in April 1981. When he confessed, he said, "It was something I had to do." He had killed at least ten black and Hispanic males, and had wounded four. Although his behavior seemed racially triggered, all he would say was that "something came over" him. Later, he seemed to suggest that he had killed 13.

Fully evaluated for mental illness and diagnosed with paranoid schizophrenia, Christopher was found incompetent, but then competent to proceed. At his trial, he was convicted of three murders, but the conviction was overturned. Eventually, he was convicted on various charges in five cases and sentenced to 58 years in prison.

Two years before his first rampage, Christopher had sought help for his mental illness. Even two weeks prior to the first shooting, he'd tried getting admitted to a psychiatric center but the psychiatrists had not considered him to be an imminent danger to himself or others.

Christopher died in prison from cancer in 1993 at the age of 37. Some people thought he had killed two taxi drivers in Buffalo on October 9 and 10, 1980, beating them to death and cutting out their hearts. However, he never admitted to these deaths or provided information on the three other murders at which he'd hinted (Warner, 2016).

Christopher is a multiple murderer. Some call him a serial killer, and he was. Some call him a spree killer, and he was also that. In a way, he was a serial-spree killer, because his spree episodes were separated by a significant period of time. His case demonstrates the difficulty of placing offenders in distinct categories, because Christopher's methods and motives fit both. Yet, he also defies some behaviors common to both.

THE SYMPOSIUM

Despite the FBI's efforts to categorize multicide into serial, spree, and mass murder, there have always been varying opinions on the number of victims, whether less will suffice or more are needed, how close or far the locations are from one another, and the time difference required to effectively distinguish one type from another.

Other researchers have focused on motivation as an equally important aspect, arguing that individuals exist who commit multiple murders over time and as separate events who are not referred to, or researched as, serial killers. Many academics and law enforcement practitioners intuitively understand the attributes of serial murder cases. Nevertheless, following a strict definition would necessarily include individuals who murder at the instruction or request of others within a hierarchy (e.g., gangs, drug cartels, and organized crime syndicates). Although meeting the definitional criteria, such cases are not generally included in serial murder research.

During the decades prior to 2005, multiple definitions were used for both serial murder and spree killing. Law enforcement, academics, clinicians, and researchers often followed operational requirements. Many felt that the FBI's definition could be improved and some resented the FBI's seemingly self-appointed role of arbiter, which made its definition the *de facto* standard. Aware of these rumblings, the FBI decided to consult with these groups to establish universally approved definitions.

The BSU, which operated under the auspices of the FBI's Training Division (Division 2), was responsible for providing training to the National Academy classes. The National Academy held four sessions per year, lasting 11 weeks each. The BSU was also teaching the new FBI agent classes, as well as numerous other groups from law enforcement agencies around the world. Besides the significant amount of time allocated to training, BSU agents were also conducting research and traveling to work operationally on complex violent crime cases, specifically serial murder, serial sexual assault, and sexual homicide. This all changed in 1994.

In response to public outcry over the standoff at Ruby Ridge, Idaho, and the Branch Davidian siege in Waco, Texas, then-FBI Director Louis Freeh created a separate division in the FBI to operationally join the critical components needed to respond to a major event or crisis. In 1994, Director Freeh created the Critical Incident Response Group (CIRG) to integrate tactical responses, investigative resources, and expertise for critical incidents that necessitate an immediate response from law enforcement authorities. CIRG would deploy investigative specialists to respond to terrorist activities, hostage takings, child abductions, serial murders, and other high-risk repetitive violent crimes. Other major incidents included prison riots, bombings, air and train crashes, and natural disasters.

Each major area of CIRG furnished distinctive operational assistance and training to FBI field offices as well as state, local, and international law enforcement agencies. Among a number of operational components that comprise CIRG, some are well known to include the Hostage Rescue Team (HRT), Crisis Negotiations Unit (CNU), Crisis Management Unit (CMU), and the NCAVC. Director Freeh also wanted the behavioral experts to be an integral unit in CIRG. The BSU remained in the Training Division to focus on training and research. A new unit, the Behavioral Analysis Unit, or BAU (after several name changes) would be created out of the BSU to become the operational component of behavioral profilers. They would consult on law enforcement cases and travel to assist those agencies in an onsite capacity if the case required it. When it was initially formed, a number of BSU Supervisory Special Agents transitioned into

CIRG to form the nucleus of the newly formed BAU. One of us, Safarik, joined the BAU shortly after its creation in CIRG.

The BAU offered to host an International Serial Murder Symposium. Along with the NCAVC, the BAU had evolved into four units, BAU-1 (Counterterrorism/Threat Assessment), BAU-2 (Crimes Against Adults), BAU-3 (Crimes Against Children), and The Violent Criminal Apprehension Program (ViCAP). Members of the BAU-2 conceived, planned, and coordinated the event.

The goal of this seminal gathering was to tap into the collective knowledge, wisdom, and experience of experts, domestic and international, who regularly dealt with serial crimes, specifically serial murder, the victims, investigation, and disposition in the legal system. The intent was to use the collective talents and experience of investigators, case managers, researchers, forensic scientists, academics, attorneys, and mental health professionals. To encourage as many invitees to attend as possible, the FBI paid for transportation and lodging. The FBI was likely the only agency that could have hosted and funded such an event. Its international reputation in law enforcement and its groundbreaking research, along with its ability to absorb the significant cost, made it the natural choice. We understood that this would likely be the first and last time such a conference would be held, so the agency believed it was important to provide the best service.

From August 29–September 2, 2005, the symposium took place at the Sheraton Riverwalk Hotel in San Antonio, Texas (Morton & Hilts, 2008). Experts from 10 countries, representing five continents, attended. Among the 140 participants, besides members of the FBI, were Steve Egger (mentioned above), Psychopathy Checklist-Revised (PCL-R) creator Robert Hare, criminologists Eric Hickey and James Alan Fox, head of Wichita's task force for the "BTK Killer" Ken Landwher, neuropsychologist Debra Niehoff, forensic psychiatrists Park Dietz and Fred Berlin, forensic entomologist Lee Goff, and several professors from the John Jay College of Criminal Justice. The primary goal was to "outline the consensus views from a variety of disciplines on the causality, motivations, and characteristics of serial murderers, which will enable the criminal justice community to generate a more effective response in the identification, investigation, and adjudication of these cases" (Morton & Hilts, 2008, p. vii).

Safarik was a contributor and panel moderator. By 2005, he had been a criminal profiler in the BAU for 10 years. There had been extensive discussions regarding definitions among him and his colleagues in the FBI and other international agencies that also had criminal profilers as part of their investigative divisions. These discussions were especially important to those engaged in research, where homicide and serial sexual assault cases from their files were being studied and serial offenders were the focus of prison interviews under Institutional Review Board (IRB) guidelines.

Safarik describes his experience of the symposium below:

Each day was organized with panel presentations and major homicide cases in the morning and early afternoon. The late afternoon was reserved for breakout groups where the attendees engaged in thoughtful and often lively discussions. BAU Adult Crimes Supervisory Special Agents led a panel of topic experts to discuss such subjects as Serial Murder Myths; Scope, Definition, and Typology; Pathology and Causality; Evaluation of Known Offenders; Media Influence in Serial Murder Investigations; Forensics in Serial Murder Cases; Prosecution of Serial Murder Cases; and Task Force and Major Case Management Issues.

The symposium members reviewed most of the definitions that were in regular use around the world, discussing the pros and cons of each. The goal was to arrive at a simple but broad definition that could primarily address law enforcement concerns but could also be used by researchers. Most felt that the definition needed to be more broadly based and inclusive. While sharing certain common themes, the definitions we discussed differed on specific requirements. The number of murders, their temporal aspect, and the primary motivations varied considerably. Previous definitions had ranged from a minimum of two victims all the way to at least 10. Most also specified a time period between the murders, to distinguish serial from spree and mass murder. The FBI's use of the term *cooling off* period was considered nebulous at best and nondescriptive at worst.

I should note that there had been at least one attempt to formalize a definition of serial murder through legislation, which had also proved problematic. In 1998, the United States Congress, passed a federal law titled Protection of Children from Sexual Predator Act of 1998 (Title 18, United States Code, Chapter 51, Section 1111). The definition stipulated three or more killings, one of which was committed in the United States, and having common characteristics that suggest a "reasonable possibility" that the crimes originated with the same "actor or actors." This law allowed the FBI to assist local law enforcement, but it was limited. No one thought it would work for serial killers everywhere.

The dynamic that drew the most animated discussion related to the number of murders that would define serial murder. Academicians and researchers wanted a definitive number, with clear inclusion criteria. Law enforcement wanted a low number to provide flexibility when deciding how to allocate resources. Recognition of unique behaviors and evidence within a multiple murder investigation, they said, could officially enable an agency to designate a case earlier in the process as a serial murder investigation.

The symposium attendees ultimately agreed that the lowest possible minimum number of victims enabled the greatest flexibility for law enforcement. Since such offenders had a number of different motivators, it seemed expedient to exclude motivation from the definition. Attendees also agreed on four attributes to be included in the definition: (1) one or more offenders, (2) two or more murder victims, (3) the murders should be occurring in separate events at different times, and (4) the time period between the murders is what separates serial murder from mass murder. Consideration of these attributes led the group to arrive at a universally agreed upon definition of serial murder: *The unlawful killing of two or more victims by the same offender(s), in separate events.*

In addition to the discussion on how to define serial murder, and more to the point of the current project, the attendees discussed at length the validity of retaining the separate category of spree murder. A number of us at the symposium, me included, thought that the concept of a spree described types of murders that were distinct from either serial or mass. We argued that the category should be retained. However, with the removal of any reference to a temporal component in the newest definition, an argument was advanced to stop using spree as a separate typology. The majority of the symposium members agreed that the spree murder category did not provide any real benefits within the law enforcement construct. Cases which had been previously designated as spree would be subsumed into either serial or mass, depending on which elements of the multicide moved it closer to one or the other:

> The general definition of spree murder is two or more murders committed by an offender or offenders, without a cooling-off period. According to the definition, the lack of a cooling-off period marks the difference between a spree murder and a serial murder. Central to the discussion was the definitional problems relating to the concept of a cooling-off period. Because it creates arbitrary guidelines, the confusion surrounding this concept led the majority of attendees to advocate disregarding the use of spree murder as a separate category. The designation does not provide any real benefit for use by law enforcement.
>
> (Morton & Hilts, 2008, p. 5)

Beyond the partnerships that were made during the symposium and the important information that resulted, the FBI also had an obligation to codify the results. This monograph, *Serial Murder: Multi-Disciplinary Perspectives for Investigators*, is freely available online on the FBI.gov website.

Although spree killer as a formal category was removed from the crime nomenclature, we find justification for reviewing this decision. By restoring the spree category and subdividing it into several identifiable subgroups, we can provide law enforcement with ways to proactively handle an ongoing spree event. Unlike the almost exclusively reactive response to both serial and mass murder, for some types of spree killers, officers can often proactively identify the offender and possibly prevent the murders of potential future victims. The following case is an example:

A SUCCESSFUL INTERVENTION

Dwight Lamon Jones once had it all: a wife, a son, and an upper middle-class life in Scottsdale, Arizona. His wife, Connie, was a radiologist and the primary breadwinner, while Jones, an Army veteran with only a GED, had become a stay-at-home father. Once their son went to school, Connie wanted Jones to find work, but he refused. He enjoyed living off her income. Trouble entered their marriage in the form of his threats and verbal abuse. This came to a head when Jones physically abused his wife. In front of their son, he threatened to kill Connie if she ever tried to leave him.

After two decades of marriage, Connie filed for divorce in May 2009, fighting for custody of their 11-year-old son. Jones disparaged her on social media and made constant threats. He assaulted administrators at his son's school, resulting in orders of harassment. The son suffered from stress-related asthma. During a standoff involving the son as a hostage, Jones threatened to end both of their lives. He finally surrendered to the SWAT team.

When Connie moved into a different house, a judge issued an order of protection and required that Jones give up his guns. That same month, Jones was arrested for disorderly conduct and given an emergency psychological evaluation for his future potential danger. The courts nevertheless gave him two hours per week of supervised visitation with his son. His instability became threatening, so Connie asked for a termination of his visitation. She believed that her $4 million insurance policy put her in jeopardy. She was aware that Jones had purchased a machete and had stalked her to learn her routes and routines. He read books about bomb-making and drew maps decorated with bodies.

The court denied her request and refused to allow her to move out of state during the separation. Her divorce came through in November 2010, with full custody. By this time, it was clear that Jones' violent behavior was a growing concern. Still, he was allowed supervised visitation. Connie was ordered to pay $6,000 per month in spousal support.

During divorce and custody hearings, Dr. Paulette Selmi and Dr. Stephen Pitt performed psychiatric evaluations in support of Connie's claims. Pitt thought that Jones posed a high degree of risk for future violence toward Connie and their son. Jones' mood disorders, along with his narcissistic, antisocial, and paranoid personality disorders, amplified his anger and sense of entitlement. He wanted control and would not easily absorb setbacks. Pitt said that Jones required excessive admiration, showed no remorse for his harm to others, and had no solid support network to help work through his anger. His paranoia might even become psychotic. "Without psychiatric intervention and treatment," Pitt's report read, "Mr. Jones' mental state is going to continue to unravel. He will become increasingly paranoid, likely psychotic, and pose an even greater risk of perpetuating violence." Although the judge ordered Jones to undergo a full psychiatric evaluation, he failed to comply and the courts did nothing about it. Connie was ordered to attend anger management classes, and she, too, did not comply.

Jones rented rooms in hotels that offered extended stays. He kept his eye on Connie. Like many men with rigid personalities, he held grudges against those who had kept him away from his son. He knew where they worked. In one court filing, it was noted, "Father has made numerous previous threats to kill mother, that if she left him ... he would wait until things settled down before taking his revenge."

Connie's behavior seemed to aggravate the situation. A court filing showed that she was in arrears for spousal payment for tens of thousands of dollars. Jones had filed motions to be paid half of the couple's joint IRA account, more than $100,000. In 2013, Connie was ordered to pay him. She waited until January 2016. The five years of spousal maintenance ended and their son reached the age of emancipation. He could decide for himself whether to see his father. There is no record of what he did, but Jones took to the Internet to express his frustration.

Onto a YouTube channel in May 2018, he loaded 18 videos spanning about 10 hours. He lashed out at "thugs," "crooks," and "lowlifes" who had joined forces with his ex-wife, who he claimed was the true abuser. He said her statements about his violence had been fabricated, and she'd managed to manipulate an entire legal team to back her up. A "biased judge" had let her attorney hire Pitt to evaluate him, and the psychiatrist had merely stated what Connie had paid him to say. Counselors had alienated his son and doctors had changed their original statements. Jones also believed his wife had hired someone to take him out. He needed to act. His last video was on May 25, 2018.

Six days later, on the afternoon of Thursday, May 31, someone overheard Dr. Pitt in a parking lot outside his office, arguing with a man before a gun was fired. Pitt died where he stood. A witness described the shooter as a white male with a round face and a dark hat. Police released a composite sketch.

The next day, 48-year-old Veleria Sharp and 49-year-old Laura Anderson were shot in the downtown Scottsdale law offices of Elizabeth Feldman, Connie's former divorce attorney. Feldman was not present.

One more day passed and life coach Marshall Levine, who shared an office with the woman who had counseled Jones' son during the custody proceedings, was found shot inside the office. Jones believed that this counselor, who was not in the office, had turned his son against him.

By this time, Connie Jones had married Richard Angelin, a former Phoenix police detective whom she had hired as a private detective and bodyguard. As he read about the murders in the local news, he spotted the connection to Connie and urged the Scottsdale police to look for Dwight Lamon Jones. Connie contacted them the following morning, Sunday, to reiterate the connections between the victims and her ex-husband, and to describe his past violent behavior. She said that ever since her divorce from Jones, she'd feared for her safety. She knew where he was currently living at an Extended Stay America hotel in Scottsdale. He drove a gold Mercedes. She and her new husband took protective precautions, aware that Jones might target them as well.

This information assisted the police to gather a team, but not before Jones had killed another couple, Mary Simmons, 70, and Bryon Thomas, 72, on Sunday, June 3. They were found shot to death on June 4, after Jones killed himself as police closed in. He'd initially shot at police but ultimately ended his life himself. His .40-caliber Glock handgun was linked to all six shootings between May 31 and June 3 at four locations.

It seemed likely that, had he not been stopped, he would have pursued other targets as well. It was clear that he'd gone looking for Connie's attorney and, not finding her, had killed the two paralegals in her office. He had also failed to kill the counselor whom he held responsible for alienating his son. In his videos, Jones had described others whom he'd believed were in a conspiracy against him. A tip, followed by quick police action, had likely cut an anger-oriented spree short.

"We started to see that Mr. Jones was visiting them in an effort to right some wrong," said Rich Slavin, assistant police chief in Scottsdale.

Although it remains unclear why Jones killed the couple in Fountain Hills, he did know one of them from playing tennis. Jones was seen dumping a .22-caliber gun that he stole from their home. From other items that Jones had dumped, it was clear that he had listened to news reports and knew that a witness had described him. He might have known that the couple had a gun he could use and had killed them to prevent them from telling anyone where he was. Although police had been searching for Jones before the couple was killed, they did not locate his car until afterward (Flaherty, 2018; Phillips, 2018).

This is the kind of spree killer for which police can prepare. Although the spree was comparatively short-lived, it appears that it could have lasted longer if police had not successfully cornered Jones. There are other cases, too, where police who acted quickly had cut a spree short. From these cases, we can form strategies for an effective response.

SPREE CATEGORIES

Criminological researchers in several areas of the social sciences who are interested in developmental, psychological, and predictive issues in homicidal events recognize value in retaining three distinct categories of multicide. Even if differences are subtle, they can be important for intervention, investigative management, and risk evaluation. They are also important for developing effective tips for law enforcement.

To achieve clarity, especially in light of the FBI's most recent definition of a serial killer, we define the major multicide categories as follows:

1) Mass murder involves at least four fatalities in a short-lived incident in one basic locale, even if the killer travels to several loosely related spots in that general area (e.g., inside a building).
2) Spree killing involves a string of at least three murders in at least two locations, arising from a key precipitating incident that continues to fuel the need to kill, and the murders occur fairly close in time.
3) Serial killers murder at least two people in two separate incidents.

We recognize that the descriptor, "fairly close in time," is vague, because it is difficult to assign time or geographic criteria that might erroneously exclude some cases. The time period for a spree lasts significantly longer than that of a mass murderer, which is generally contained to a range of minutes to hours on a single day. The longer the spree lasts, the more it resembles serial murder. Hence, to accommodate these issues, we formed a category for mixed types. In addition, for those spree killers who seem to overlap mass murderers, we designated a category for movement in tight locations.

We realize that many lists of spree killers included offenders with only two victims, but we think this does not adequately capture the nature of a spree.

As mentioned before, the serial and mass murder categories have been grouped into subcategories, but spree has not. Serial killers are often grouped by motive, such as power, greed, anger, sex, and fame (Ramsland, 2006). For example, Ted Bundy and Belle Gunness were both predatory serial killers, but Bundy was sexually compelled while Gunness focused on financial gain. Similarly, mass murderers might be grouped by motives like anger or ideology, or by target type, such as family, the workplace, a group of people, or a country. Often, mass murderers hope to make a public statement or wreak revenge, and they might expect to die in the process, or be arrested (Capellan et al., 2019; Ramsland, 2005).

Those multicidal murderers who take longer than a few hours to commit their murders and who appear to be driven by impulse, desperation, or a mission are often labeled as spree killers. Basically, spree killers stay on the move, killing along the way, until the spree ends with a suicide, capture, or police shooting. Spree killers try to stay alive for a longer period than mass murderers and might even believe they'll get away. (Some have.) With both types, however, their identity is generally known.

As we collected cases of spree killers, we could see clear groupings based on motive, behavior, and mental state. Categorizing spree killers allows for data analytics that identifies the types of killers that can be effectively identified in an investigation and possibly stopped before they achieve their destructive goals. This is why we believe that the FBI's reason to eliminate spree as a form of multicide is incorrect. When law enforcement view spree as a homogenous category, they overlook the group for which they can effectively prepare. Via categories, we present an improved way to understand spree killers.

Few other researchers have done this. In his overview of Canadian multiple killers, Mellor (2013) offered four categories for spree killers: Utilitarian, Exterminator, Signature, and Marauder. (No Canadian killer fit the Marauder category.) Under these categories, he created a chart to list traits, factual background such as marital status, and key behaviors during the spree. He admits that this approach could be improved upon.

From our database of 359 spree cases involving 419 killers from 43 countries, we devised seven primary categories: anger/revenge, mission-inspired, desperation, mental illness, robbery/thrill, movement in tight locations, and spree crossovers. Five are further divided into subcategories, for a total of 15 (see below).

Many had identifiable targets, due to grudges or a defined sense of mission, and many of these sprees lasted long enough for law enforcement to mobilize and predict where the killer would go. This supports the need to understand spree killers as a distinct type of multicide, standardize the definition, identify motivators, and provide tools for response strategy. In addition, we believe that creating spree killer subcategories will inspire more research in criminology for improved comprehension of these killers' diverse triggers.

HOW THE BOOK IS ORGANIZED

Chapters 2 through 8 each focus on one of the seven categories:

1) Anger and Revenge: Targeted; Targeted and Random-Opportunistic; Random-Opportunistic
2) Mission Killers: Psychotic and Nonpsychotic

3) Desperation
4) Mental Illness
5) Robbery and Thrill: Team and Lone Operators
6) Movement in Tight Locations: Targeted; Targeted and Random-Opportunistic; Random-Opportunistic
7) Mixed Multicides: Spree/Mass; Spree/Serial, and Spree/Mass/Serial

Each chapter offers extended case studies to show the dynamics, followed by summaries of other similar cases.

Chapter 9 provides a detailed analysis from our database for trends and comparisons on such items as age, race, gender, motivation, and spree duration.

Chapter 10 discusses cases in which the offender fell short of qualifying as a spree killer but clearly intended to take enough victims to do so. Chapter 11 offers cases with unique circumstances that were not included in the database but which are nevertheless worth consideration.

Not only is there sufficient diversity among spree killers to form classifications similar to those devised for mass and serial but some subtypes offer distinct utility for identification, tracking, and warning potential targets. The final chapter uses such cases to offer tools for law enforcement.

SUMMARY

Criminologists and psychologists tend to place offenders in distinct categories, the better to study their development, motives, and behavior. Law enforcement needs categories in order to assign resources, and the needs of these groups can conflict. Although the FBI decided in 2005 that the spree category was no longer relevant, criminologists have retained it. Once we examine spree killers more closely and place them into categories, we see that the FBI's reasoning does not apply to all spree killers. Therefore, restoring the spree category and standardizing the definition offers benefits for all relevant criminal justice communities.

REFERENCES

Altman, J., & Ziporyn, M. (1967). *Born to raise hell*. New York, NY: Grove Press.

Capellan, J. A., Johnson, J., Porter, J. R., & Martin, C. (2019). Disaggregating mass public shootings: A compariative analysis of disgruntled employee, school, ideologically motivated, and rampage shooters. *Journal of Forensic Sciences*, *64*(3), 814–823.

Castledon, R. (2011). *Spree killers: The enigma of mass murder.* London, UK: Futura.

Cawthorne, N. (2009). *Spree killers: Devastating massacres by unpredictable gunmen.* West Sussex, UK: Summersdale.

Cimino, A. (2010). *Spree killers: The world's most notorious gunmen and their deadly rampages.* London, UK: Quercus.

Crockett, A. (1991). *Rampage: Spree killer case files.* New York, NY: Pinnacle.

Douglas, J., Burgess, A., Burgess, A., & Ressler, R. K. (1992). *Crime classification manual.* San Francisco, CA: Jossey-Bass.

Egger, S. (1998). *The need to kill: Inside the world of the serial killer.* Upper Saddle River, NJ: Prentice Hall.

Flaherty, J. (2018, June 6). Days before shooting started, scottsdale murder suspect sought media attention. *Phoenix New Times.*

Jensen, K. (2015). *Shocking spree killers: True, horrific, puzzling stories of cold-blooded murderers.* Breinigsville, PA: Scottsdale Book.

Lunde, D. T. (1976). *Murder and madness.* San Francisco, CA: San Francisco Book Co.

Megargee, E. I., & Bohn, M. J. (1979). *Classifying criminal offenders: A new system based on the MMPI.* London: Sage Publications.

Mellor, L. (2013). *Rampage: Canadian mass murder and spree killing.* Toronto, ON: Dundurn.

Morton, R. J., & Hilts, M. A. (Eds.).(2008). Serial murder: Multi-Disciplinary perspectives for investigators. Washington, DC: Federal Bureau of Investigation, U.S. Department of Justice.

Munn, C. (1992). The Investigative Support Unit's role in assisting law enforcement. In J. Douglas, A. Burgess, A. Burgess & R. Ressler (Eds.), *Crime classification manual.* New York, NY: Lexington.

Newton, M. (1992). *Serial slaughter: What's behind America's murder epidemic?* Port Townsend, WA: Loompanics Unlimited.

Pantziarka, P. (2002). *Lone wolf: True stories of spree killers.* London, UK: Virgin.

Parker, R. (2012). *Rampage: Spree killer case files.* Toronto, Ontario: R. J. Parker.

Phillips, K. (2018, June 4). Suspect in Arizona killings fatally shoots himself in hotel room as officers close in, police say. *The Washington Post.*

Ramsland, K. (2005). *Inside the minds of mass murderers.* Westport, CT: Praeger.

Ramsland, K. (2006). *Inside the minds of serial killers.* Westport, CT: Praeger.

Reinhardt, J. M. (1960). *The murderous trail of Charles Starkweather.* Springfield, IL: Charles C. Thomas.
Ressler, R. K., & Shachtman, T. (1992). *Whoever fights monsters.* New York: St. Martin's Press.
Warner, G. (2016, July 2). A new look at the 22-caliber killer. *The Buffalo News.* Retrieved from buffalonews.com/2016/07/02/a-new-look-at-the-22-caliber-killer/

CHAPTER 2

Anger and Revenge

We divided this category into three subtypes: Targeted; Targeted and Random-Opportunistic; and Random-Opportunistic. In other words, some spree killers who have a grudge or seek revenge know exactly who they want to kill, while others have a more generalized need to act out or punish. In some cases, they target one or more people but then extend their spree randomly or in an opportunistic circumstance. We use 'opportunistic' to indicate that people became victims because of where they were rather than who they were. They might have worked at a targeted workplace, for example, or attended a targeted place of worship. "Random" denotes that anyone along the path of a spree can be a target; they're just in the wrong place at the wrong time.

The first category, Targeted, includes those spree killers who are more easily identified and potentially stopped. The Anger/Revenge category, with all three subtypes, represents 30.6% of the spree killers in this database. With rare exceptions, this type of killer goes solo. Also rare in this category are females. We should mention that many spree killers who engage in short-lived sprees in tightly related locations are also motivated by anger and/or revenge, but we have placed them into a different category. They are covered in Chapter 7, Movement in Tight Locations, with the same three subcategories.

We explore several cases of each subcategory below in detail, with references, before we summarize other similar cases. "Unk" or a blank area means the information was unclear or unavailable.

Total: 110 cases, 114 killers

Targeted: 67 cases, 69 killers

Targeted and Random-Opportunistic: 33 cases, 34 killers (1 female)

Random-Opportunistic: 10 cases, 11 killers

ANGER/REVENGE: TARGETED

Dwight Lamon Jones

Age/race-ethnicity: 56/Black

Victims: 6 dead

Place/number of locations: Phoenix, Arizona/4

Date: May 30–June 4, 2018/4 days

Weapon: firearm

Ended in suicide

The case details are in Chapter 1. He is a classic revenge-compelled spree killer who targeted his victims. He killed six people in 4 days, four of which were related to his contentious divorce and child custody hearings. The other two appear to have been acquaintances from whom he stole a gun. Quick intervention seems to have protected other people against whom Jones held a grudge, notably his wife and her current husband.

Christopher Dorner

Age/race-ethnicity: 33/Black

Victims: 4 killed, 3 wounded

Place/number of locations: California/3

Date/duration: February 3–12, 2013/9 days

Weapon: firearms

Ended in suicide

On February 3, 2013, Monica Quan and her fiancé Keith Lawrence were fatally shot in their car in their condo's parking garage in Irvine, CA. A prime suspect was former police officer Christopher Dorner, who had posted a warning to Quan's father, LAPD Captain Randal Quan, that there would be consequences for him and his family if Dorner were dismissed from the LAPD. Quan had unsuccessfully represented Dorner in his disciplinary hearing. In late 2011, Dorner's final appeal was denied and he was let go.

Dorner had joined the LAPD in 2005, after completing a stint in the U.S. Navy Reserve. In 2007, after a mediocre performance review from his probation trainer, Teresa Evans, Dorner filed a complaint against her for using excessive force on a mentally ill man whom they had placed under arrest. An investigation found that the arrestee might have been kicked, but his statements were incoherent. Dorner's complaint was dismissed. The next year, Dorner was fired for making false statements. He believed this was retaliation. Evans said that Dorner had told her during his training that once it was over, he was going to sue the LAPD.

Outraged over this insult to his integrity, Dorner appealed, but each time the Court backed the LAPD. Dorner viewed this as the result of racism. He penned a lengthy manifesto to express his frustration, rage, and vow for revenge, declaring "unconditional asymmetric warfare." He named 40 targets related to those whom he believed had a hand in his demise. He said he intended to make a big splash. He would clear his name and make sure that people did not forget. "Unfortunately, this is a necessary evil that I do not enjoy but must partake and complete for substantial change to occur within the LAPD and reclaim my name" (Dorner, 2013). He urged journalists to pursue the truth and asked only that the LAPD admit its error.

On February 1, Dorner was honorably discharged from the Navy as a Lieutenant. He sent a package of his complaints and evidence of his shooting accuracy to television journalist Anderson Cooper on CNN. Then he committed the double homicide. On February 4th, he posted his manifesto online. He made it clear that he expected to die during his rampage. No one knew who was next, but officials did know whom Dorner expected to kill.

A man flagged down two officers on protection detail for a potential target to say he had seen Dorner at a gas station in Corona. They followed a truck, but the driver fired at them, grazing the head of one. Twenty minutes later in Riverside, two officers were ambushed and shot; one died.

Early the next morning, a man who looked like Dorner tried to steal a boat in San Diego. Dorner's vehicle was found burning on a remote fire trail near Big Bear Lake. Officers went door to door in the area to try to locate the fugitive.

On Feb 9, LAPD Chief Charlie Beck used the media to inform Dorner that there would be another review of his disciplinary case. He probably knew that this was a ploy, because he had much bigger problems now. A large reward was offered and Dorner was called a domestic terrorist. Charges were filed for murder and attempted murder.

Dorner took a couple hostage in their remote cabin. He stole their truck and left. The wife got free from her bindings and alerted the police. San Bernardino County Sheriff's Department chased Dorner to a remote cabin and surrounded him. He continued to shoot. Two officers were wounded and one was killed. They used a demolition vehicle to knock down walls and the cabin burst into flames, possibly from pyrotechnic gas canisters the police had tossed. They heard a single gunshot. Then ammo exploded, keeping them out. Finally, they entered and found Dorner's charred remains. An autopsy showed that he'd died from a self-inflicted gunshot. His arsenal included five semiautomatic handguns, a .308-caliber bolt-action rifle with a scope, a .223-caliber semiautomatic rifle, and high-capacity magazines and suppressors.

Gang Lu

Age/race-ethnicity: 28/Asian

Victims: 5 dead, 1 wounded

Place/number of locations: Iowa City, Iowa/2 buildings, 5 locations

Date/duration: November 1, 1991/1 hour

Weapon: firearm

Ended in suicide

The University of Iowa in Iowa City had won a worldwide reputation in 1959 when Dr. James Van Allen discovered the Earth's radiation belts. The school attracted students who intended to focus on physics. Gang Lu, 28, was one of them.

Lu had come from China. He did well and earned top grades to achieve his doctoral degree, but his performance did not win the Spriestersbach Dissertation Prize, which would have earned him $2,500 and ensured his continued residence for two more years. To make matters worse, the prize went to a fellow countryman, Linhua Shan.

Blaming several key people for his failure, Lu planned his suicidal revenge. On November 1, 1991, he entered Van Allen Hall to attend a meeting of the physics research group in Room 309 between professors and doctoral students. They were sitting ducks. Lu walked up to his academic advisor, Professor Christoph Goertz, and shot him in the head. He then turned the gun on Linhua Shan. Professor Robert Smith tried to flee but was hit in the back and arm. Smith was incapacitated.

Lu went looking for others on his list. He headed down to the second floor and entered the office of the department chair, Dwight Nicholson. Lu aimed and fired, killing the man. He then returned to 309. Two researchers were trying to help Smith. Lu ordered them to leave. When they complied, Lu shot Smith several more times, killing him.

But Lu was not finished. He wanted to kill university administrators. That building, Jessup Hall, was across the street. Inside, he told a temporary secretary, Miya Rodolfo-Sioson, that he wanted to see the Associate Vice President for Academic Affairs, T. Anne Cleary.

When Cleary emerged from her office, Lu fatally shot her and then shot the secretary (who survived). Next door was the president's office. Lu found it locked. The president was away. Foiled, Lu climbed to the second floor and entered room 203. There, he shot himself.

A postmortem investigation found that Lu had been a demanding person who had tantrums when crossed. Some believed he had psychological problems. Certainly, he had the rigid personality common to mass murderers, and he was reportedly a loner (Mann, 1992). He wrote a long statement to be read after his death, which listed his life story and his grievances against the specific people he had targeted (Chen, 1995).

Ronald Gene Simmons

Age/race-ethnicity: 47/Caucasian

Victims: 16 dead, 4 wounded

Place/number of locations: Russellville, Arkansas/4

Date/duration: December 23–28, 1997/5 days

Weapon: firearm, asphyxiation

When Simmons gunned down several people on the morning of December 28, 1987, in Russellville, Arkansas, he was winding down. What appeared to have been an incident of workplace violence turned out to be far worse.

With a .22-caliber pistol, Simmons shot a receptionist at a law office in the head, and then moved on to the Taylor Oil Company. He shot two men there and two more in a nearby convenience store. He ended his spree in the Woodline Motor Freight Company, where he wounded a woman and took another hostage. When police arrived, Simmons gave up peacefully.

Rumors held that Simmons was infatuated with receptionist Kathy Kendrick, 25, and that she had rebuffed him, so they assumed this had been the revenge shooting of a jilted man. Officers went to where Simmons lived on 13 acres outside town to notify his family. The place seemed eerily still. Finding an unlocked window, the officers entered. The smell hit them at once.

Simmons' son and daughter and their spouses lay dead. All had been shot, but Simmons' 6-year-old granddaughter had been smothered. The officers returned to town to get more resources.

The next day while searching the property, investigators came across disturbed earth over which lay barbed wire and a piece of sheet metal. They dug down and unearthed a body. Then another. They kept digging until they found the remains of seven people: Simmons' wife, two sons, three daughters, and 3-year-old granddaughter. Another search team found two more corpses in the trunks of junked cars: Simmons' infant grandsons.

The adults had been shot and the children asphyxiated. A coroner determined that they had been killed a few days earlier, just before Christmas. Simmons had just committed the largest family massacre in the country. Every person who had lived under Simmons' roof, as well as grown children returning at his invitation for the Christmas holiday, were dead. To police, it appeared to have been a planned ambush.

Simmons was charged with 16 counts of first-degree murder and four counts of attempted murder. He was taken for a psychiatric examination. Known for his obsession with order and control, he had kept his family mostly captive in a run-down building surrounded by junk cars. No mail came for them, no calls, and no friends.

Records turned up charges of incest in New Mexico, where Simmons had once lived. He had impregnated his 15-year-old daughter, Sheila, and before he could be arrested, he had fled with his family to Arkansas. Once Shelia was able to leave, she got married and moved out. Apparently, Simmons had viewed this as a betrayal, triggering the massacre. He had believed that Sheila was his soulmate

Despite having hallucinations while incarcerated, Simmons was declared competent to stand trial and was convicted of the two murders he had committed in town. He wanted to be executed, and hoped this could be accomplished before the trial for killing his family. When he was sentenced to die, he refused to appeal, so on June 25, 1990, Simmons was given a lethal injection (Marshall & Williams, 1991).

George Banks

Age/race-ethnicity: 40/biracial Caucasian and Black

Victims: 13 dead, 1 wounded

Place/number of locations: Wilkes-Barre and Jenkins Township, Pennsylvania/3

Date/duration: September 25, 1982/less than 2 hours

Weapon: firearm

Banks, a prison guard dressed in Army fatigues and carrying a semiautomatic AR-15 rifle, began eliminating members of his family around 2:00 a.m. on September 25, 1982, in Wilkes-Barre, Pennsylvania. Two stepchildren hid, surviving to witness the horror as he broke into their trailer and killed their mother, grandmother, sister, and half-brother. That same night he killed nine others, including two bystanders, one of which survived.

Arrested and arraigned, Banks' attorney indicated that he was mentally incompetent. Banks was on leave from his job because he had threatened to commit suicide and had expressed some paranoid ideation about his food being poisoned.

Dr. Michael J. Spodak, Chief of Psychiatry at Baltimore County General Hospital in Maryland, had examined the defendant for his competence to stand trial and found him remorseful over killing his children but preoccupied with conspiracy issues. Spodak diagnosed Banks as "terminally paranoid" and incompetent to stand trial.

However, psychiatrist Robert Sadoff found him competent. Jurors heard how Banks was the child of a black father and white mother and although he was married to a black woman who had separated from him, at the time of the crime he had lived with three white women in a run-down house. In all, he had killed four women with whom he'd had children, seven children (five were his), an elderly woman, and a man he did not know. Associates indicated that he hated both races whose heritage he shared. He did not like being pushed around and had said things that suggested he felt persecuted by whites and blacks alike. He had been in a dispute over child custody with the woman in the trailer home and had a history of battering the others.

The jury convicted him of 12 counts of first-degree murder and sentenced him to death. In 2001, his death sentence was overturned on a technicality. In 2004 and 2010, he was found incompetent to be executed (Worden, 2011).

James Schnick

Age/race-ethnicity: 36/Caucasian

Victims: 7 dead

Place/number of locations: Mansfield, Missouri/2

Date/duration: September 25, 1987/1–2 hours

Weapon: firearm

On Sept 25, 1987, Schnick fatally shot his brother-in-law, Steve Buckner, at his farm, along with his wife and four kids. Dropping Buckner's body at a cemetery half a mile away, he drove the body of their 14-year-old son, Kirk, in Buckner's truck to his own house, where he killed his wife before inflicting wounds on himself. He staged the scene to look as if Kirk had burst in and started shooting. He stabbed the body and placed the gun in the boy's dead hand. Then he called for help, claiming he'd saved his own two children. The gun proved to be the murder weapon.

It was a chance discovery that Kirk was left-handed that blew open the case. Police were already uneasy over the fact that no cartridge casings had turned up in either location or on Kirk, despite 18 shots fired. Also, the Buckner's truck had blood in it, as if used to haul Steve Buckner to the cemetery, but he'd been too large for Kirk to carry. In addition, Kirk's wounds didn't support Schnick's account. Schnick's wounds had been superficial, despite his dramatic reaction, and he'd received $100,000 in life insurance on his wife and the title to his brother-in-law's farm. He also had a mistress. Pressured, he confessed to the seven murders. However, the reason he gave for the slaughter was that Steve Buckner had raped his sister – Schnick's wife – when they were kids, so this was payback. Her psychological problems had caused their marriage to fail. (In reality, his mistress had told his wife about the affair, causing trouble in the marriage.)

Mark O. Barton

Age/race-ethnicity: 44/Caucasian

Victims: 9 dead, 13 wounded or injured

Place/number of locations: Stockbridge, Georgia/3

Date/duration: July 28–29,1999/2 days

Weapon: hammer, firearm

Ended in suicide

Barton bludgeoned his wife and two children from his first marriage with a hammer and typed a rambling confession. He then went to two brokerage houses where he'd lost money during 2 weeks of day trading and shot four people in one place and five in the other. Thirteen were wounded. Estranged from his wife, Barton had suffered financial losses. After a police pursuit, he shot and killed himself. He had also been a suspect in the double homicide of his first wife and her mother in 1993.

Dakota Theriot

Age/race-ethnicity: 21/Caucasian

Victims: 5 dead

Place/number of locations: Ascension and Livingston Parishes, Louisiana/2

Date/duration: January 26, 2019/1hour

Weapon: firearm

Deputies were called to a trailer in the city of Gonzales for a domestic incident. They found Theriot's parents dying. His father told them that Dakota had shot them. In the next parish, Theriot had killed his girlfriend and her brother and father. He was apprehended the next day in Virginia. See Chapter 12 for more details.

Ernest Ingenito

Age/race-ethnicity: 26/Caucasian

Victims: 5 dead, 4 wounded

Place/number of locations: Piney Hollow, New Jersey/3

Date/duration: November 17, 1950/1 hour

Weapon: firearm

On the evening of November 17, 1950, Ingenito drove to the Mazzoli home to confront his ex-wife Theresa. He demanded to see their children. She fled and he shot her. His mother-in-law, Pearl, ran across the street to her parents' home. Ingenito followed, shooting Pearl's mother, brother, and sister, who was pregnant, then wounding a 9-year-old girl. He found Pearl in a closet and fatally shot her. Ingenito then drove to another New Jersey town and wounded his ex-wife's aunt and uncle.

Luke Woodham

Age/race-ethnicity: 16/Caucasian

Victims: 3 dead, 7 wounded

Place/number of locations: Pearl, Mississippi/2

Date/duration: October 1, 1997/2 hours

Weapon: firearm

Woodham was enraged when his girlfriend broke up with him. He stabbed his mother and went to school with a rifle and a pistol. There, he killed his former girlfriend and another girl. Seven other students were wounded before he ran out of ammunition and was disarmed.

Joseph Harris

Age/race-ethnicity: 35/Caucasian

Victims: 4 dead in spree, 1 dead 3 years earlier

Place/number of locations: Ridgewood, New Jersey/2

Date/duration: November 15, 1988; October 10, 1991/a few hours

Weapon: samurai sword, firearm

In 1984, Harris invested $10,000 with Roy Ellison's firm, an investment company. When the company failed the following year, Harris wanted his investment back. The company ignored him. Harris went to the Ellison residence dressed as a ninja warrior. He handcuffed and blindfolded Ellison and his family in the master bedroom. He raped Ellison's wife and two daughters before fatally shooting him. He was not arrested.

On October 10, 1991, Harris dressed again like a ninja and went on a spree. A former postal worker, he went to his supervisor's home and killed her with a samurai sword, then shot her fiancé. From there, he went to the postal facility and killed two mail handlers on the night shift. Harris left a handwritten two-page letter complaining about postal authorities and vowing revenge. The note referred to the massacre at an Oklahoma post office in August 1986, where an employee facing dismissal pulled guns from his mailbag, killing 14 people, and injuring six.

Edwards tried an insanity defense, saying the ninja spirit had made him kill, but he was convicted.

Carl Robert Brown

Age/race-ethnicity: 51/Caucasian

Victims: 8 dead, 3 injured

Place/number of locations: Miami, Florida/multiple, with another intended

Date/duration: August 20, 1982/half an hour

Weapon: firearm

Brown got into numerous disputes with people. On August 19, 1982, Brown had a heated argument with Jorge Castalleda at Bob Moore's Welding & Machine Service Inc. over a $20 repair of a lawnmower. He stated he would return and kill everybody. The next day, he purchased several weapons and ammunition. He invited his 10-year-old son to go with him to "kill a lot of people," but first, he rode his bicycle to the welding shop. There, he shouted that he would send everyone "to Germany." He walked through the building, shooting everyone he saw. Three escaped to get help. Brown got on his bicycle, heading to another target location where he'd had a dispute. However, an armed man pursued him, shooting at him. Brown returned fire, so the pursuer ran him down with a car. Brown died from his injuries.

Howard Franklin Stewart

Age/race-ethnicity: 37/Caucasian

Victims: 6 dead

Place/number of locations: Lebanon, Missouri, and Corsicana, Texas/2

Date/duration: September 1987/6 days

Weapon: firearms

Ended in suicide

In 1987, Stewart was fired from a job in emergency services that specialized in train wrecks. A few months later, his wife threw him out of their home, barring him from seeing his two sons. He trained two pitbulls to be vicious and constantly wore camouflage clothing. Having served in the military, he shaved his head and asked people to call him Rambo. On September 9, he went to his parents' home in Lebanan, MS. A week later, he had an argument with a relative, so he hitchhiked to Corsicana, TX. George and Carol Brewer picked him up. They owed him money. He shot them and caught a ride with Steve Vestal, killing him as well. On September 18 Stewart boarded a bus to Corsicana. He went fishing and shooting for 2 days before killing his former supervisor. He returned to his former home to shoot his wife's current boyfriend before killing her (she'd been warned). When police arrived, he shot himself in the head.

Efren Valdemoro

Age/race-ethnicity: 38/Asian

Victims: 5 dead

Place/number of locations: Hercules and Vallejo, California/3

Date/duration: August 28–31, 2010/4 days

Weapon: hands

Valdemoro met Cindy Tran at a Vallejo beauty salon. In August 2010, Valemoro got into a fight over his girlfriend with two men in Hercules, California, who lived in her house. He killed both, leaving one body in the house and hiding the other behind a false wall in a closet. He'd beaten and strangled them. Then two women disappeared from Vallejo. Their bodies were found 6 days later in a house where Valdemoro sometimes lived. He'd often fought with their husbands. Finally, Valemoro also kidnapped Tran from the salon and strangled her.

Christopher Chubasco Wilkins

Age/race-ethnicity: 37/Caucasian

Victims: 3 dead

Place/number of locations: Forth Worth, Texas/2

Date/duration: October 26, 2005/2 days

Weapon: firearm

Wilkins killed a man in a dispute over a pay phone. The next day, he shot and killed a man who had cheated him, along with the man's friend, who was shot because he was there.

Ian Stawicki

Age/race-ethnicity: 41/Caucasian

Victims: 5 dead, 1 wounded

Place/number of locations: Seattle, Washington/2

Date/duration: May 30, 2012/5 hours

Weapon: firearm

Ended in suicide

Stawicki's history was dotted with failure, rejection, delusions, assaults, and an interest in guns. In 2012, he stopped at Cafe Racer, a Seattle coffee shop, from which he had been barred. He killed a man to block the exit and started shooting others. Four died at the scene. He shot a woman to hijack her car. His spree ended 5 hours later in suicide. He'd been diagnosed with autism spectrum disorder and learning disabilities. He'd received a head injury while in the Army.

Bradley William Stone

Age/race-ethnicity: 35/Caucasian

Victims: 6 dead, 1 wounded

Place/number of locations: Lansdale & Souderton, Pennsylvania/3

Date/duration: December 15, 2014/2 hours

Weapon: knife, firearm

Ended in suicide

On December 15, 2014, Stone grew tired of clashing with his ex-wife over the custody of their two children. He killed his ex-wife's sister, brother-in-law, and daughter, wounding their son before he went to kill his mother-in-law and grandmother-in-law. His final victim in another town was his ex-wife. He took his two young daughters away and dropped them off with a neighbor. Most of the victims were shot, although some were also stabbed with a knife. Stone failed in an attempted carjacking and fled into the woods. After an extensive manhunt, Stone was found dead on the day after the killings in the woods near his home. He had committed suicide by overdosing on drugs.

Richard Starry

Age/race-ethnicity: 60/Caucasian

Victims: 4 dead

Place/number of locations: Robstown, Texas/2

Date/duration: July 2018/less than an hour

Weapon: firearm

Ended in suicide

Starry used a handgun to fatally shoot his adoptive brother and step-brother. He then went to an eldercare home down the road where he killed his father, stepmother, and himself.

Darrell Wayne Ferguson

Age/race-ethnicity: 23/Caucasian

Victims: 3 dead (claimed he killed 5 others)

Place/number of locations: Dayton, Ohio/2

Date/duration: December 26–27, 2001/2 days

Weapon: boots, knife

Following his conviction for burglary, Ferguson served time in a drug treatment program and received a pass on December 21, 2001. His murder spree began 4 days later when he attacked and killed a disabled relative with a kitchen knife. He pawned two televisions and a radio to buy cocaine. The next day, he broke into the home of an elderly couple who were former neighbors and beat and stomped them to death with steel-toed boots.

Daniel Andrew Bowler

Age/race-ethnicity: 26/Black

Victims: 3 dead

Place/number of locations: Richmond, Virginia/3

Date/duration: June 2, 2005/less than an hour

Weapon: firearm

Bowler shouted racial slurs before fatally shooting a black male and robbing him. He then traveled to a strip mall a few miles away and fatally shot two men at two adjacent businesses, one of Middle Eastern descent and the other Korean. Police Chief Rodney Monroe said these were grudge killings.

Carey Dyess

Age/race-ethnicity: 73/Caucasian

Victims: 5 dead

Place/number of locations: Wellton, Arizona/3

Date/duration: June 4, 2011/1–2 hours

Weapon: firearm

Ended in suicide

Divorced 4 years earlier, Dyess fatally shot five people before ending his own life. His ex-wife and her current partner were among the victims. He was angry at her, and his victims had all played a role in his contentious divorce. After he killed her, he drove away and word spread for others to be on the lookout. Dyess went to the office of his wife's divorce attorney, about to retire, and shot him. The other two victims were friends of his ex-wife. The community had lived in fear of Dyess for a decade, although he had claimed that some of the victims had harassed him.

William Ray Bonner

Age/race-ethnicity: 25/Black

Victims: 7 dead, 9 wounded

Place/number of locations: Los Angeles, California/6

Date/duration: April 22, 1973/1 hour

Weapon: firearms

Bonner was an unemployed service station attendant. His spree began at home after an argument with his grandmother. Enraged he went outside and fired shots at two teens who had come with her. Leaving them wounded, he went back inside and killed the grandmother. Taking her car, Bonner drove to a gas station where he had once been employed and approached two people he knew. He killed one and wounded the other. He went to another gas station to shoot a former colleague. From there, he went to the home of someone with whom he'd had a recent dispute. He killed one person and wounded two others. Carrying a grudge for being shortchanged at a liquor store, he killed the shop owner and wounded a customer. His next target was another liquor store, where he wounded two employees. Finally, he killed a girl who had just broken up with him.

William James Ramos

Age/race-ethnicity: 39/Caucasian

Victims: 3 dead

Place/number of locations: Antioch, California/3

Date/duration: March 6–7, 1991/1 day

Weapon: firearm

Ramos killed his girlfriend the day before he killed the daughter and sister of his ex-wife. He apparently had control issues, as he had attempted to kill a former girlfriend in 1976 by shooting her. He also made threats against law enforcement and carried out several assaults. A prison psychiatrist found that he had paranoid personality disorder and difficulty controlling his temper, due to PTSD from serving in Vietnam.

Hugh G. Miller

Age/race-ethnicity: 33/Caucasian

Victims: 3 dead

Place/number of locations: Burlington County, New Jersey/3

Date/duration: April 7, 1995/6 hours

Weapon: hands, firearm

While Miller argued with his girlfriend over her desire to break up, he beat and strangled her. After killing her, Miller visited his friend, Keith Tiesman, who taunted him about his failed relationship. Miller shot him in the head. He then drove to the home of his mother and confessed. When she urged him to turn himself in, he shot and killed her.

John Merlin Taylor

Age/race-ethnicity: 52/Caucasian

Victims: 3 dead, 2 wounded

Place/number of locations: Escondido, California/2

Date/duration: August 10, 1989/1 hour

Weapon: firearm

Ended in suicide

Taylor, a postal worker armed with enough ammunition for an extended siege, shot his wife to death at their residence before driving to a post office where he killed two coworkers and wounded two others before ending the spree with a gun blast to his head.

Lawrence Michael Hensley

Age/race-ethnicity: 30/Caucasian

Victims: 4 dead, 2 wounded

Place/number of locations: Sidney, Ohio/3

Date/duration: July 8, 1999/5 days

Weapon: firearm, knife

Hensley began his spree by shooting and stabbing three teenage girls at his residence. He fled with his wife, while neighbors who heard the shots called police. During the search, officers found Molotov cocktails, so they called in the Army Explosive Ordinance Disposal Unit. Hensley drove to the home of Brett Wildermuth, their Bible study teacher, where Hensley shot the man. Five days later, he shot and wounded a motorist. Hensley was a compulsive flasher, so authorities speculated that he had killed the kids to prevent them from reporting his inappropriate behavior. Another woman at his home was also wounded but had managed to escape. Rumors held that Hensley had tried luring kids into his house for sexual purposes and had once been into devil worship. He allegedly killed Wildermuth because he viewed him as a rival in a religious cult.

Nikolay Soltys

Age/race-ethnicity: 27/Caucasian

Victims: 6 dead

Place/number of locations: Sacramento, California/3

Date/duration: August 20, 2001/3 hours

Weapon: knife

Soltys, a Ukrainian immigrant, stabbed his pregnant wife to death, believing she had disrespected him. He drove to his uncle's home and murdered his aunt and uncle and their two grandchildren, who were both nine. The final stop was his mother's house to pick up his 3-year-old son. Driving to a field, he cut the boy's throat. Soltys hid from police for 10 days but was cornered in his mother's backyard.

Ramon Salcido

Age/race-ethnicity: 28/Hispanic

Victims: 7 dead, 2 wounded

Place/number of locations: Sonoma and Cotati, California/4

Date/duration: April 14, 1989/3 hours

Weapon: firearm, knife

Salcido was going through a divorce and about to lose his job and custody of his three young daughters. He thought his wife was having an affair with his coworker, so he reacted. After drinking and taking cocaine, he slashed the throats of his three daughters and dumped them in an isolated area (one survived). He drove to his mother-in-law's house, where he fatally shot her and his wife's two sisters. Returning home, he killed his wife. From there, he went to his workplace to shoot his coworker. His last stop was the home of another supervisor, wounding him before he fled to Mexico. He was arrested there.

John M. Goins

Age/race-ethnicity: 48/Caucasian

Victims: 6 dead

Place/number of locations: Stockton and Galt, California/3

Date/duration: March 18, 1926/1 day

Weapon: firearm

Ended in suicide

Goins began his spree by killing his wife and her sister over his impending divorce. He then went to the law offices to find the attorney, who was away, so he went to the attorney's house and shot the man's wife. News spread, but Goins fled to Galt, 20 miles away, where a man lived against whom he held a grudge. There, he killed three more. When police chased him, he killed himself. Police found his list of people he had planned to kill had he not been stopped.

Charles Smith

Age/race-ethnicity: 53/Black

Victims: 4 dead, 3 injured

Place/number of locations: Joliet, Illinois/2

Date/duration: July 23, 1997/3 hours

Weapon: firearm

Ended in suicide

Smith fatally shot his ex-girlfriend in her car, then drove with the body to the home of her sister and brother-in-law. There he killed his girlfriend's daughter and in-laws. He raped a 13-year-old girl who was staying there and tried unsuccessfully to strangle two other children. He hanged himself in the basement. Allegedly, Smith had a grudge against the family because they disapproved of his biracial relationship with the victim.

Orlando T. Ganal

Age/race-ethnicity: 37/Asian

Victims: 4 dead, 4 injured or wounded

Place/number of locations: Honolulu, Hawaii/2

Date/duration: August 25, 1991/5 hours

Weapon: fire, firearm

Ganal was upset with his wife over her affair with a coworker. He also thought she was turning their son against him. Late at night, he drove to his in-laws' home where his wife and son were living. He shot all four, but his wife and son survived. Ganal moved on to the home of the brother of his wife's lover and torched the house. Two children died. Ganal was arrested that morning.

Leo Held

Age/race-ethnicity: 39/Caucasian

Victims: 6 dead, 6 wounded

Place/number of locations: Lock Haven, Pennsylvania/4

Date/duration: October 23, 1967/1–2 hours

Weapon: firearm

Held drove his kids to school, dropped his wife at her job and showed up at the paper mill where he worked. He brought two weapons, fatally shooting five supervisors who were part of his car pool, and wounding four others. Then he went to a local airport and wounded a switchboard operator who was part of his car pool. Next he went home and shot two neighbors, one of whom survived. The police surrounded his house and shot him. Before he died in the hospital, he gave his reasons for shooting people. All had irked him in some way. He had intended one more but had failed to get to this man.

Lynwood Drake

Age/race-ethnicity: 43/Caucasian

Victims: 6 dead, 2 injured

Place/number of locations: Morro Bay, California/3

Date/duration: November 7–8, 1992/11 hours

Weapon: firearm

Ended in suicide

Upset over being evicted, Drake traveled to three separate towns to kill people, including his landlord and those who had assisted in the eviction proceedings. He then killed people at the Oak Card Parlor, where he had lost money and had been barred. He took another former landlord hostage and had planned to kill two more people, his pastor and the daycare worker, but could not get his car started. He was on the phone with a hostage negotiator when he killed himself. "I have been persecuted my whole life by people," his suicide note read. "They refused to help. Damn the American family to hell. God forgive me."

Mary Ann Holder

Age/race-ethnicity: 36/Caucasian

Victims: 5 dead, 1 wounded

Place/number of locations: Pleasant Garden, Greensboro, North Carolina/3

Date/duration: November 20, 2011/1–2 hours

Weapon: firearm

Ended in suicide

On the morning of November 20 in her home, Holder shot her son Robert and his 15-year-old girlfriend, along with Holder's niece and nephew. Holder then drove to the GTCC Aviation Center near the airport and shot Randal Lamb, her former boyfriend, in the arm. Picking up her son Zach from a friend's house, Holder shot him in her car before turning the gun on herself. She left two suicide notes in different handwriting, expressing remorse. She had written a $10,000 check to the wife of her boyfriend to settle a lawsuit for "alienation of affection." There was evidence that if a sheriff's deputy had not arrived on the scene when

Holder killed Zack Smith, her next stop would have been her daughter's home in Greensboro.

Alan Eugene Miller

Age/race-ethnicity: 34/Caucasian

Victims: 3 dead

Place/number of locations: Pelham, Alabama/2

Date/duration: August 5, 1999/2 hours

Weapon: firearm

Miller shot coworkers at Ferguson Enterprises before driving five miles to shoot another man at the place where he had formerly worked. He had been resentful of assignments to another driver, and was then laid off. He had a history of disputes, especially with the men he had killed.

Alexander Pogosyan and Michael Martinez

Age/race-ethnicity: 18 and 18/Caucasian and Hispanic

Victims: 5 dead

Place/number of locations: Aurora, Colorado/2 or 3

Date/duration: September 7, 1998/1 hour

Weapon: firearm

Pogosyan and his friend Michael Martinez armed themselves with shotguns, put bandanas over their faces, and went on a murderous rampage during Labor Day. They were apparently gunning down people who angered them, but Martinez was found dead, shot 13 times. No one has been charged in his death, although Pogosyan was a key suspect. If Pogosyn killed Martinez, then it would be six murders in three locations over 3 hours.

Kenneth Eugene Turrentine

Age/race-ethnicity: 41/Black

Victims: 4 dead

Place/number of locations: Tulsa, Oklahoma/2

Date/duration: June 4, 1994/1 hour

Weapon: firearm

Turrentine suspected his girlfriend was having an affair behind his back. He thought his sister knew about it and was conspiring to cheat him out of money to buy drugs. He obtained a .22 pistol and drove to his sister's home to confront her. When she denied his accusations, he shot her in the head. He then went to his girlfriend's house and shot her and her two children. He turned himself in.

Austin Smith

Age/race-ethnicity: 30/Black

Victims: 4 dead

Place/number of locations: Phoenix, Arizona/2

Date/duration: April 13, 2019/1 hour

Weapon: firearm, baseball bat

Smith confronted his wife about an affair he thought she was having with his brother. When she denied his allegation, he fatally shot her and their 5-year-old daughter. When his 7-year-old daughter began to cry, he beat her to death with a bat. Austin went looking for his brother and ran into a friend who tried to persuade him he was delusional. Smith shot the man. When he tried to flee, police arrested him.

Adam Moss

Age/race-ethnicity: 23/Caucasian

Victims: 7 dead

Place/number of locations: Sioux City, Iowa/2

Date/duration: August 27–29, 2001/2 days

Weapon: hammer, knife

At 3:00 a.m., Moss beat his girlfriend to death with a hammer and cut her throat. He then killed her five children with the hammer. He hid for the day before going to his former boss's home to beat and stab him to death. It took police a day to locate Moss hiding behind a woodpile.

Dale Burr

Age/race-ethnicity: 63/Caucasian

Victims: 3 dead

Place/number of locations: Iowa/3

Date/duration: December 9, 1985/2 hours

Weapon: firearm

Ended in suicide

Burr was deep in debt. Feeling the pressure, he killed his wife before driving to the Hills Bank & Trust. When he could not cash a check, he fetched his shotgun and returned. Entering the office of the bank president, he shot the man in the face. He also aimed at other bank officers, but he accidently ejected the second shell. Unable to shoot, he left and drove to the farm of Richard Goody, who had won a judgment against Burr's son. Burr shot Goody in the face. Sheriff's deputies tried to arrest him, but he committed suicide.

Anthony Bell

Age/race-ethnicity: 25/Black

Victims: 5 dead

Place/number of locations: Baton Rouge, Louisiana/2

Date/duration: May 21, 2006/2 hours

Weapon: firearm

Bell entered the Ministry of Jesus Christ Church in Baton Rouge and shot four of his in-laws. He kidnapped his wife and three children, driving three miles to an apartment complex where he shot his wife to death in the parking lot. Police responding to the shooting arrested Bell in his apartment without incident.

Terry Todd Wedding

Age/race-ethnicity: 27/Caucasian

Victims: 4 dead

Place/number of locations: Depoy, Kentucky/2

Date/duration: June 26, 1999/1 day

Weapon: firearms, baseball bat

Wedding was angry that his parents and cousin had recommended that he be committed for a short stay in Western State Hospital. He convinced his father to accompany him to visit the grave of his grandmother. Once there, he killed his father with a baseball bat. He then took his mother to the same location and shot her. The following morning, he shot his cousin (a police officer) and the cousin's wife. Wedding surrendered to police later that morning.

Shon D. Miller

Age/race-ethnicity: 22/Black

Victims: 4 dead

Place/number of locations: Ascension Parish, Louisiana/two

Date/duration: March 10, 1999/half an hour

Weapon: firearm

Miller, an unemployed welder went looking for his estranged wife where she lived with her mother. He blamed her for losing his job. When he failed to find her, he shot her mother. He then drove to the church where he believed his wife would be with their 2-year-old son. There, he killed them both, along with a man sitting next to his wife. Three hours later, police arrested him.

Kenneth Lee Myers

Age/race-ethnicity: 47/Caucasian

Victims: 4 dead

Place/number of locations: Aiken County, South Carolina/2

Date/duration: July 2, 2011/1 hour

Weapon: firearm

Ended in suicide

Meyers took a shotgun and drove to his ex-wife's home, killing her, her sister, and their mother. He then drove four miles to the home of his ex-girlfriend and killed her. He stole her car. Pursued by police, Meyers returned to the first crime scene where he committed suicide. He had a "hit list" of people he would kill if his life fell apart. His four victims were on it. Police likely interrupted his plans to kill others.

Michael Cummings

Age/race-ethnicity: 25/Caucasian

Victims: 7 dead, 1 wounded

Place/number of locations: Westmoreland, Tennessee/2

Date/duration: April 27, 2019/Unk, possibly 1 day

Weapon: firearm

In response to a 911 call, police found the bodies of six of Cummings' relatives (including his parents) in one house, plus one wounded, and one more body in another house. Cummings was arrested after a brief shootout when he emerged, heavily armed, from the woods. He had a criminal history, including aggravated arson and aggravated assault. He had been given probation on the condition that he get a mental health evaluation, which he had ignored. On an earlier assault, in 2017, he had said, "If I get out of jail, I'll go down there and do it again," and later, when authorities asked about it, he said that "when I get out, I'll finish the job." He appeared to show the markers for future violence.

Malcolm George Baker

Age/race-ethnicity: 45/Caucasian

Victims: 6 dead, 1 wounded

Place/number of locations: Australia/3

Date/duration: October 27, 1992/2 hours

Weapon: firearm

The shootings started when Baker broke the window of his ex-girlfriend's apartment, killing her and her younger sister, along with the sister's friend. Their father, Thomas Gannon, 43, who had been visiting, was shot in the street. Baker then drove to Bateau Bay, where he arrived at his son's home. He shot the young man in the backyard. Baker's next stop was the home of a couple with whom he had had a confrontation 2 years earlier. He killed them both. At 11:00 p.m., Baker walked into Toukley police station and handed over his 12-gage pump-action shotgun.

Xiong Zhenlin

Age/race-ethnicity: 35/Asian

Victims: 8 dead, 4 wounded, 9 intended

Place/number of locations: China/2

Date/duration: January 24, 2009/15 hours

Weapon: ax, hammer

Xiong had wanted to marry Zhu Deqing, but when she refused, he killed her and a 2-year-old boy with an ax. While searching Zhenlin's junkyard, police discovered the bodies of three men and three women. All had been employees at his salvage operation. Others were hurt. When captured, Xiong told police he had planned to kill nine other people with whom he had fought in the past, including his ex-wife.

Mohammed Merah

Age/race-ethnicity: 23/Black

Victims: 7 dead, 5 wounded

Place/number of locations: Toulouse, France/3

Date/duration: March 11–19, 2012/9 days

Weapon: firearm

On March 11, Merah shot and killed a soldier whom he lured to a gym in a ruse to buy a motorcycle. Four days later, Merah killed two soldiers and critically injured a third outside a shopping center north of Toulouse. On March 19, Merah attacked a Jewish school in Toulouse, opening fire in the schoolyard. The first victim was a rabbi and teacher, along with the teacher's two sons. Inside, he shot at staff, parents, and students. He rode off, but was located 3 days later and died in a shootout.

Gustavo Pissardo

Age/race-ethnicity: 22/Hispanic

Victims: 5 dead

Place/number of locations: São Jose dos Campos, Brazil/2

Date/duration: September 29, 1994/22 hours

Weapon: firearm

Pissardo, a student, had a bad headache. His father took him to the hospital where he was given an injection and sent home. At midnight he woke up and found his mother and his sister watching TV. He retrieved a revolver and fatally shot both, along with his father. He then staged the scene by undressing the females to make it look like a rape and robbery. He drove his father's truck nearly 100 miles to where his grandparents lived, killing them. He spent 4 days with his girlfriend before turning himself in.

Joseph Rosario Bilodeau

Age/race-ethnicity: 38/Caucasian

Victims: 6 dead, 2 injured

Place/number of locations: Quebec City, Quebec/3

Date/duration: October 25, 1934/3–4 hours

Weapon: firearm

Bilodeau had been fired, so he was angry. He gunned down two 18-year-old cousins in the woods. He then drove back to lure his cousin and two older sisters to the same area, where he killed them. Two hours later, he went into the post office from which he'd been fired and killed the divisional superintendent and wounded his former supervisor and the chief clerk.

Erminio Criscione

Age/race-ethnicity: 27/Caucasian

Victims: 6 dead, 6 wounded, 1 intended

Place/number of locations: Switzerland/4

Date/duration: March 5, 1992/2 hours

Weapon: firearm

Criscione had disputes with his coworkers, so he went out early one morning with his assault rifle and shot his best friend. At another house, he fatally shot four people and wounded three. In another place, he killed two more before reaching his boss's home. When he discovered the man was not home, he shot his wife in the leg and said, "Tell him I'll be back." However, the police had caught up. After 2 days in jail, he committed suicide.

Ozan Selamet

Age/race-ethnicity: 50/Caucasian

Victims: 6 dead

Place/number of locations: Belgium/2

Date/duration: January 19, 2002/2 days

Weapon: hands, firearms

Selamet strangled or shot three of his sons and a daughter one night when they arrived for a visit. He drove with the bodies to his ex-wife's home, where he gunned down his eldest daughter and his wife's ex-lover. He told his ex-wife that he wanted her to live with the memory of their dead children.

Pere Puig Punti

Age/race-ethnicity: 57/Caucasian

Victims: 4 dead

Place/number of locations: Catalonia, Spain/2

Date/duration: 2010/less than an hour

Weapon: firearm

A builder shot dead his two bosses in a café in Catalonia, Spain after being told he was going to be let go. He then drove to a bank and killed deputy bank manager Rafael Turro and a cashier, because the bank had evicted him over his debt.

Diego Loscalzo

Age/race-ethnicity: 38/Hispanic

Victims: 6 dead plus a fetus, 2 wounded

Place/number of locations: Buenos Aires, Argentina/3

Date/duration: February 2017/less than 2 hours

Weapon: firearm

The Hurlingham massacre began when Loscalzo argued with his wife Romina, a police officer, and shot her with her service weapon. Romina's sister and her husband ran to help and ended up fatally shot. A neighbor was also killed. Loscalzo fled on a motorcycle to his mother-in-law's home. When his brother-in-law confronted him outside, Loscalzo killed him before firing on a vehicle in which three people were sitting, killing one and wounding the others.

Marcos Feruglio

Age/race-ethnicity: 25/Hispanic

Victims: 4 dead, 3 wounded

Place/number of locations: Sauce Viejo and Santa Fe, Argentina/2

Date/duration: December 24–25, 2016/2 days

Weapon: knife

Feruglio was arrested in December 2016 in Argentina accused of stabbing four family members of his former partner on Christmas Eve. On Friday, while looking for his wife, he killed his former mother-in-law and her current husband. On Saturday, he entered a building and killed his former father-in-law and a former sister-in-law, and wounded his ex-wife, her new partner, and another woman. He had been angered by their accusations of domestic violence.

Ljubiša Bogdanović

Age/race-ethnicity: 60/Serbian

Victims: 13 dead, 1 wounded

Place/number of locations: Serbia/5

Date/duration: April 9, 2013/less than an hour

Weapon: firearm

Ended in suicide

Former factory worker Bogdanović, 60, shot and killed his 83-year-old mother and his 42-year-old son, and wounded his wife with a shot to the head. He then entered four neighboring houses, killing five men, five women, and a 2-year-old child, most of whom were shot in the head while they were sleeping. He was related to most of them. The police were called. Bogdanović shot himself in the head, dying 2 days later.

Joseph Gautsch

Age/race-ethnicity: 36/Caucasian

Victims: 6 dead

Place/number of locations: Mauterndorf and Salzburg, Austria/3

Date/duration: November 22, 1997/a few hours

Weapon: firearm

Ended in suicide

Joseph Gautsch, 36, a mechanic, began his spree by shooting the headmaster of a school at Mauterndorf, who had assisted with the divorce mediation between Gautsch and his ex-wife. Then he killed his ex-wife, her husband, and their 3-year-old child. Finally, he invaded the home of a couple with whom he had lived when he had financial difficulty and shot them before killing himself.

Genildo Ferreira de França

Age/race-ethnicity: 27/Hispanic

Victims: 15 dead, 2 wounded

Place/number of locations: Santo Antônio do Potengi, Rio Grande do Norte, Brazil/7

Date/duration: May 21–22, 1997/2 days

Weapon: firearm

Ended in suicide

Angry at people who owed him money, Ferreira had planned to commit murder for over a year. He hoped to become famous. On his list were 20 people, including one who had spread rumors that he was gay. On May 21, he killed his ex-wife's boyfriend. He then picked up three associates and drove to the home of his former father-in law to execute him and another man. He visited two more men, killing both. He picked up his girlfriend and shot his ex-wife. During the night, he said good-bye to members of his family. The next day he went to kill his parents, but police intervened. He wounded two officers. Ferriera fled to the home of his mother-in-law and killed her. When police surrounded him, he shot himself. His suicide note explained things:

> The reason I am writing these few lines is not to justify the wrong I have done, but it is only in this way that I can prove to the entire world, and can challenge those who wanted to prove that I was a homosexual, I was not, nor am I going to be [a homosexual] because of this claim, which is the reason for this tragedy. I don't feel like a normal person, after these lies have been told about me. It was difficult to live unaccepted in society, because of a single caboclo who told lies about me but now is dead.

Chippa Mateane

Age/race-ethnicity: 42/Black

Victims: 8 dead, 3 wounded

Place/number of locations: Tarlton, South Africa/3

Date/duration: April 3, 2006/1 hour

Weapon: firearm

In 2006, senior police officer Mateane fatally shot three women and a 1-year-old child and wounded another woman in Tarlton, South Africa, before going to the Kagiso police station in Krugersdorp to shoot four officers. He fled in a police car to Sebokeng, where he shot his brother before police killed him in a shootout. Jealousy appeared to have sparked the rampage. He left a note that stated: "I am not to blame. I am important … I deserve to be loved by you. I deserve to be treated with respect. And I will still love you forever."

Mutsuo Toi

Age/race-ethnicity: 21/Asian

Victims: 30 dead, 3 injured

Place/number of locations: Okayama, Japan/multiple

Date/duration: May 1938/1 hour

Weapon: ax, firearm

Ended in suicide

Toi used an ax and a shotgun to kill 30 people and injure three more before killing himself. He began by cutting electricity to a village during the evening to make it dark. At 1:30 a.m., he decapitated his grandmother with an ax. Using flashlights strapped to his head, he roamed through the village for over an hour, entering homes to kill his neighbors. He thought his neighbors had begun to treat him badly and had formed a plan of revenge, although the murder of his grandmother was to spare her.

Kumatarō Kido and Yagorō Tani

Age/race-ethnicity: 36 and Unk/Asian

Victims: 11 dead

Place/number of locations: Osaka, Japan/2

Date/duration: May 25, 1893/several hours

Weapon: firearms, knives

Ended in double suicide

Angry over losing his common-law wife to another man, Kido and his pupil, Yagorō, went after the man's family. They killed four people in one home and five in another, which included the wife and her mother. Afterward, they committed suicide together.

Mika Muranen

Age/race-ethnicity: 23/Caucasian

Victims: 3 dead

Place/number of locations: Kotka, Finland/2

Date/duration: April 18–19, 1994/2 days

Weapon: firearm, crossbow

Muranen, a military conscript, returned to his barracks from a holiday. He stole a RK-62 assault rifle and went to his hometown, Kotka, Finland. There, he retrieved a crossbow. The next day, he killed two neighbors with whom he'd been feuding. The following day, he killed a mailman with the assault rifle. Police chased him, and he returned fire but was wounded and caught.

Leonardas Zavistonovičius

Age/race-ethnicity: 58/Caucasian

Victims: 9 dead, 2 wounded

Place/number of locations: Draučiai, Lithuania/5+

Date/duration: February 15, 1998/half an hour

Weapon: firearm

Beaten to death by survivors

Zavistonovičius took a hunting rifle and a Czech carbine with telescopic sight. Within the next half-hour, he entered four homes and killed nine neighbors and their relatives with single shots to the head or chest. He tried to ambush four men gathering wood. When they emerged from the woods, Zavistonovičius wounded two, but was beaten to death by the other two. Zavistonovičius suffered from a paranoid delusional disorder that had caused difficult relations between him and his neighbors, although he had passed psychiatric exams to keep renewing his gun licenses.

Shi Yuejun

Age/race-ethnicity: 35/Asian

Victims: 12 dead, 5 wounded

Place/number of locations: Tonghua, Jilin Province, China/5

Date/duration: September 24/29, 2006

Weapon: knife

Shi had a grudge against people whom he believed had humiliated him. On September 24, he killed Li Zhenjun in his home, as well as Wang Yuliang, a health inspector who had once punished him. He also killed Wang's wife and parents, and wounded Wang Yuhong, one of Wang's relatives. Shi then drove to Liuhe County, where he killed shop owner Liu Guohua, who had refused to sell his meat, and wounded Liu's wife and Wang Gangyin, who had paid him low wages. On another stop,

Yuejun killed shop owner and slaughterhouse supervisor Yu Hongyong, who had also punished him. Before he fled, he wounded Yu's wife. He went into hiding until September 27, when he murdered Sun Honglian and his wife in their secluded home near Tonggou. Two days later, he killed three villagers and wounded another. He was captured that day.

Fredrik von Sydow

Age/race-ethnicity: 24/Caucasian

Victims: 4 dead

Place/number of locations: Stockholm, Sweden/2

Date/duration: March 7, 1932/1 hour

Weapon: flatiron, firearm

Ended in suicide

Swedish politician Hjalmar von Sydow, his cook, and his maid were beaten to death with a flatiron at von Sydow's home. Police issued a warrant for von Sydow's son, Fredrik. After dining with friends at a restaurant, Fredrik fatally shot his wife and himself. Fredrik, addicted to drugs, was in financial difficulty. He'd stolen his father's wallet, which contain about $762.00.

Amara ben Ahmed

Age/race-ethnicity: 54/Middle Eastern

Victims: 7 dead

Place/number of locations: Edough, Algeria/2

Date/duration: May 27, 1937/2 hours

Weapon: firearm

After getting divorced from his ninth wife, Amara wanted to marry a 16-year-old girl, but she refused him. He implored her again on May 26, 1937, but she stood firm. Ahmed threatened to get his rifle and kill everyone, but the girl and her three brothers ignored him. Angry, he made good on his threat. He returned to the girl's home and killed all four. He set fire to the home, and then went to the other end of the village. There he killed a woman who had repeatedly made fun of him, along with her husband and sister. Ahmed set this home on fire, too.

Then he confessed what he'd done to a friend before fleeing into the mountains. He was not caught.

Wilhelm Brückner

Age/race-ethnicity: 31/Caucasian

Victims: 9 dead, 1 injured

Place/number of locations: Hassenberg and Lindenberg, Germany/3

Date/duration: June 6–7, 1925/1 night

Weapon: knife, ax

Ended in suicide

During the night, Brückner cycled to Lindenberg. He waited for his brother-in-law, Hugo Birnstiel, and lured him into a forest, where he hit him with a piece of iron on the back of his head. The young man survived. Brückner returned to Lindenberg to where his estranged wife was living with her parents. He cut her throat, then returned to Hassenberg. He entered the house of his sister where he was living, killing her, her husband, their five children, and his mother by smashing their skulls with an ax and cutting their throats with the kitchen knife. He hanged himself next to his mother's bed.

Unknown German

Age/race-ethnicity: 20/Caucasian

Victims: 3 dead, unknown number injured

Place/number of locations: Etching and Freising, Germany/2

Date/duration: February 19, 2002/1 hour

Weapon: firearm, bomb

Ended in suicide

The rampage began when this camouflage-wearing male entered a small factory in Etchings from which he had recently been fired and shot his former boss and foreman. From there he took a taxi to a school 12 miles away and fatally shot the principal before setting off two bombs that injured more people. He shot another teacher before ending his own life.

ANGER/REVENGE: TARGETED AND RANDOM-OPPORTUNISTIC

Charles Starkweather and Caril Ann Fugate

Age/race-ethnicity: 19 and 14/Caucasian

Victims: 10 together; Starkweather – one more dead 7 weeks before

Place/number of locations: Wyoming, Nebraska/5

Date/duration: January 21–29,1958/8 days

Weapon: firearm, knife

Late in 1957, Starkweather had trouble paying his rent. On December 1, he placed a bandana over his face, robbed a service station, and killed the attendant. No one suspected him. Still in financial trouble, he formed a plan to take his 14-year-old girlfriend, Caril Ann, to a place in the mountains, but her mother and stepfather forbid him to see her. On January 21, 1958, Starkweather quarreled with them, killing them and their other daughter. After a lifetime of being bullied, along with a head injury that made it difficult for him to work, he'd had enough. Starkweather and Caril Ann stayed in the house for nearly a week before their spree began.

They first shot a family friend, but the other six victims were random. Each involved stealing a car or other goods, but in a home invasion, Starkweather got revenge for having been a garbage man for the wealthy. This triple homicide was equally motivated by anger. As Starkweather killed victim #11 in Wyoming to steal his car, the police came along. Caril Ann turned on Starkweather, claiming he'd held her against her will, although evidence contradicted her. Starkweather made several confessions, sometimes taking the blame and other times sharing equal responsibility with Fugate. He would now become famous, as he thought he deserved. He did not want any talk of an insanity defense, because "no one remembers a crazy man." He had enjoyed the feeling of power that killing had conveyed.

Dr. James Melvin Reinhardt, a professor of sociology and criminology at the University of Nebraska, was allowed to interview Starkweather as he sat in prison awaiting trial. He called Starkweather a "chain killer." Reinhardt viewed Starkweather as suffering from hopelessness, being paranoid, and having an unrealistic assessment of the world around him. He seemed enraged over not having what he believed he deserved (Reinhardt, 1960).

Michael McLendon

Age/race-ethnicity: 28/Caucasian

Victims: 10 dead, 6 wounded

Place/number of locations: Geneva County, Alabama/7

Date/duration: March 10, 2009/1 hour

Weapon: firearms

Ended in suicide

McLendon was depressed over his parents' divorce, his inability to qualify for the military, and his loss of a job. He made a list of people whom he held accountable for his failures. He shot his mother and three dogs and set the house on fire. In another town, he killed his uncle, two cousins, and a visiting neighbor with a child. (His aunt escaped.) Next door, he killed his maternal grandmother. He then shot three people randomly from his car, killing them. He led police on a chase, wounding one, before he committed suicide. None of the people on his list were among those shot, but police thought he had intended to find them before he was finished.

Paul Devoe III

Age/race-ethnicity: 43/Caucasian

Victims: 6 dead

Place/number of locations: Texas to New York/3

Date/duration: 2007/2 days

Weapon: firearm

Devoe left behind six bodies as he made his way from Texas to New York in 2007. After fighting with an ex-girlfriend, he shot a bartender in Marble Falls and then killed another former girlfriend, her current boyfriend, her daughter, and a friend of her daughter's in Austin before stealing a car. On the run, he shot an elderly woman, apparently to switch cars. He went to the home of a former coworker in New York, where police arrested him.

Maksim Gelman

Age/race-ethnicity: 23/Caucasian

Victims: 4 dead, 5 wounded or injured

Place/number of locations: Brooklyn, New York/7

Date/duration: February 11–12, 2011/28 hours

Weapon: knife, car

Just after 5:00 a.m., Gelman killed his stepfather after an argument with his mother about driving their car. Gelman took the vehicle and sped off in it, running over a crossing guard. He decided to take down "rats" before he was caught. He killed the mother of a female friend and waited to ambush the young woman, fatally stabbing her. When he fled, he rammed a car and stabbed the driver. He stole the man's car and ran over a pedestrian, killing him. He hailed a cab and stabbed him. He approached another car and stabbed the driver, stealing the car. He boarded a train and stabbed the ticket seller. By now, his picture had been published in the newspaper and passengers recognized him. He tried getting off, but police were waiting.

Earl M. Forrest

Age/race-ethnicity: 53/Caucasian

Victims: 3 dead, 2 wounded

Place/number of locations: Platte County, Missouri/2

Date/duration: December 9, 2002/1 hour

Weapon: firearm

Forrest had been drinking. He went to Harriet Smith's home and demanded that she buy a lawn mower and mobile home for him in exchange for Forrest introducing her to a source for methamphetamine. Something went wrong and Forrest shot a guest of hers, killing him. Then he fatally shot Smith. He grabbed $25,000 worth of methamphetamine and returned to his own home. Police came after him, engaging him in a shootout. Forrest killed Deputy Joann Barnes and wounded two others.

Joseph Ferguson

Age/race-ethnicity: 20/Caucasian

Victims: 5 dead

Place/number of locations: Sacramento, California/3

Date/duration: September 8, 2001/1 day

Weapon: firearms

Ended in suicide

Despondent over a break-up and suspension from his employment, Ferguson armed himself and made phone calls to Burns Security employees saying he was going to Old Sacramento to kill more people than fellow Sacramento spree killer, Nikolay Soltys. He went to a city maintenance yard and shot two women. Then Ferguson headed to a city-run marina where he killed two more Burns employees. Next was the Sacramento Zoo. He handcuffed a former coworker to a tree and stole her car. Employees were escorted to safe houses. However, Ferguson arrived at the home of a Burns supervisor who had not been evacuated, and filmed a video suicide message before killing the supervisor and stealing his car. In the video, Ferguson said he would soon kill himself.

Joseph C. Palczynski

Age/race-ethnicity: 31/Caucasian

Victims: 4 dead

Place/number of locations: Baltimore, Maryland/2

Date/duration: March 7–8, 2000/2 days

Weapon: firearm

Palczynski terrorized residents in suburban Baltimore by killing four people and taking a family of three as hostage in a 4-day standoff. An unemployed electrician, he had a record of domestic violence and related crimes. George and Gloria Shenk had provided a haven for Palczynski's estranged girlfriend, so he came after her and killed them. A neighbor tried to intervene and was shot. The next day, Palczynski killed a woman to steal her car. For 10 days, Palczynski was the subject of an intense manhunt. He had taken his terrified girlfriend to a hotel. A police car showed up and she was able to escape. Palczynski fled into the woods. On March 17, Palczynski penetrated a police barrier and ran to the home of his girlfriend's mother, her boyfriend, and their 12-year-old son, holding them hostage until he died in a shootout with police.

Kenneth Tornes

Age/race-ethnicity: 32/Black

Victims: 5 dead (also the chief suspect in an earlier triple homicide)

Place/number of locations: Jackson, Mississippi/2

Date/duration: April 24, 1996/6 hours

Weapon: firearm

An 8-year veteran firefighter, Tornes was angry at his estranged wife. He shot her in the head. While police investigated, he went to the fire station to carry out punishment for a grudge he had carried for years over how he was treated. He looked for anyone wearing a white shirt, signaling a supervisor. In the end he killed four fire chiefs and captains. Police pursued him to a local mall and wounded him before placing him under arrest.

Phillip Carl Jablonski

Age/race-ethnicity: 45/Caucasian

Victims: 4 dead

Place/number of locations: California and Utah/3

Date/duration: April 22–27, 1991/6 days

Weapon: firearm, knife, duct tape

Jablonski had murdered his first wife in 1978. While in prison, he married Carol Spadoni. When he got out in September 1990, she did not want to be near him. He took classes at a community college to satisfy parole requirements. Here, he met Fathyma Vann. On April 22, 1991, she was found shot in the head and sexually assaulted, lying naked in a ditch with the words "I Love Jesus" carved in her back. Her ears and eyes had been removed. The following day, Carol Jablonski and her mother were murdered at their home. Jablonski was arrested for these murders and also charged with the robbery and murder of a woman in Utah on April 27.

Matthew John Murray

Age/race-ethnicity: 24/Caucasian

Victims: 4 dead, 5 wounded

Place/number of locations: Arvada and Colorado Springs, Colorado/2

Date/duration: December 9, 2007/12 hours

Weapon: firearms

Ended in suicide

On December 9 around 12:30 a.m., following a Christmas banquet, Murray knocked on the door of the Youth With a Mission Center to request overnight accommodations. When he was turned away, he opened fire, killing the center's director of hospitality and staff member and wounding two others. He fled, driving to the New Life Church in Colorado Springs. After the 11 a.m. service ended, Murray opened fire in the church parking lot shooting four people. He entered the main foyer where he shot another man. A woman shot back, hitting him several times, whereupon he killed himself. According to investigators, Murray had descended into anti-Christian derangement over a period of several months, and his web-postings had become increasingly violent and hateful.

Darnell Collins

Age/race-ethnicity: 33/Caucasian

Victims: 7 dead, 3 wounded

Place/number of locations: June 17–21, 1995/New Jersey and New York/6

Date/duration: 5 days

Weapon: firearm

Collins, an ex-convict from Atlantic City, killed seven people and injured three others, two critically, before being shot and killed by the police in Nutley, New Jersey. His victims were acquaintances and strangers, including his ex-girlfriend, who had a restraining order, and her mother. Authorities surmised that a domestic squabble ignited the spree, exacerbated by drugs.

William Bryan Cruse

Age/race-ethnicity: 60/Caucasian

Victims: 6 dead, 10 wounded

Place/number of locations: Palm Bay, Florida/4

Date/duration: April 13, 1978/7 hours

Weapon: firearms

Cruse had developed delusions about his neighbors thinking he was gay, and he thought kids who came on his lawn were targeting him. On April 23, 1987, after a quiet dinner, Cruse saw a boy run across his lawn. He grabbed his guns and went out into the streets. He shot a boy playing basketball before driving to a local Publix supermarket to shoot customers. He killed three people in the parking lot but could not enter the store. Frustrated, he drove to a Winn-Dixie. A cop arrived and Cruse killed him. He then killed a second officer who'd fired at him and missed. Cruse entered the supermarket and started shooting. He took a woman hostage inside the store for 6 hours before finally surrendering. He pled not guilty by reason of insanity, claiming he did not recall hurting anyone, but he was convicted.

Pablo Antonio Serrano-Vitorino

Age/race-ethnicity: 40/Hispanic

Victims: 5 dead

Place/number of locations: Kansas and Missouri/2

Date/duration: March 7, 2016/3 days

Weapon: firearm

Serrano-Vitorino, a Mexican national, shot his neighbor and three other men who were in the neighbor's home in Kansas City, Kansas. The next day, he shot a man in Missouri. He pulled his rifle on a person at a gas station but did not shoot. This helped police to locate him and place him under arrest.

John Zawahri

Age/race-ethnicity: 24/Caucasian

Victims: 5 dead, 4 wounded

Place/number of locations: Santa Monica, California/3

Date/duration: June 7, 2013/1 hour

Weapon: firearm

Zawahri killed his father and brother before setting his house on fire. He carjacked a driver, shooting a woman who tried to intervene. He ordered the driver to take him to the Santa Monica College campus. Along the way, he shot randomly, wounding three people and killing two. With his AR semiautomatic rifle, Zawahri arrived on campus, killing a woman outside the library. Entering, he opened fire. Police arrived and shot him, stopping his rampage. He had a suicide note on him that expressed remorse for killing his relatives.

Alofa Time

Age/race-ethnicity: 51/Asian

Victims: 3 dead

Place/number of locations: Boise, Idaho/2

Date/duration: June 15, 2006/4 hours

Weapon: knife, vehicle

On June 15, 2006, Time went to the home of his estranged wife where he killed and cut her head off. He took her severed head with him in his truck. While driving down a county road with the intention of committing suicide, he crossed into oncoming traffic, killing a woman and her daughter. The head of his decapitated wife rolled onto the freeway. Time, not killed, was arrested at the scene.

John Felton Parish

Age/race-ethnicity: 49/Black

Victims: 6 dead, 4 injured

Place/number of locations: Grand Prairie, Texas/4

Date/duration: August 9, 1982/half an hour

Weapon: firearms

Armed with a carbine, semiautomatic pistol, and a revolver, Parish entered the Western Transportation Company building to discuss a payment dispute with his supervisor. When he failed to get what he sought, Parish killed the man, as well as two others, before stealing a truck and driving half a block to the Western Transportation Company office. There he killed two and wounded a third. He took a hostage but let her go. Parish next drove four miles to the Jewel T warehouse, where he killed a district sales manager. In the shipping office, he killed the warehouse supervisor and wounded the shipping supervisor. Parish left the building and approached an 18-wheeler tractor-trailer. The driver jumped out, breaking his foot. Hijacking the truck, Parish fled, chased by police. An officer at a barricade shot him and was injured. Parish crawled out of his overturned vehicle, shooting at the officers, and went into a building, where he was killed.

Lonnie Davis

Age/race-ethnicity: 21/Black

Victims: 3 dead, 2 intended

Place/number of locations: Seattle, Washington/2

Date/duration: May 26, 1999/1 hour

Weapon: knife, posthole digger

Davis killed his mother and 18-month-old nephew in their home with a paring knife. He drove away, running down a motorcycle rider. David fled on foot into a nearby neighborhood, where he killed a woman in her home with a posthole digger and critically injured another. He barricaded himself inside an empty house. A sniper killed him.

Eliseo Hernandez Moreno

Age/race-ethnicity: 24/Hispanic

Victims: 6 dead

Place/number of locations: Fort Bend County, Texas/3

Date/duration: October 11, 1983/a few hours

Weapon: firearm

The spree began in College Station with the slayings of his brother-in-law, Juan Garza, and Mr. Garza's wife, because they refused to help him find his estranged wife. When a state trooper pulled Moreno over for a violation, Moreno fatally shot him. Also gunned down in another town were a retired nurse, her sister, and her brother-in-law. Moreno was on his way to the Rio Grande Valley to kill his wife when he was arrested.

Carl Drega

Age/race-ethnicity: 62/Caucasian

Victims: 4 dead, 3 injured

Place/number of locations: Colebrook, New Hampshire and Vermont/3

Date/duration: August 19, 1997/1 day

Weapon: firearms

Drega had issues with authority dating back to 1970. When a state trooper stopped him for having too much rust on his car, Drega killed the man. He then killed another officer who arrived to help. Drega stole the police car and drove to the district court to kill a judge. He also killed a news editor who struggled with him for the gun. Drega returned to his property and set his house on fire. He wounded a Fish and Game warden. Police converged on him in his hiding place in Vermont, killing him in a shootout, but not before he had wounded two of them.

Ibrahim Shkupolli

Age/race-ethnicity: 43/Caucasian

Victims: 5 dead

Place/number of locations: Leppävaara District of Espoo, Finland/2

Date/duration: December 31, 2009/several hours

Weapon: firearm

Ended in suicide

Shkupolli discovered that his girlfriend was having an affair with a coworker at the Prisma supermarket where she worked. He went to her apartment and stabbed her to death. He then went to the market to hunt down her boyfriend. Shkupolli entered the Prisma and began firing. He killed four employees, including the lover, before going home to shoot himself.

Michel Van Wijnendaele

Age/race-ethnicity: 28/Caucasian

Victims: 7 dead, 3 wounded

Place/number of locations: Bogaarden, Belgium/3

Date/duration: May 12, 1987/5 hours

Weapon: firearm

Ended in suicide

At approximately 2:00 p.m., Van Wijnendaele used a .22-caliber rifle to shoot six members of the De Crem family on their farm. One survived. At a neighboring farm he killed a woman and her son, because they had witnessed the shooting, and then fled in his car. While police set up roadblocks, he drove to Denderwindeke, where 3 hours later he shot and wounded both of his parents-in-law. Police in Brugelette eventually spotted Van Wijnendaele. A car chase ensued. When, cornered, the shooter killed himself.

Éric Borel

Age/race-ethnicity: 16/Caucasian

Victims: 15 dead, 4 injured

Place/number of locations: Sollies-Pont and Cuers, France/3

Date/duration: September 23–24, 1995/1 day

Weapon: hammer, firearm

Ended in suicide

Borel shot his stepfather four times and smashed his head with a hammer. He did the same to his half-brother. When his mother came home, he shot her (and possibly hit her with a baseball bat). Packing a bag with food, supplies, and ammunition, he walked several miles to Cuers the next day, where he killed a close friend for refusing a favor. He then went on a random shooting spree in the street, hitting anyone he saw. He aimed for the head and if he did not get it right, he shot again. When police arrived, Borel shot himself. His mother had been rigid and abusive, and he had had frequent quarrels with his stepfather.

Guy Martel

Age/race-ethnicity: 41/Caucasian

Victims: 7 dead, 5 injured

Place/number of locations: Ille-et-Vilaine and Cotes-du-Nord, France/multiple

Date/duration: June 19, 1985/3 hours

Weapon: firearm

On June 19, Martel argued with his father, then took his .22-caliber rifle and drove to the home of his uncle, wounding him. Martel then drove to Dr. Launay's office. There he entered the room of Launay's colleague, Michel Lhommelet, and killed him with four shots. He next went to a gym and killed a manager. Moving on, he went to his father's home and killed him. Then he killed another uncle and wounded a brother. Finally, he shot three strangers. Spotting a police helicopter, Martel drove into Cotes-du-Nord, wounding two strangers along the way. When asked after his arrest about the reason for shooting strangers, he explained that at first he had business with his family and a few others, but upon realizing that it was easy to shoot people, he simply continued. Martel had been under treatment at a mental hospital.

Vernon Reynolds

Age/race-ethnicity: 43/Caucasian

Victims: 4 dead, 5 wounded

Place/number of locations: North Wales, United Kingdom/2

Date/duration: December 31, 1991/1 hour

Weapon: knife, car

Ended in suicide

Taxi driver Vernon Reynolds, kicked out of his house, showed up there to discover his wife holding a party. He was told to leave. Instead, he retrieved a knife from the kitchen and stabbed her to death. Then he went after others, injuring five. He fled, driving down a country road. Aware the police were after him, he saw a car carrying three men. Reynolds deliberately ran into it, killing them and himself.

Tian Mingjian

Age/race-ethnicity: 31/Asian

Victims: 28 dead, 30–80 wounded

Place/number of locations: Beijing, China/3+

Date/duration: September 20, 1994/2 hours

Weapon: firearms

Tian armed himself with a Type 81 assault rifle and killed the regimental political commissar on the drill ground. He also killed three other military officials who were trying to stop him and injured at least 10 more before fleeing. He hijacked a jeep and forced the driver to head toward Beijing. The driver crashed the car and tried to escape, but Tian killed him. Then he shot people at random on his way to the embassy district. Police engaged in a gun battle with him, and he killed seven. Eventually, heavy police fire forced Tian to flee into a dead end, where a sniper killed him.

Carel Delport

Age/race-ethnicity: 36/Caucasian

Victims: 9 dead, 19 injured

Place/number of locations: Ladysmith, KwaZulu-Natal, South Africa/multiple

Date/duration: January 20, 1992/1 day

Weapon: firearms

The shooting began at the family farm after Delport had an argument with his father about the sale of three calves. When his father showed him the money he had received, Delport armed himself with a .357 Magnum revolver and killed the man. Delport next shot the housemaid in the kitchen and set fire to the mattress in his room and his car, which eventually burned down the house. Outside, he killed two men who were there to buy the calves, and then drove to his stepmother's house to set her car on fire. When he could not find it, he shot randomly at people in the street, killing five and wounding 11. When police arrived, he fled toward Newcastle and shot at commuters in a bus, wounding six. Delport was eventually arrested after a shootout that resulted in two wounded officers.

Campo Delgado

Age/race-ethnicity: 52/Caucasian

Victims: 30 dead, 15 injured

Place/number of locations: Bogota, Colombia/4

Date/duration: December 4, 1936/5 hours

Weapon: knife, firearm

Delgado entered the bank to close his account. Then he purchased a revolver and ammunition. The next day, he went to the apartment of a girl to whom he was giving English lessons, stabbing her and her mother. He returned to his own home and killed his mother, setting her body on fire. Gun in hand, he ran through the apartment building shouting that the place was on fire. Seven people who opened their doors to his knock were shot to death. Delgado went to a pizzeria he frequented. He had a meal and several drinks. After paying his bill, he shot the other diners point-blank, killing 20 and wounding 12. A police officer killed him at the scene.

Mark Hobson

Age/race-ethnicity: 34/Caucasian

Victims: 4 dead

Place/number of locations: North Yorkshire, England, United Kingdom/2

Date/duration: July 10–18, 2004/8 days

Weapon: hands, knife, hammer, ligature

On July 10, Hobson beat his girlfriend in their apartment with a hammer. On July 18, he lured her twin sister to the apartment, sexually assaulted her and strangled her to death. Her boyfriend discovered both bodies. Hobson subsequently stabbed and beat an elderly couple in their home, 25 miles from the first murders. He was arrested after an 8-day manhunt. Discovered notes showed that the first two murders had been planned, and he had a kill list that included four other people.

Kevin Weaver

Age/race-ethnicity: 24/Caucasian

Victims: 4 dead

Place/number of locations: Bristol, England/2

Date/duration: March 28, 1988/a few hours

Weapon: firearm, hammer

When Weaver's sister refused to loan him her car, he entered her bedroom and hit her with a hammer. When his mother came home, he bludgeoned her to death as well. He cleaned up and turned on the gas taps in the house. He also planted a shotgun cartridge triggered by a tripwire. This he left as a booby-trap for police. Weaver then put three shotguns and hundreds of rounds of ammunition into a golf bag and set off to kill a girl who had turned down his proposal. He spared her but killed two others at her workplace. Weaver was arrested and confined in a psychiatric facility, considered to have maniacal jealousy.

Derrick Bird

Age/race-ethnicity: 52/Caucasian

Victims: 12 dead, 11 wounded or injured

Place/number of locations: Cumbria, England/numerous

Date/duration: June 2, 2010/6 hours

Weapon: firearm

Ended in suicide

In the early hours of 2 June, Bird drove to his twin brother's home and shot him 11 times with a .22 rifle, killing him. He then went to the home of the family solicitor, Kevin Commons, whom Bird killed. Retrieving another gun, Bird drove to a taxi rank in Whitehaven and called over a man he with whom he had conflicts. Bird shot and killed him. He shot three other taxi drivers, a passenger, and three pedestrians, killing two. Driving away, he found other victims, killing some and wounding others. When his car broke down, he went into the woods and killed himself.

Mattias Flink

Age/race-ethnicity: 24/Caucasian

Victims: 7 dead, 1 wounded

Place/number of locations: Falun, Sweden/2

Date/duration: June 11, 1994/less than 1 hour

Weapon: firearm

On June 11, 1994, Second Lieutenant Mattias Flink consumed alcohol before he put on his field uniform, picked up his AK-5 assault rifle, and went to a park in Falun, Sweden. There he shot a woman who had just broken up with him, as well as five other members of the Women's Auxiliary Services. Nearby, he shot a cyclist and a security officer. Flink tried to go home via an abandoned railway, but police discovered him. After exchanging fire with them, Flink was hit. Police arrested him.

Jin Ruchao

Age/race-ethnicity: 41/Asian

Victims: 108 dead, 38 injured

Place/number of locations: Shijiazhuang Hebei, China/4

Date/duration: March 16, 2001/2 hours

Weapon: bombs

In March 2001, Jin Ruchao rode in taxis to set a series of bombs in four apartment buildings in Shijiazhuang Hebei, China that killed 108 people and injured 38 others. He said he was angry at his lover, ex-wife, and her family, who lived in the targeted buildings. Two men who supplied him with ammonia nitrate were also convicted and executed with him. Jin said he had acted alone.

Bulelani Vukwana

Age/race-ethnicity: 29/Black

Victims: 11 dead, 6 injured

Place/number of locations: East London, South Africa/5+

Date/duration: February 9, 2002/several hours

Weapon: firearm

Ended in suicide

After a quarrel with his girlfriend over her decision to end their relationship, Vukwana traveled to several places and shot 17 people, killing 11 and injuring six. Some victims were random, but he also killed his girlfriend, a friend of hers, and her father. He killed one person who arrived to help. He then shot randomly at motorists and pedestrians. When police cornered him, he killed himself.

ANGER/REVENGE: RANDOM-OPPORTUNISTIC

Jason Brian Dalton

Age/race-ethnicity: 45/Caucasian

Victims: 6 dead, 2 wounded

Place/number of locations: Kalamazoo County, MI/3

Date/duration: February 20, 2016/6 hours

Weapon: firearms

On the morning of February 20, 2016, Dalton went to several gun stores, purchasing a jacket designed for carrying a concealed weapon. That afternoon, he answered a call for a pick-up. He'd been driving for Uber for a couple of weeks to supplement his income as an insurance adjuster. He had wanted to be a police officer and was disappointed that it had not worked out. Married and the father of two, Dalton had no psychiatric history or a history of violence. Neighbors had noticed Dalton seeming more paranoid. He thought it was all right to pick up passengers while his dog was in his car, which suggests a lack of professional protocol. At 4:00 p.m., Matt Mellen got in. Dalton took a call from his son and, without warning, began driving recklessly at 75 mph. He drove through stop signs and sideswiped another car before Mellen managed to open a door and escape. He called 911 to report the erratic Uber driver in the silver Chevrolet Equinox. A BOLO went out, with the license plate number.

Dalton went home to get his Glock 19 9-mm. handgun and a bulletproof vest. He then went to pick up a fare that he could not locate. In a parking lot of a condo complex, he drove up to a woman to ask if she was the person who had called him and then he shot at her with 15 rounds, hitting her four times. She survived.

Dalton struck another vehicle and went home to change cars with his wife, going back out in a dark blue Chevrolet HHR. He lied about how his Equinox had been damaged, saying another driver had fired a shot at him. He also told her that he could not tell her what was going on, but that it would be on the news that night. He drove around but came back to switch handguns, because the Glock had malfunctioned. He picked up several Uber riders without incident. Then at 10:00 p.m., Dalton walked up to a father and son who were looking at a truck at a Kia dealership and fatally shot them both before driving off. Witnesses called 911.

Ten minutes later and five miles away, Dalton walked up to a woman in a van parked at a Cracker Barrel and asked her for a dollar to "make

America great again." She refused and he shot her. Three other women and a teenage girl in an adjacent car started screaming. Dalton shot them all. Only the girl survived.

Dalton drove off and picked up more fares, also without incident. Some asked him if he was the Uber driver who was shooting people. He always denied it.

The police eventually identified Dalton's car and ordered him to stop. He surrendered without incident. During interrogation, he eventually told officers that the Uber mobile app had possessed him, indicating whom he should shoot. By the time the police stopped him, the "possession" had supposedly dissipated. The app had gone from black back to red, so he had not drawn his gun on them.

Dalton's attorney said he would enter a plea of not guilty by reason of insanity. However, two separate psychiatrists failed to find anything to support this. Dalton had planned for his murders, had lied about them, had told his wife he'd be on the news, and had picked up many other people that day without incident. He had no record of mental illness and had shown none after that day. The insanity plea was withdrawn and Dalton stopped his trial during jury selection to plead guilty.

Dalton had once been a suspect in some shootings on two interstates, and his wife stated that she had once found their cat dead on their bed. Another person stated that Dalton had said he was going to strangle it and leave it there. Aside from his report of the Uber app becoming the devil to command him to kill, no other motive ever surfaced. However, he had not been sleeping well and he apparently had issues with frustration and anger (Burke, 2019).

Ernest Moore

Age/race-ethnicity: 25/Unk

Victims: 4 dead, 1 wounded

Place/number of locations: Cameron County, Texas/2

Date/duration: July 7, 1988/1 hour

Weapon: firearm

Moore fatally shot a mother and daughter in a predawn attack at their home, allegedly for harboring his former girlfriend. He then ambushed law officers searching for him, killing two border patrol agents. Moore was shot four times and was hospitalized, where he later died.

Jon Frederick Thanos

Age/race-ethnicity: 41/Unk

Victims: 3 dead, 1 wounded

Place/number of locations: Worcester and Baltimore Counties, Maryland/3

Date/duration: August 31–September 2, 1990/3 days

Weapon: firearm

On Friday afternoon, August 31, Thanos kidnapped a cab driver in Salisbury, stuffed the driver in the trunk, and drove around for several hours before abandoning the vehicle. Later, he hitchhiked along Route 50 when a high school student picked him up. Thanos took the student into the woods and shot him to take his car. The next day, Thanos wounded a clerk at a convenience store and killed a couple at a gas station. Police chased and arrested him. He told police, "I'm miserable and I want to die, but I don't have the wherewithal to do it myself. I wanted to get in a running gun battle with police." When asked why he had killed the others, Thanos replied, "I'm pissed off at the world." At his trial, he taunted his victims' families by saying he wanted to dig up their bodies and defile them.

Alan Winterbourne

Age/race-ethnicity: 33/Caucasian

Victims: 4 dead, 5 wounded

Place/number of locations: Oxnard, California/2

Date/duration: December 2, 1993/1 hour

Weapon: firearm

Frustrated with an extended failed job search, Winterborne went on a shooting rampage at the unemployment office. After a police chase, he killed one of the officers. He died in the shootout.

James Rodney Johnson

Age/race-ethnicity: 42/Caucasian

Victims: 4 dead, 1 wounded

Place/number of locations: Cooper and Moniteau Counties, Missouri/3

Date/duration: December 8–9, 1991/2 hours

Weapon: firearm

Johnson argued with his wife and adult daughter. He forcibly took his daughter from the house at gunpoint but soon returned. His wife had called for help. Deputy Sheriff Roark responded and contacted Johnson, who shot him. Johnson then left the house and drove to the residence of County Sheriff K. Jones and fired multiple shots through his front window, striking his wife. Johnson then went to the home of Sheriff Borts and shot him four times, but Borts survived. Johnson then went to the Moniteau County Sheriff's Office. When officers ran out to respond to the attack on Borts, Johnson killed Sheriff Charles Smith and Deputy Sheriff Sandra Wilson. Johnson escaped and hid at a local residence where he held the residents hostage until he was arrested.

Mitchell Carlton Sims and Ruby Padgett

Age/race-ethnicity: 25, 20/Caucasian

Victims: 3 dead, 2 injured, more intended

Place/number of locations: Hanahan, South Carolina, Glendale, California/2

Date/duration: December 3/10, 1985/1 week

Weapon: firearm

Terminated from a Domino's Restaurant, Sims developed an abiding hatred against the chain. He hooked up with Ruby Padgett, 5 years his junior, and invaded the pizza parlor that had let him go. They held two employees at gunpoint and tortured both before Sims shot them, execution-style. One survived long enough to reach a police station. Sims and Padgett drove to California. On December 10, Sims ordered a Domino's pizza from his motel room. Deliveryman John Harrington was stripped, gagged with a washcloth, and drowned in the bathtub. Sims wore the dead man's uniform when he returned to the restaurant, looted its safe, and left two employees locked in the freezer, bound in a way that forced them to stand on tiptoe to avoid hanging themselves. They survived. Sims and Padgett had traveled to Las Vegas to pick their next target but were arrested in the delivery driver's car.

Tim Kretschmer

Age/race-ethnicity: 17/Caucasian

Victims: 15 dead, 9 wounded

Place/number of locations: Winnenden, Germany/5+

Date/duration: March 11, 2009/3 hours

Weapon: firearm

Ended in suicide

Dressed in black camouflage gear, Kretschmer burst into his former high school in Winnenden, Germany, brandishing a 9-mm Beretta he'd stolen from his father's gun collection. In one classroom, he shot five students in the head. In the next classroom, he killed two more and wounded nine (two later died). He moved on to the Chemistry laboratory where he killed the teacher. When police arrived, Kretschmer fled, killing two teachers as he exited. Leaving campus, he killed a caretaker at a nearby psychiatric hospital. He remained under the radar for several hours before forcing a man to drive him 25 miles to a Volkswagen car showroom, where he killed a salesman and a customer. He fired multiple times at the police who'd followed him, wounding two. When an officer shot him in the leg, he shot himself in the head, recording the whole thing on his phone. Krestschmer had been treated in a psychiatric facility for depression. A former friend described him as lonely, frustrated, and feeling rejected.

Christo Brian Fortune

Age/race-ethnicity: 31/Caucasian

Victims: 4 dead, 9 wounded

Place/number of locations: Postmasburg, South Africa/multiple

Date/duration: July 1, 2002/Unk (1–2 hours)

Weapon: firearm

Fortune, a Postmasburg police officer, went on a random shooting spree in 2002. Drunk one night, he argued with his wife over her intent to divorce him and her perceived infidelity. He was also unemployed and highly stressed. He hit his wife and attempted to strangle her. She broke free and ran with their three children. Leaving, he threatened a police officer with a knife to acquire firearms from a safe, taking three. He then randomly shot people in the streets and in a shop, a grocery, and a tavern. He hijacked two cars and killed a driver. Police arrested him after a shootout.

Woo Bum-Kon

Age/race-ethnicity: 27/Asian

Victims: 56 dead, 35 wounded

Place/number of locations: South Gyeongsang Province, South Korea/ multiple

Date/duration: April 26, 1982/10 hours

Weapon: grenades, firearms

Ended in suicide

Woo had an argument with his live-in girlfriend, Chun Mal-soon, on April 26, 1982, after she swatted a fly on his chest. Enraged, he left the house and went to the police station in Pusa, South Korea, where he reported for duty. He began drinking heavily. He went home at 7:30 p.m., beating his girlfriend before going to the reservists' armory to gather weapons. Two hours later, Woo shot his first victim and entered the local post office, where he killed three more. He next went to Torongni, where he threw a grenade and shot at passers-by, killing six. He proceeded from village to village, exploiting his position as a police officer to gain entry to the houses. He killed several people in a marketplace before making his way toward Pyongchon-Ni, where he killed more families. In one home, he killed 18 people who were attending a wake. He took hostages when police arrived, killing them and himself with two grenades.

Wang Xiwen

Age/race-ethnicity: 32/Asian

Victims: 7 dead, 12 wounded

Place/number of locations: Hadan, China/4+

Date/duration: November 17, 1980/6 hours

Weapon: firearms, grenades

Xiwen was a police officer in the Handan municipal public security sub bureau. He lost out on a promotion because he and his wife did not adhere to the family planning policy. In the evening of November 17, 1980, he broke into the office of the director, pried open a drawer, and stole a pistol and ammunition. Subsequently, he broke into the armory and took a light machine gun, eight rifles, 28 hand grenades, and 2,700 rounds of ammunition. For the next 6 hours he paced through the streets of Handan, shooting people, and throwing grenades. When he was finally arrested, police realized he'd shot 460 rounds and detonated 26 grenades.

REFERENCES

Burke, M. (2019, February 5). Michigan Uber driver who murdered 6 people in shooting rampage sentenced to life in prison. *NBC News.* Retrieved from https://www.nbcnews.com/news/us-news/michigan-uber-driver-who-murdered-6-people-shooting-rampage-sentenced-n967231

Chen, E. (1995). *Deadly scholarship: The true story of Lu Gang and mass murder in America's heartland.* New York, NY: Birch Lane Press.

Dorner, C. (2013, February 4). To America (manifesto). Retrieved from https://web.archive.org/web/20130227045151/http://laist.com/2013/02/07/christopher_dorners_manifesto_in_fu.php

Mann, J. (1992, June 7). The physics of revenge. *The Los Angeles Times.*

Marshall, B., & Williams, P. (1991). *Zero at the bone.* New York, NY: Pocket.

Reinhardt, J. M. (1960). *The murderous trail of Charles Starkweather.* Springfield, IL: Charles C. Thomson.

Worden, A. (2011, March 26). Mass murderer judged unfit for execution. *Philadelphia Inquirer.*

CHAPTER 3

On a Mission

Mission killers have a sense of purpose for their rampages, sometimes clearly articulated but sometimes disjointed and delusional. Although there are many different motives for mission-based murder, we subcategorize the nature of these motives as psychotic and nonpsychotic. The former involves a major psychiatric disorder, according to criteria in *The Diagnostic and Statistical Manual of Mental Disorders* (fifth edition), and the latter is usually a hate-inspired crime or an act of terror, often viewed by the killer as a noble cause. Some sprees arise from a group mission, but most mission spree killers are lone agents who act out what they imagine is consistent with a certain ideology or goal.

We start with the psychotic mission killers, who show a wider range of reasons for their violent assaults. Longer case summaries display the development of the mission, while the brief summaries identify other spree killers who fit these categories.

Total: 31 cases, 38 killers

Psychotic: 13 cases, 18 killers

Nonpsychotic: 18 cases, 20 killers

MISSION: PSYCHOTIC

Psychotic disorders comprise a cluster of severe mental conditions characterized by specific symptoms, such as impairments of thought or mood. These conditions involve the ability to respond appropriately, comprehend reality as others know it, behave appropriately, and make oneself understood. Several different conditions can display psychotic symptoms, such as severe depression, bipolar disorder, schizophrenia, some forms of borderline personality disorder, and some types of substance abuse or exposure to environmental toxins. A person with psychotic symptoms such as fixed delusions and hallucinations cannot function well in daily life. They may adopt a suspicious and hostile manner. Delusions of paranoia or grandiosity may trigger acting out against others, especially when coupled with auditory command hallucinations. In many cases, the delusions have a religious or ideological context, triggering crimes of hate, punishment, or elimination (American Psychiatric Association, 2013).

Paranoid schizophrenia appears to be implicated most often in violence, especially reactive or defensive. Typically developing during adolescence or early adulthood, this perceptual and thinking disorder can have positive or negative symptoms. Hallucinations, disorganized thinking, and delusions show up as "positive" manifestations, such as auditory commands, and "negative" symptoms such as diminished emotions and life engagement. Delusions that form as paranoid beliefs can trigger violence. Sometimes these individuals fail to recognize their illness, a condition called anosognosia, and thus seek no treatment. They might also have an accompanying major mood disorder, such as depression, which becomes schizoaffective disorder. Schizophrenia affects 1–2% of the population (Levy, Kelly, & Ray, 2018).

Delusional disorders, overlapping schizophrenia, are somewhat different and can show up in either psychotic or nonpsychotic mission killers. Developing later in life, delusions are characterized by one or more false beliefs. To be merely a delusional disorder rather than schizophrenia, the beliefs must be non-bizarre, i.e., the imagined situation or condition might conceivably occur. These individuals appear to function normally, but if the subject of their delusion comes up, they show an abnormally passionate attachment to it (Levy et al., 2018). For example, a person laid off from a job might attach a motive, such as racism or genderism, which has no basis in fact. This person might then decide that all of his subsequent bad luck is connected to the person who made the lay-off decision. The delusion might become more elaborate, with the employer being in league with some larger agency such that the delusional individual's future employment in any other similar workplace is in jeopardy. This belief in a broader conspiracy can become paralyzing and lead to a sense of helplessness that launches an act of reactive or preemptive violence.

Besides these chronic conditions, an individual might have a brief psychotic disorder for reactive psychosis, which involves a sudden onset of hallucinations, delusions, and speech disorganization. In addition, someone in the manic phase of a bipolar disorder can also trigger a violent attack, although it is rare. So can exposure to certain types of environmental toxins. However, paranoid schizophrenia is present in most of the psychotic mission killers on our list.

Richard Trenton Chase

Age/race-ethnicity: 28/Caucasian

Victims: 6 dead

Place/number of locations: Sacramento, CA/3

Date/duration: December 29, 1977–January 27, 1978/1 month

Weapon: rifle, handgun, knife

Mission: need to treat an imagined physical disorder

Weapons: rifle, handgun, bludgeoning

Often categorized as a serial killer, given the sense of desperation in his disorder, Chase's crimes had a spree quality. He'd suffered for years from paranoid schizophrenia with somatic delusions. Having been institutionalized, he was on supervised released, but his parents had failed to act as his guardians. His mother said he scared her. Unsupervised, he killed animals and humans to alleviate his imagined conditions. He once had entered an emergency room to find the person who had "stolen" his pulmonary artery. He'd also complained to doctors that the bones were coming out through the back of his head.

Chase began to catch and torture cats, dogs, and rabbits, killing them to drink their blood. Arming himself, on December 29, 1977, he tried out his new rifle on a man in the neighborhood who was unloading his car. On January 23, 1978, he walked into the home of Teresa Wallin, who was 3 months pregnant. He shot her twice and dragged her body into a bedroom. Using a knife, he cut her open and removed several body parts. Then he retrieved a yogurt container from the trash to fill with her blood so he could drink it.

On January 27, Chase entered another home, where he murdered Evelyn Miroth, her male friend, and her 6-year-old son. Chase grabbed her infant son from his cradle, smashed the boy's head, and took the body. At home, he consumed some of its organs.

The police closed in and arrested him. In prison, he told another inmate that he needed the blood of his victims because he had blood poisoning and he'd grown tired of hunting for animals to use their blood. He drank other people's blood, he claimed, because he feared that his was disintegrating (Ressler & Schachtman, 1992).

Chase was convicted of six counts of first-degree murder and given a death sentence. He died in December 1980 from an intentional drug overdose.

Herbert Mullin

Age/race-ethnicity: 25/Caucasian

Victims: 13 dead

Place/number of locations: Santa Cruz, California/7

Date/duration: October 13,1972–February 13, 1973/4 months

Weapon: bat, firearms, knife

Mission: agentic: paranoid ideology about saving California with human sacrifice

The body of an adult male was found on October 13, 1972, lying off a road outside town. The victim was a vagrant known as Lawrence "Whitey" White. Someone had bludgeoned him to death.

The perpetrator would turn out to be Herbert Mullin, who would insist that the killing was necessary and also voluntary: White had agreed to become a human sacrifice for a greater good. As a modern-day Jonah, Mullin's goal involved 13 "willing sacrifices" that would protect California from a massive natural disaster. He also killed a hitchhiker and a priest, believing he had halted an earthquake that a self-styled prognosticator had recently predicted.

For several months, Mullin had unsuccessfully tried to enlist in the Marines, believing that he could more easily kill the number of people he needed to complete his task. Then he thought of someone who really *should* die: Jim Gianera, a high school acquaintance who'd introduced him to drugs. Between Gianera and his wife, and three people who lived in Gianera's former home, Mullin killed five. He believed he needed just five more.

His next opportunity arrived on February 1, 1973. He hiked into Henry Cowell State Park and saw a plastic-covered hut where he knew no one was permitted to camp. He returned the following day, confronting four adolescent boys who defied him. He fatally shot them all. That made 12.

On February 13, Mullin allegedly heard his father's voice order him to kill, so he went out and shot the first person he saw: Fred Perez, 72, a former professional boxer. This time, there was a witness and Mullin was arrested. In his mind, however, he had accomplished his mission.

In Mullin's apartment, police found a biography of Albert Einstein, a Bible, a coat missing a button like the button found at the Gianeras' house, and news clippings about the recent murders. A pistol from Mullin's car proved to be one murder weapon and a rifle in his possession proved to be another. More evidence implicated him until a strong case could be made against him for most of the murders.

Raised Catholic, Mullin had been a normal child. He had done well in school and played sports. When the family had moved to Santa Cruz, Mullin found a girlfriend, met Jim Gianera, and developed a strong friendship with Dean Richardson.

During the summer of 1965, just after high school graduation, Dean was killed in a car accident. This incident seemed to have been a factor in Chase's developing mental illness. During a stint in college, he studied Eastern religions and renounced his Catholic faith. Then he dropped out and dabbled with drugs. In 1969, Mullin was diagnosed with schizophrenia. However, under new laws that favored civil rights, he'd been able to leave treatment.

Mullin claimed to believe that certain actions that could prevent mass natural disasters would ensure for him an elevated reincarnated life. He said the main reason for his killing spree had been to prevent a catastrophic earthquake. He'd hear a command hallucination in his father's voice, urging him to kill, and became obsessed with charts about birth and death rates. Each person who died, he believed, protected millions of others. Mullin viewed himself as God's chosen one to save the people of California. He would "sing the die song," which he thought had persuaded 13 people to either kill themselves or allow themselves to be killed (Lunde & Morgan, 1980).

Mullin was found guilty of several counts of first-degree and second-degree murder. He remains incarcerated in prison in California, having been denied parole 10 times.

Dawn Godman, Glen Helzer, Justin Helzer

Age/race-ethnicity: 30, 28, 26/Caucasian

Victims: 3 dead

Place/number of locations: Concord, CA/2

Date/duration: July 30, 2000/5 days

Weapon: knife/hammer

Mission: agentic, religious ("Children of Thunder")

An ambitious mission formed among three people in California in 2000. Stockbroker Glenn Taylor Helzer, 33, felt guided to raise $1 million to fund a group called "Transform America" that would open the door to Christ's return to Earth. During manic phases of his bipolar disorder, Helzer expected to also take over the Mormon Church. He enlisted his brother, Justin, and a young woman, Dawn Godman, whom they had met at a murder mystery event, to play parts in his "Children of Thunder" plan. They all moved into a house together in Concord.

Helzer had identified people from among his former clients from whom he could steal the funds. Because he expected to eliminate them afterward, he purchased three Rottweilers to consume the remains. The group launched the plan on July 30, 2000.

The brothers kidnapped Annette and Ivan Stineman. Glenn forced them to take Rohypnol and sign over checks for $100,000. According to Godman, who cut a deal with prosecutors, the brothers tried to suffocate the couple, but they fought back. Glenn cut Annette's throat while his brother smashed Ivan's head against the floor. They dismembered the bodies.

Selena Bishop, 22-year-old daughter of a Blues musician, was dating Glenn. She innocently deposited the checks. Then Glenn and Justin bludgeoned her to death with a hammer before dismembering her. The next morning, Glenn fatally shot Bishop's mother and the mother's boyfriend. Godman told police after the trio's arrest that she had held the three severed heads while Justin smashed the teeth with a hammer and a chisel.

This killing trio then put the body parts into nine black duffel bags and dumped them in the Mokelumne River. One by one, the bags rose to the surface and were turned over to police. A woman who'd initially provided an alibi for the Helzers and kept their weapons in a safe finally told police. All three were convicted and the Helzers were given the death penalty. Godman got a lighter sentence. Justin committed suicide in 2013.

Christopher Bryan Speight

Age/race-ethnicity: 40/Caucasian

Victims: 8 dead

Place/number of locations: Appomattox, Virginia/3

Date/duration: January 19–20, 2010/2 days

Weapon: firearm

Mission: agentic: service to a higher power

The incident began on January 19, 2010, when police were called to a road outside Appomattox on a report of a man who required medical attention. When police arrived, security guard Christopher Bryan Speight shot at them and fled to a wooded area. Police found Speight's sister and her husband and son shot dead in a house. Four other people lay dead outside, with a final victim on the road. Speight surrendered on January 20.

Speight was found to be incompetent to stand trial. He told the court that Jennifer, an Egyptian goddess, had ordered him to shoot his family to get rid of demons. He had killed the others to prevent them from saving his target victims, because Jennifer had demanded that their bodies must decompose. Speight had shot the three Sipes in the house 2 days before killing the others, who had apparently arrived to help. In a plea deal on February 15, 2013, Speight was sentenced to five life terms. His mental condition made him ineligible for the death penalty.

Jennifer San Marco

Age/race-ethnicity: 44/Caucasian

Victims: 8 dead

Place/number of locations: Goleta, California/3

Date/duration: January 30, 2006/less than 3 hours

Weapon: firearm

Mission: hate; self-defense against an imagined conspiracy

Ended with suicide

In 2006, Jennifer San Marco passed through a security station to enter the mail processing plant building where she had formerly worked. She had just killed a former neighbor in another location. Armed with a 9-mm Smith & Wesson pistol, she took an employee's badge. She shot two people in the car park before entering the building to shoot four more. The she turned the gun on herself, ending her life. San Marco was suffering from paranoid schizophrenia and she also had held a grudge against minority workers at the post office for over two years, whom she believed had conspired against her.

Susan Atkins, Patricia Krenwinkle, Leslie van Houten, Charles "Tex" Watson

Age/race-ethnicity: 21, 22, 20, 23/Caucasian

Victims: 7 dead, plus an unborn child

Place/number of locations: Los Angeles, California/2

Date/duration: August 8–9,1969/2 days

Weapon: knives

Mission: agentic, groupmind manipulation, noble cause

On July 27, Charles Manson directed three of his followers to kill musician Gary Hinman for not turning over his assets to the group. They stabbed him to death and wrote "Political piggy" on a wall. When Bobby Beausoleil was arrested on August 6 in Hinman's stolen car, Manson announced to his "family" of followers the start of his Helter Skelter revolution. Inspired by the Beatles' song, he had preached that blacks would rise up to massacre whites and reclaim the earth.

During the night of Saturday, August 8, at the home of film director Roman Polanski, Manson's disciples slaughtered five people in a blood-drenched spree, including Polanski's 8-months-pregnant wife, Sharon Tate.

The next evening, August 9, they entered the home of Leno and Rosemary LaBianca, stabbing both to death. The killers had carved "War" into Leno's chest and used his blood to write "Death to Pigs," "Rise," and "Healter Skelter [sic]" on the walls.

In October, Susan Atkins bragged in jail about her involvement. This led the police to her associates, an odd collection of unemployed hippies living on Spahn ranch outside Los Angeles, led by Charles Manson. It became clear that Manson had urged his followers to go on a killing spree, telling them to make it look like the job of black militants. Some of his followers claimed to believe his notion that he was Christ.

Prosecutor Vince Bugliosi made the case that Manson was the group mastermind. The jury convicted Manson, Atkins, and Krenwinkel of seven counts of first-degree murder. Leslie Van Houten was convicted on two counts. In a separate trial, Watson was convicted for his part.

This case straddles psychotic and nonpsychotic, but the delusional nature of Manson's ideas, along with his extreme methods of brainwashing to form his band into a group-mind before he sent them to kill, places their acts into the psychotic category. However, the jury decided that they knew what they were doing.

Michel Hayes

Age/race-ethnicity: 26/Caucasian

Victims: 4 dead, 5 wounded

Place/number of locations: Salem-Winston, NC/9 (one location over time)

Date/duration: July 17, 1988/45 minutes

Weapon: firearm

Mission: kill demons

With a history of bullying, substance abuse, and petty crime, Hayes annoyed his parents so much that they threatened to withdraw their financial support. Angry, he shot nine people in front of their moped shop in 45 minutes, killing four. Under arrest, he said he had believed the people were demons that he had to kill. Hayes' attorneys convinced a jury that he was psychotic at the time of the killings, as he had been diagnosed with antisocial personality disorder and schizophrenia. Winning an insanity acquittal, Hayes was committed to a psychiatric institution. He was released in 2012.

Louis D. Hastings

Age/race-ethnicity: 39/Caucasian

Victims: 6 dead, 2 wounded

Place/number of locations: Glennallen, Alaska/2

Date/duration: March 1, 1983/1 hour

Weapon: firearm

Mission: interrupt the population growth and save the Alaskan wilderness

An unemployed computer programmer, Hastings moved to Alaska in 1980. There, his business and marriage failed. He withdrew. Frustrated with the growth in population from the trans-Alaska pipeline, he began to plan an attack. He wanted to destroy the pipeline and block more people from coming. He planned it for when the daily mail was flown in. Most residents usually went to greet the plane, he knew. He planned to shoot them all and hijack the plane to go destroy the pipeline with a fuel truck, which would kill him as well. He figured that, with everyone dead and his body burned, no one would know that he had been the killer. It did not go as planned, but he did kill several people at the airstrip and some in a nearby house.

Shi Yuejun

Age/race-ethnicity: 37/Asian

Victims: 13 dead, 4 wounded

Place/Number of locations: China/5

Date and duration: September 24–29, 2006/5 days

Weapon: knife

Mission: revenge against everyone who had humiliated him

Yuejun had a list of people whom he had decided had humiliated him. On the morning of September 24, 2006, he drove to Ermi in Tonghua County where he killed five people and wounded one. He moved on to another county, where he killed a shop owner who had once refused to sell his meat. He wounded the man's wife, as well as a man who had paid him low wages. In another town, he killed two more men and wounded a woman. Police went after him, setting up roadblocks. On 27 September, Yujun murdered another couple before moving into another area to kill on the morning of September 29. He was eventually captured. Yuejun was said to have had serious psychological problems

Christian Dornier

Age/race-ethnicity: 30/Caucasian

Victims: 15 dead/7 wounded

Place/number of locations: Luxiol, France/2

Date/duration: July 12, 1989/half an hour

Weapon: firearm

Mission: payback, family annihilation

Dornier fatally shot a man who had come to inspect cattle on his family's farm. Then he shot his father and sister. His father managed to run for help, but Dornier pursued and shot him again. When he came back, his mother was calling the police, so he killed her. Having annihilated his family, Dornier drove into the village and shot people at random. Finally, he was stopped. Found to be suffering from schizophrenia, he was sent to a psychiatric institution. Although he offered no motive for his sudden violence, police discovered that his father had decided against giving him the farm, due to his unstable behavior.

Marcello Palma

Age/race-ethnicity: 33/Caucasian

Victims: 3 killed

Place/number of locations: Toronto, Canada/3

Date/duration: May 20, 1996/2 hours

Weapon: firearm

Mission: revenge against prostitutes

The spree began with the murder of a prostitute who apparently had argued with Palma. Later, two more were shot on different corners. The same gun was used in all three murders. The perpetrator turned out to be a successful, married businessman who was under a psychiatrist's care and had repeatedly threatened to kill himself. He had also been having sexual contact with prostitutes, including males and transvestites. He was arrested on June 1 without incident. He pleaded not guilty by reason of insanity. He'd once revealed a violent hatred of prostitutes to a psychiatrist. He'd selected Victoria Day because he thought fireworks would mask his gunshots. He was found guilty.

Denis Lortie

Age/race-ethnicity: 59/Caucasian

Victims: 3 killed, 13 wounded

Place/number of locations: Quebec City, Quebec, Canada/3

Date/duration: May 8, 1984/4 hours

Weapon: firearms

Mission: destroy the government

On May 7, 1984, Lortie left the CFS Carp military base, pretending that he needed time off to arrange a divorce. Instead, he rented a car to drive to Quebec City and take a tour of the Parliament Building. The next day at 9:30 a.m., Lortie walked into CJRP radio station, identified himself as "Mr. D," and dropped off a sealed envelope with an audiotape for a host. He told them not to open it until 10:30, but they ignored him and discovered his plan of violence. Lortie entered the Parliament Building dressed in combat fatigues. He shot and mortally wounded a receptionist, then killed a messenger in the corridor. Lortie entered a smoking room and wounded a person inside before he found the location of the Assembly Chamber. However, instead of looking at his watch for the start of the 10 a.m. meeting, Lortie timed his attack by listening to the radio. He waited for the station's host, André Arthur, to end his segment. But due to Lortie's envelope, he ended his broadcast 20 minutes early, so the chamber was mostly empty. Lortie killed two and wounded 11 others, but he was unable to assassinate his intended targets.

The National Assembly's Sergeant-at-arms faced off with Lortie and persuaded him to talk. At 2:15 p.m., Lortie surrendered to officers of the SQ, Quebec City Police, and the National Assembly security. According to psychiatrist Pierre Mailloux, Lortie suffered from paranoid schizophrenia and had organized his crime during a psychotic episode, believing that he was acting on instructions given to him from God.

Daniel Gonzalez

Age/race-ethnicity: 25/biracial Caucasian and Hispanic

Victims: 4 dead, 2 wounded

Place/number of locations: Woking and Tottenham, England/5

Date/duration: September 2004/3 days

Weapon: knife

Mission: to become a famous serial killer

In September 2004, at the age of 25, Gonzalez decided to "become a famous serial killer" after viewing the horror films, *A Nightmare on Elm Stree*t and *Friday the 13th*. He told police he was walking the streets with a knife, looking for the opportunity to "carve up someone." He confronted 61-year-old Peter King, who was walking his dog with his wife. King fought him off. Later that day, Gonzalez headed up to Woking near London. Wearing a hockey mask like the character Jason Voorhees, he fatally stabbed Marie Harding, as she was walking home.

On September 16, Gonzales traveled to Tottenham, where he drank for hours. At 5:30 a.m., he used two stolen knives to kill Kevin Molloy. An hour later, he broke into a house and wounded Koumis Constantino. He tried again in Highgate, entering the home of an elderly couple, Derek and Jean Robinson, stabbing them both to death. When someone called the police after seeing Gonzales naked and covered in blood, he was arrested. Convicted, he received life in prison. He wrote about his experiences in letters to himself, saying that his brief rampage was "one of the best things I've done in my life." A year after his conviction, he committed suicide.

MISSION: NONPSYCHOTIC

Some spree killers develop a mission based on an ideology that justifies murder via the idea that they are serving a higher cause. They think that only violence will bring attention to the cause or they believe that the first act of violence will inspire others to rise up and follow their example, inciting a widespread rebellion. This is often in the service of a religious belief or a political ideology. Some spree killers merely act from hate, targeting a specific group for punishment and elimination. Delusional elements are present, but not to the grandiose degree that we see in the psychotic killers. Yet their beliefs can be elaborate and extreme.

Elliot Rodger

Age/race-ethnicity: 22/biracial – Caucasian and Malaysian

Victims: 6 dead, 14 wounded

Place/number of locations: Isla Vista, California/8

Date/duration: May 23, 2014/4 hours

Weapons: knives, firearms, car

Mission: punishment for perceived wrongs

Ended in suicide

Elliot Rodger used YouTube to air his grievances and make angry threats. On May 23, 2014, he went into action. First, he fatally stabbed his two male roommates and a friend of theirs. He went out to get coffee before uploading his final video and emailing his 107,000-word manifesto, "My Twisted World." He planned to knock on the door of the Alpha Phi sorority at the University of California at Santa Barbara, and, once inside, kill the women. However, when he arrived, no one answered the door. He shot and killed two female students outside, wounding another. Frustrated, he drove down the road, firing into shops, including the Isla Vista Deli Mart, killing a man inside. Then Rodger raced through town, shooting at people or ramming them with his car. Responding officers wounded him, and the violent spree ended when Rodger crashed into a parked vehicle and shot himself in the head.

Despite growing up with privilege as the son of a successful British filmmaker, Rodger had been angry over his lack of success with a certain type of woman who would have given him status. Since the age of eight, Rodger had seen multiple therapists and was receiving psychiatric care. From his writings, it appeared that he'd been planning the attack for a year.

During the investigation, it came out that on April 30, 2014, Rodger's parents had asked the police to make a welfare check after they'd seen his earlier YouTube rantings. Officers had gone to his apartment, but he'd convinced them him he was fine.

Rodger's last video had captured his mood:

> It all has to come to this. Tomorrow is the day of retribution, the day in which I will have my revenge against humanity, against all of you. For the last eight years of my life, ever since I hit puberty, I've been forced to endure an existence of loneliness, rejection, and unfulfilled desires all because girls have never been attracted to me. Girls gave their affection, and sex and love to other men but never to me. I'm 22 years old and I'm still a virgin. I've never even kissed a girl. I've been through college for two and a half years, more than that actually, and I'm still a virgin. It has been very torturous. College is the time when everyone experiences those things such as sex and fun and pleasure. Within those years, I've had to rot in loneliness. It's not fair. You girls have never been attracted to me. I don't know why you girls aren't attracted to me, but I will punish you all for it. It's an injustice, a crime, because ... I don't know what you don't see in me. I'm the perfect guy and yet you throw yourselves at these obnoxious men instead of me, the supreme gentleman.

In his manifesto, Rodger had stated that in his "War on Women," he "will attack the very girls who represent everything I hate in the female gender: The hottest sorority of UCSB." He wanted to "quarantine all [women] in concentration camps. At these camps, the vast majority of the female population will be deliberately starved to death. That would be an efficient and fitting way to kill them all off." Then he planned to kill his mother and half-brother. He'd despised his Malayasian mother for preventing him from being an elite white man.

Rodger had referred to an "Incel" rebellion arising from an Internet-based group of disgruntled males who called themselves "Involuntary Celibates." The Incels build community by reinforcing their anger, resentment, and entitlement. Women, they think, should not be free to make their own sexual choices. This only contributes to the social oppression that they view as their lot. They are "subhumans," viewing themselves as "beta males" instead of "alpha males," because the social system is supposedly rigged against them. Some adhere to an elaborate sociological explanation for their failure in which these women ("Stacys") are attracted only to hyper-muscular males ("Chads"). Because it is not their fault that genetics has disadvantaged them, they find this situation unjust and they blame women. "Society has become a place for worship of females," one incel member wrote on a message board, "and it's fucking wrong, they're not Gods they are just a fucking cum-dumpster."

Rodger's example has inspired other violent incidents. Alek Minassian killed 10 people and injured 16 by driving a van down a busy street in Toronto. He had pledged allegiance to the "Incel Rebellion." He apparently believed that his attack would trigger a massive wave of similar assaults. In Tallahassee, Florida on November 3, 2018, 40-year-old disgruntled military veteran Scott Paul Beierle entered a yoga studio, shooting six people and pistol-whipping a seventh. Two died. Beierle then killed himself. He, too, had aligned with Elliot Rodger.

Marc Lépine

Age/race-ethnicity: 25/Caucasian

Victims: 14 dead, 16 wounded

Place/number of locations: Montreal, Canada/4

Date/duration: December 6, 1989/30 minutes

Weapons: firearms, knife

Mission: hate ideology, anti-feminist

Ended in suicide

Lépine went to the École Polytechnique, the engineering school at the University of Montreal, to make his political statement and exact his revenge for a lifetime filled with anger, pain, and failure. Beaten by his father, he nevertheless accepted his father's view that women were second-class. He was unprepared for a world in which women were getting educated, acquiring opportunities, and becoming independent. He began to feel as if women were pushing him out of his own rightful opportunities. Someone, he believed, had to teach them a lesson and he decided that it would be him.

His plan took months, but his long-standing hatred held him to it. He purchased a Ruger semiautomatic Mini-14.223-caliber rifle and a banana clip loadable to 30 rounds. Weapons gave Lépine a feeling of confidence and power. Through his readings he had become acquainted with the tale of Corporal Denis Lortie (described above), who'd killed three government employees and wounded 13.

In 1986, Lépine had been rejected by the École Polytechnique. He'd let his financial resources run out. He was ready to die and wrote a long suicide note. He wanted to die a political death, a sacrifice in the name of killing as many feminists as he could, to show other women their place.

"Because I decided to send *Ad Patres* [to the fathers] the feminists who have always ruined my life," he jotted in this letter. "For seven years my life has brought me no joy, and being utterly weary of the world, I have decided to stop those shrews dead in their tracks." It came out later that he had made a list of 19 women mentioned in newspapers whom he wanted to target.

Lépine shaved his head in preparation and dressed in a shirt that featured a skull design. He strapped on a hunting knife and grabbed his new rifle. His target was the École Polytechnique.

Just after 5:00 p.m., he went to a classroom in which 60 students had gathered for a lecture. He ordered the students to separate into male and female groups. He told the men to leave and cornered the nine women, killing six. Striding through the halls, Lépine shot at people. He took the stairs down to the first-floor cafeteria, shooting diners and killing several.

Lépine went to the third floor via a broken escalator, where he shot a woman, entered another classroom, and killed more female students there. When one young woman begged for help, he plunged his hunting knife into her chest. Then, he used the rifle to kill himself (Weston & Aubry, 1990).

Tamerlan Tsarnaev and Dzhokbar Tsarnaev

Age/race-ethnicity: 26 and 25/Caucasian

Victims: 5 dead, 280 injured

Place/number of locations:/3

Date/duration: April 15–18, 2013/3 days

Weapon: pressure cooker bombs, firearm

Mission: terrorism

The 117th annual Boston Marathon was run on Patriots' Day, April 15, 2013. At 2:49 p.m. two bombs detonated about 210 yards apart at the finish line on Boylston Street near Copley Square. The explosions killed three civilians and injured an estimated 280 others. On April 18, the Tsarnaev brothers fatally shot Sean A. Collier of the MITPD in a failed attempt to steal his gun. Early on April 19, Tamerlan was killed after a carjacking brought police. Dzhokbar drove the car over his brother and fled. BPD officer Dennis Simmonds received hand-grenade injuries, from which he eventually died. That evening, a Watertown resident noticed that the tarp was loose on his parked boat. He saw a body lying inside the boat in a pool of blood. A police helicopter verified movement with thermal imaging. The figure inside poked at the tarp, drawing police fire. Dzhokbar was arrested and tried. Convicted, he was sentenced to death. He had said that he and his brother were going to next hit Times Square in Manhattan. Tamerlan was also implicated in a triple homicide in 2011 in Waltham, Massachusetts.

Mark James Robert Essex

Age/race-ethnicity: 23/Black

Victims: 9 dead, 13 wounded

Place/number of locations: New Orleans, Louisiana/2

Date/duration: January 7, 1973/10 hours

Weapon: firearm

Mission: hate ideology

In New Orleans, on January 7, 1973, former sailor-turned-black-radical Mark Essex started shooting. The siege lasted 10 hours and was racially motivated. It followed an attack he had made on police headquarters on New Year's Eve, fatally wounding a cadet and killing another officer. He told a bystander he wanted to shoot white cops. On January 7, Essex shot a grocer and fled in a stolen car. Moving through the Howard Johnson Hotel on Loyola, he set fires on several floors and shot first responders. Police killed Essex at the scene.

Richard Baumhammers

Age/race-ethnicity: 34/Caucasian

Victims: 5 dead, 1 wounded

Place/number of locations: Pittsburgh, Pennsylvania/4

Date/duration: April 4, 2000/2 hours

Weapon: firearm

Mission: hate ideology

At 1:30 p.m., Baumhammers walked to the home of his next-door neighbor in Pittsburgh, a 63-year-old Jewish woman named Anita "Nicki" Gordon and fatally shot her before setting her house on fire. An immigration attorney with delusional ideas about immigrants, Baumhammers drove to the Beth El Congregation in Scott Township, where Gordon, a friend of his parents, had been a member. He fired into the windows of the synagogue, then spray-painted two red swastikas on the building. A short distance from the synagogue at the India Grocer in Scott Town Center, he shot 31-year-old Anil Thakur and store manager Sandeep Patel, paralyzing him. Baumhammers next drove to the Ahavath Achim Congregation in Carnegie where he shot out the synagogue's glass windows. At Robinson Town Center, about 10 miles from his home, he walked into Ya Fei Chinese Cuisine and fatally shot Chinese restaurant manager Ji-ye Sun and Theo "Tony" Pham, a Vietnamese American cook. Baumhammers ended at the C.S. Kim School of Karate in Center Township, where Garry Lee, a 22-year-old African-American was exercising with a friend, George Thomas II. Baumhammers initially pointed the gun at Thomas, but turned and killed Lee. Reportedly, Baumhammers had hoped to form a political party to act against immigrants. He viewed Oklahoma City bomber Timothy McVeigh and Adolf Hitler as his heroes.

Nidal Hasan

Age/race-ethnicity: 48/Caucasian

Victims: 13 dead, 32 wounded

Place/number of locations: Fort Hood, Texas/3

Date/duration: July 31, 2009/10 minutes

Weapon: firearm

Mission: Muslim ideology

On July 31, 2009, Hasan entered a gun store to ask for "the most technologically advanced weapon ... with the highest standard magazine capacity." He purchased an FN five-seven pistol the next day. On November 5, Hasan entered the Soldier Readiness Preparation Center at Fort Hood. He was getting set to be deployed to Afghanistan and apparently had fretted about shooting fellow Muslims.

He went to the first desk and asked to see Major Parrish. After bowing his head, he shouted, "Allahu Akbar" and opened fire, spraying bullets in the Center. Hasan roamed the building, shooting as he went. Outside, he wounded several soldiers. He went around the building, now locked against his reentry. When he ran out of bullets and tried to reload, he was felled by five shots. In 10 minutes, he'd killed 13 and wounded 32. Taken into custody, Hasan was tried and sentenced to death.

On the Internet, Hasan had compared a suicide bomber to a soldier who throws himself on a grenade to save his colleagues – a noble cause sacrifice. Between December 2008 and June 2009, the FBI had intercepted emails between him and terrorist Anwar al-Awlaki.

Ali Muhammad Brown

Age/race-ethnicity: 29/Black

Victims: 4 dead

Place/number of locations: Seattle, WA and West Orange, New Jersey/3

Date/duration: April 27–June 25, 2014/2 months

Weapon: firearm

Mission: terrorism, retaliation

Brown confessed to killing Ahmed Said, Dwone Anderson-Young, and Leroy Henderson in Seattle and Brendan Tevlin in New Jersey, between April 27 and June 25, 2014. Previously, Brown had been convicted in 2005 of bank fraud in support of terrorism. Brown said he was guided by his faith and that the killings were "just," as retaliation for U.S. government actions in Iraq, Syria, and Afghanistan. His shooting spree involved killing gay men. When Brown was arrested on July 18, he possessed a notebook on how to carry on warfare and evade authorities.

Nathaniel Mitchell

Age/race-ethnicity: 24/Black

Victims: 4 dead, 4 injured

Place, number of locations: Portsmouth, Virginia/4

Date/duration: December 2015/1 month

Weapon: firearm

Mission: raise social status

Hoping to improve his status as a member of the Nine Trey Gangsters, Mitchell went with another gang member to kill three people, and then shot a young mother on his own. The victims were not rival gang members but ordinary people in the community.

Frazier Glenn Miller

Age/race-ethnicity: 73/Caucasian

Victims: 3 dead, 2 wounded

Place, number of locations: Overland Park, Kansas/2

Date/duration: April 13, 2014/less than 1 hour

Weapon: firearm

Mission: hate ideology

Miller shot people outside the Jewish Community Center and outside a retirement home, Village Shalom, nearby. All victims were Christians. Others had been shot at, including one person who was Jewish, but escaped without wounds. Miller was found later outside an elementary school nearby. He had shouted "Heil Hitler" numerous times during the shooting and during his arrest. Miller admitted that he'd begun planning the shootings in late March when he became convinced that he was dying from emphysema. During his trial, he raised bizarre religious objections. Miller was commonly known as an American domestic terrorist and former leader of the defunct North Carolina-based White Patriot Party (formerly known as the Carolina Knights of the Ku Klux Klan). He is an advocate of white nationalism and a proponent of anti-Semitism.

Ronald Taylor

Age/race-ethnicity: 39/Black

Victims: 3 dead, 2 injured

Place/number of locations: Wilkinsburg, Pennsylvania/3

Date/duration: March 1, 2000/1 hour

Weapon: firearm

Mission: hate ideology

Taylor became enraged over a broken door in his apartment. He set his apartment on fire and fatally shot a maintenance worker because he was white. He went out to the Burger King and shot a former Catholic priest, then crossed the street to a McDonald's and shot a man entering the parking lot in his van. Inside the restaurant, Taylor shot the assistant manager and a customer in the drive thru. When he encountered black customers, he assured them he was only after white men. Police who arrested him found anti-white and anti-Semitic writings in his apartment.

Brenton Harrison Tarrant

Age/race-ethnicity: 28/Caucasian

Victims: 49 dead, 48 wounded

Place/number of locations: Christchurch, New Zealand/3

Date/duration: March 15, 2019/36 minutes

Weapon: firearms

Mission: hate ieology and dissension

Inspired by an American conservative commentator and the hate murders of Dylan Roof, and enraged by attacks on white Europeans, Tarrant posted a 74-page manifesto to align himself with European white supremacy groups. He then entered Christchurch's Al Noor Mosque, live-streaming his 17-minute attack that left 41 dead, because he wanted the world to see his actions. He yelled, "Let's get this party started" before he entered and sprayed bullets around the room. He hoped to survive to keep spreading his message that immigrants had to be kept out of white cultures. He went back to his car to reload and entered the mosque to eliminate survivors. He also shot a woman outside in the street. Tarrant then drove to Linwood mosque to shoot more, killing seven.

He had selected New Zealand to show that no place was safe. A member of a working-class family in Australia, he was employed as a personal trainer. He thought that China most aligned with his fascist political views and claimed that Anders Breivik, killer of 77 in Norway, had given his blessing to this attack. Tarrant plotted his attack for 2 years, after witnessing immigrant violence in Europe. On his wish list was to destabilize the West and cause a civil war in America over gun laws. The number 14 on his rifle appeared to refer to "14 words" that inspire white supremacy. When someone in the second mosque tackled him and took his gun, Tarrant fled and was soon pulled over by two community police officers and arrested. In court, he used a hand gesture that signaled alignment with white supremacy.

Ferdinand Gamper

Age/race-ethnicity: 38/Caucasian

Victims: 6 dead

Place/number of locations: Merano, Italy/6

Date/duration: February 8–March 1, 1996/3 weeks

Weapon: firearm

Mission: hate ideology

Ended with suicide

The "Monster of Mareno" started shooting people on February 8, 1996, usually in the back of the head. He killed 61-year-old Hans-Otto Detmering, an official for the Deutsche Bundesbank, and his Italian mistress, Clorinda Cecchetti. On February 14, he shot a 58-year-old farmer, Umberto Marchioro in the head. Two weeks later, he shot 36-year-old accountant Paolo Vecchiolini, who was walking with his girlfriend. In Riffian on March 1, two notes were left near the sixth shooting victim, which showed anti-Italian racist comments. Police identified and cornered Gamper, who then shot himself.

Ahmed Ibragimov

Age/race-ethnicity: 43/Caucasian

Victims: 34+ dead, 20 injured

Place/number of locations: Mekenskaya, Chechen, Russia/5+

Date/duration: October 5 and 8, 1999/3 days

Weapon: firearm

Mission: hate ideology

On October 8, 1999, a battle between Chechen government rebels and the Russian Army occurred in the Mikenskaya area. Afterward, Ibragimov approached people on a bench, took out a Kalashnikov rifle and killed four of them. He then went throughout the village, shooting people he thought were Russians. Stealing a bike, he rode to houses occupied by Russians, and shot them. In less than an hour, Ibragimov had killed at least 34. Reportedly, he had killed several members of a family in another village 3 days prior.

Satoshi Uematsu

Age/race-ethnicity: 26/Asian

Victims: 19 dead, 26 injured

Place/Number of locations: Kanagara, Japan/numerous rooms in a care home

Date/duration: July 26, 2016/a few hours

Weapon: hammer/knife

Mission: hate ideology, noble cause

The "Sagamihara stabbings" occurred at a care home for the disabled. Uematsu had worked there for 3 years as a caregiver, but he adhered to Nazi philosophies that people with serious disabilities should be eliminated. Right after he expressed such sentiments to coworkers, he quit and wrote a letter to the speaker of Japan's House of Representatives.

Uematsu argued in support of euthanasia and offered himself as the right person for the job. "I envision a world where a person with multiple disabilities can be euthanized with an agreement from the guardians," he wrote, "when it is difficult for the person to carry out household and social activities." He said he could "wipe out a total of 470 disabled individuals" by targeting two facilities during the night shift, "when staffing is low. The act will be carried out speedily, and definitely without harming the staff. After wiping out the 260 people in two facilities, I will turn myself in." In his mind, this was a noble gesture, because funds for the disabled could be redirected to improving the world's economy and preventing a Third World War.

Police brought Uematsu in and officials committed him for mental evaluation. He admitted that he appreciated Hitler's philosophy about eliminating certain types of people. After 2 weeks, the staff thought he'd improved, so they released him in March 2016, but police warned his prior employer to be vigilant. Uematsu formed a plan.

In July, he packed a hammer, bindings, and a bag of knives and returned to the facility. He targeted the women's section, where he figured it would be easier to overcome the night staff, who were all female. With his hammer, he broke in and tied up the staff with zip-ties to prevent any interference. He took their keys to enter the patients' rooms. Stabbing each disabled person in the neck, Uematsu murdered 19 and injured 26. Then he turned himself in, telling police, "It is better for the disabled to disappear."

Florence Rey and Audrey Maupin

Age/race-ethnicity: 19 and 22/Caucasian

Victims: 4 dead, 4 wounded or injured

Place/number of locations: Nanterre, France/4

Date/duration: October 4, 1994/2 hours

Weapon: firearms

Mission: inspire anarchy

Florence Rey lived with Audry Maupin, a former professor from the faculty of medicine at Nanterre. The French secret police had them under observation for their anarchist views. Their spree began on October 4, 1994, at 9:25 p.m. The couple climbed the fence of the Porte de Pantin car park to steal the security guards' firearms. They then entered a taxi with a passenger inside, ordering the driver, Dialoo, to take them to the Place de la République. Dialoo saw a police patrol car, so he rammed it at full speed, injuring an officer. The two others jumped out and were killed when Rey and Maupin opened fire. Maupin shot Dialoo, but the passenger escaped. The couple hijacked a car and ordered the driver, Jacky Bensimon, to drive to the Bois de Vincennes. When a motorcycle cop drew close behind, Maupin killed him. On arrival, they encountered a roadblock so Maupin ordered Bensimon to drive through it. The car went into a spin, throwing Bensimon out. The police opened fire, fatally wounding Maupin. They arrested Rey, who went to trial in 1998 and was convicted as an accomplice.

Marthinus Jacobus Stapelberg

Age/race-ethnicity: 22/Caucasian

Victims: 5 dead

Place/number of locations: South Africa/multiple

Date/duration: 1995–1996/3 months

Weapon: firearm

Mission: hate ideology

A police officer, Marthinus was convicted of five counts of murder and three of attempted murder, theft, and robbery. He told the Johannesburg High Court that the film *Natural Born Killers* had influenced him. He'd killed because he "hated blacks."

Barend Hendrik Strydom

Age/race-ethnicity: 23/Caucasian

Victims: 8 dead, 16 wounded

Place/number of locations: Pretoria, Gauteng Province, South Africa/8

Date/duration: November 15, 1988/less than 1 hour

Weapon: firearm

Mission: Protect farmers from encroachment

On the afternoon of November 15, 1988, right-wing extremist Hendrik Strydom donned camouflage-style army fatigues and set out for central Pretoria. He carried a 9-mm pistol, two magazines, and 200 loose bullets. At around 3 p.m. he walked to Strjdom Square, chosen for its association with Prime Minister J.G. Strydom, and shot random black people. He shot one person on Church Street and headed toward Prinsloo, where he shot two more people. After walking three blocks, shooting randomly, Strydom turned down Struben Street and entered Sato Engineering to reload. A pedestrian followed him and grabbed his gun. According to the killer, the shootings were to "show the world that there are boere [farmers] in the southern part of Africa who will fight to protect what is theirs." He was disappointed that he had not killed more. He believed he was doing God's work. In court, he received eight death sentences.

Mark Moore

Age/race-ethnicity: 31/Black

Victims: 4 dead

Place/number of locations: Toronto, Canada/3

Date/duration: September 10/29/November 4, 2010/35 days

Weapon: firearms

Mission: terror, enhance reputation as a serious gangster rapper

Moore shot four people at random in three places, seemingly choosing a location where he once had been shot in the face and disfigured. The Crown suggested the shooting happened because Moore wanted to prove that his name "shakes the streets." Days after the final victim was shot dead on November 24, Moore texted Williams: "got him in the Cedar that dude that rob us."

REFERENCES

American Psychiatric Association. (2013). *Diagnostic and statistical manual of mental disorders (DSM-5)*.Washington, DC: Author.

Levy, K. N., Kelly, K. M., & Ray, W. J. (2018). *Case studies in abnormal psychology*. Los Angeles, CA: Sage.

Lunde, D., & Morgan, J. (1980). *The die song: A journey into the mind of a mass murderer*. New York, NY: W. W. Norton.

Ressler, R. K., & Schachtman, T. (1992). *Whoever fights monsters*. New York, NY: St. Martin's Press.

Weston, G., & Aubry, J. (1990, February 7). The making of a massacre: The Marc Lepine story, part I. *The Ottawa Citizen*.

CHAPTER 4

Deadly Desperation

This category is as close as we come to killers who seem to snap. A sense of "nothing to lose" seems to fuel their rush, which is often irrational and suicidal. Generally, police know their identity. Some have (or claim to have) a mental illness, but what drives them is the sense that they must keep moving until they are stopped, or they end it. Their victims are more often random than targeted, although some have killed a family member or someone against whom they have a grudge, which precipitates their spree. They know that they have no recourse. Of the cases in this category, one in three killed or attempted to kill themselves to end the spree. Desperate killers often target people with modes of transportation they can steal, but theft is not their primary motivator. Aware that law enforcement will be searching for them, they often move from one vehicle to another in order to stay ahead of their pursuers. Needing resources, they might invade homes or commit armed robberies, often adding to their killing toll.

Total: 25 cases, 26 killers

Jean-Claude Romand

Age/race-ethnicity: 38/Caucasian

Victims: 5 dead, 1 injured (a suspected homicide 4 years earlier)

Place/number of locations: Prévessin-Moëns, Clairvaux, and Paris, France/3

Date/duration: January 9–11, 1993/3 days

Weapon: firearm, rolling pin, hands

Romand launched his spree when he could no longer bear the pressure of discovery of the fraud he had perpetrated on his family over the past

18 years. With his money depleted and no ability to repay those whom he had scammed, he believed he would have to kill them all.

The fraud started when he was too embarrassed to admit that he had dropped out of medical school at the end of his second year. Instead, he'd pretended that he'd passed an examination and continued to "register" for the next 12 years, borrowing papers and lecture notes, and even pretending to take exams. He finally left when a school official grew suspicious.

To those close to him, Romand posed as a successful medical professional and researcher for the World Health Organization (WHO). To accomplish the façade, he went to public areas for WHO and took items that bore the organization's logos. Acquiring medical books and journals, he pretended to be a lecturer and to go on business trips. Instead, he drove around recreation areas and sat alone. He forbade his wife from calling him at the office, so she never discovered his lack of a position.

He'd devised a scheme to acquire and live off funds from friends and family by telling them that he was investing their money in successful foreign ventures. His wife's salary and the sale of an apartment also supported his family. Romand had learned early that lying was better than facing the truth. His mother had suffered from extreme anxiety, so he'd often told lies to ease her worries.

In 1988, the lies caught up with him when his father-in-law wanted access to some of his invested money. The man "accidentally" fell to his death. Four years later, Romand's ex-mistress in Paris asked for the 900,000 francs that she had given him to invest, and some of his friends and associates were asking tough questions about his supposed results. He was in a corner, running low on funds. He considered killing himself. He knew there was another option.

Removing 2,000 francs from the bank on January 9, 1993, he purchased gas canisters, a stun wand, ammunition, and a suppressor for the rifle he had borrowed from his father. Later that day, Romand fatally beat his wife with a rolling pin, then slept in the bed with her body. He spent the day watching cartoons with his two children before shooting them. The next day, he traveled 50 miles to join his parents for a meal. He then shot them and their dog. Finally, he went to see his former mistress. On their way to a dinner engagement, he used the stun wand and gas canisters on her and attempted to strangle her, but she fought back and survived. Romand returned home and watched TV for a while, surrounded by the bodies of his wife and children. His final act was to set fire to the house and take an overdose of expired sleeping pills. However, firefighters rescued him before he burned to death.

Romand was tried in 1996. He gave a full statement during his testimony. Sentenced to life imprisonment with eligibility for parole, he was diagnosed with narcissistic personality disorder and mythomanic tendencies (an excessive or abnormal propensity for lying and exaggerating) (Carrere, 2000).

Christopher Wilder

Age/race-ethnicity: 39/Caucasian

Victims: 8 dead, 2 injured (also suspected in earlier murders)

Place/number of locations: cross country, Florida to California to New Hampshire/numerous locations

Date/duration: March 24–April 13, 1984/3 weeks

Weapon: firearm, hands, knife

Elizabeth Kenyon, a teacher in Miami, Florida, disappeared on March 4, 1984. Her parents told police about Wilder, a former boyfriend whom Beth had declined to marry. He ran a construction business and had been associated with another missing woman, Rosario Gonzales, who had vanished on February 26. When Wilder heard that he was a suspect in Kenyon's disappearance, he withdrew money, got into his 1973 Chrysler New Yorker sedan, stole his partner's credit card, and left. Generally called a serial killer, due to his actions over these 3 weeks, he had stepped up his violence as he raced to leave the United States. Each time he killed, it was to acquire a car or assault someone along the way. He always left in a hurry, which made it difficult for the FBI to locate and arrest him. No matter what he did during other times in his life, this period shows a sense of desperation.

Wilder seemed to count on the act of moving to prevent capture. Yet, he also seemed unable to control his urge to "collect" young women to torture and kill. Perhaps he thought his life was over and he had nothing left to lose. On April 3, the FBI placed Wilder on its "Ten Most Wanted" list and issued a nationwide alert. The media dubbed him "The Beauty Queen Killer." It is likely that he was aware of this.

When he took the time to kill out of lust, Wilder's MO was to pose as a photographer looking for a model. He would lure potential victims with flattery about their beauty and the promise of a career, and then invite them to see his portfolio. Once alone, he would force them into his car to transport to another destination. A survivor held captive for a day said that Wilder had made her perform sexual acts before raping her. He'd used an electrical cord with open copper wires to her feet to shock her. Then he'd glued her eyes shut with Superglue. She'd managed to lock herself in the bathroom and make enough noise to make him flee.

At one point in California, Wilder abducted a 16-year-old girl whom he ordered to help him lure others. With her, he drove back across the country, heading to Maine. There, after killing another woman for her car, he let his hostage go.

Wilder entered New Hampshire on his way into Canada. An officer spotted the stolen car and in their struggle over Wilder's gun, Wilder was fatally shot. Found in his possession were handcuffs, rolls of duct tape, rope, the adapted electrical cord, and a novel by John Fowles called *The Collector*. Therapists who had treated Wilder over a period of time knew that he had nearly memorized this book as a slave manual. It featured a lonely entomologist who abducts a beautiful woman named Miranda, to hold her captive in a locked dungeon he has prepared on his isolated property. He has the delusion that he can make her love him.

An investigation into Wilder's background turned up suspicion in other murders. His childhood in Australia had been stable, although he did some window-peeping. He was also arrested with a group of friends for the gang-rape of a girl on the beach. Pleading guilty, he had received a year of probation with counseling and electroshock therapy. Shortly after this treatment, he had begun to envision shocking girls while having sex. Psychologists noted his need to dominate women and his desire to turn them into unwilling sex slaves (Gibney, 1984).

Kipland Kinkel

Age/race-ethnicity: 15, Caucasian

Victims: 4 dead, 24 wounded or injured

Place/number of locations: Springfield, Oregon/2

Date/duration: May 21, 1998/12–15 hours

Weapon: firearms

Kinkel had been expelled from school in Springfield, Oregon, for having a gun in school. He returned the next day, armed with a knife, handgun, and a semiautomatic rifle. Entering the cafeteria, he started shooting. He killed one student and wounded eight others, one of whom later died. The stampede hurt 15 more. Kinkel was disarmed and taken to the police station, where he withdrew a hidden knife. He claimed he wanted to die and begged the police, "Just kill me." He knew what else they would soon find.

Officers went to his home when his parents did not answer the phone and discovered that both were dead. Kinkel had shot them and booby-trapped the house with five homemade bombs, one of which he'd placed beneath his mother's corpse. An investigation turned up trouble between Kinkel and his parents, especially his father. Bill Kinkel had apparently decided to send his troublesome son to a military school for some discipline. Both parents were teachers and Kinkel had trouble with dyslexia. He believed that he was a disappointment to them. At school, he had developed the reputation for being "dangerous" and hung out with kids who were involved in petty theft. Fascinated with explosives, he also collected guns, hiding his stash from his parents. Briefly, he went on Prozac for depression, but when he was doing better, he stopped taking it. He fell in love and then lost the girl. He became obsessed with the soundtrack for a film version of *Romeo and Juliet* that glorified violence and suicide.

He started his spree by killing his father at home, shooting him from behind. He dragged the body into the bathroom and waited for his mother to come home. When she did, he claimed he'd told her he loved her before he'd shot her six times. Overnight, Kinkel talked on the phone with friends. The next day, he drove his parents' car to school. In less than a minute, he shot 48 rounds into his classmates. When taken into custody and questioned about why he'd done this, he just kept saying through tears, "I had no other choice … I had to." He'd asked the cops to shoot him, so he might have expected to die. This would be a suicide-by-cop scenario, but he remained alive.

Although he was 15, Kinkel was certified to be tried as an adult. He'd initiated an insanity defense but dropped it. During the sentencing phase, a brain scan was introduced as evidence to mitigate what he had done, and Dr. Richard Konkel, a neurologist, testified that it showed areas of decreased activity consistent with recent research on childhood schizophrenia.

Kinkel pleaded guilty to four counts of first-degree murder and 24 counts of attempted murder. He was sentenced to 112 years in prison without parole (Kellerman, 1999; Langman, 2014). Without having killed his father, it is unlikely that he would have taken weapons to school to kill his classmates, despite admiring some of the earlier school shooters.

Walter Earl Durand

Age/race-ethnicity: 26/Caucasian

Victims: 4 dead

Place/number of locations: In and around Powell, Wyoming/3

Date/duration: March 13–24, 1939/11 days

Weapon: firearm

Ended with suicide

One spring morning, Durand ignored the requirement for a hunting license and was arrested and jailed for poaching elk, resisting arrest, and killing a calf. He received a 6-month sentence in Cody, Wyoming. Two days later, he escaped this jail. He forced a deputy to drive him to his parents' home in nearby Powell before killing him. As a 10-man posse chased Durand into the mountains, he shot and killed two officers. A larger posse formed. Desperate, Durand came out of the woods after 10 days to rob a bank. He took hostages, one of whom was killed when townspeople shot at Durand and he returned fire. A teenager hit him in the chest, forcing him back into the bank, where he shot himself.

James Pough

Age/race-ethnicity: 42/Black

Victims: 11 dead, 6 wounded

Place/number of locations: Jacksonville, Florida/3

Date/duration: June 17–18, 1990/2 days

Weapon: firearms

Ended in suicide

Pough was angry that a General Motors Acceptance Corporation car loan office had repossessed his 1988 red Pontiac. Known to fly into rages, he'd abused his wife and threatened to kill people. He'd been arrested in 1971 for manslaughter after shooting his best friend during an argument. His wife left him in 1990. On June 17, Pough killed a pimp and a prostitute. Ten minutes later in another area, he shot at and wounded two teens after asking them for directions. The next day, with "nothing to lose," he robbed a convenience store. Then he visited his mother's grave and called in sick to work. He went to the loan office and killed the receptionist before walking through the office and shooting others. Finally, he killed himself.

Jimmy Earl Whitt

Age/race-ethnicity: 23/Caucasian

Victims: 4 dead, 1 wounded

Place/number of locations: Greenville and Foley, Alabama/4

Date/duration: June 14, 1994/8 hours

Weapon: stolen police pistol

Ended with suicide

Whitt shot a police officer and a store clerk during a holdup. He then gunned down a deputy with the Pearl River County Sheriff's Department, on a stretch of I-59. He drove to Mobile, where he stole a car at gunpoint and then drove east on I-10. At the Loxley exit, Whitt shot an Alabama PSC officer, and then headed south toward Foley, where he shot a woman at a McDonald's drive-in window to steal her car. When FBI agents caught up, Whitt placed the pistol to his temple and pulled the trigger.

Jordan Witmer

Age/race-ethnicity: 21/Caucasian

Victims: 3 dead, 1 wounded

Place/number of locations: Harrisburg, Pennsylvania/2

Date/duration: January 26, 2019/1–2 hours

Weapon: firearm

Ended in suicide

Witmer was drinking at P.J. Harrigan's Bar and Grill at the Ramada Hotel, near Penn State University with his former girlfriend, 21-year-old Nicole Abrino. Home for a few weeks before ending a 3-year stint in the Army, he'd been at the bar for about 2 hours. There is some suggestion from witnesses that he was angry. Around 10:30 p.m., Witmer got into an argument with Abrino. Two other patrons, Dean Beachy, 61 and his son, 19-year-old Steven, tried to intercede. From Ohio, they were in town for an animal auction. Witmer fatally shot both before shooting Abrino in the chest. He fled, crashing his car about two miles from the bar. He ran to the nearby home of George McCormick, broke a sliding glass door by shooting it, and fatally shot McCormick inside. McCormick's wife locked herself in the bedroom and called police. Witmer then turned the gun on himself. The killings stunned Witmer's family. They said he'd left the Army's active-duty status on good terms and had planned to join the reserves. He'd also hoped to become a police officer.

Mark Newton Spotz

Age/race-ethnicity: 35/Caucasian

Victims: 4 dead

Place/number of locations: Schuylkill, York, and Cumberland counties, Pennsylvania/4

Date/duration: January 31–February 3, 1995/4 days

Weapon: firearm

Spotz fatally shot his brother during a fight over a gerbil at their mother's home, then fled with his girlfriend, killing three women during carjackings within 48 hours in Schuylkill, York, and Cumberland counties. The girlfriend, an unwilling accomplice, left when she could. Spotz surrendered to police in a motel room.

Melvin Keeling

Age/race-ethnicity: 43/Caucasian

Victims: 3 dead

Place/number of locations: Ohio, Indiana/2

Date/duration: September 2005/2–6 hours

Weapon: firearm

Ended in suicide

In September 2005, Keeling fatally shot 13-year-old Katelind Caudill in her bedroom, because she'd revealed to authorities that he'd sexually abused her friend, Keeling's stepdaughter. A few hours after killing her, he fatally shot two convenience store clerks in Indiana. Keeling was wanted on charges of rape and gross sexual imposition involving a child in an unrelated case. He shot himself with a gun he'd redeemed from a pawnshop.

Ernest D. Jamison

Age/race-ethnicity: 34/Black

Victims: 3 dead

Place/number of locations: Tennessee, Missouri, Illinois/3

Date/duration: June 19, 1995/1 day

Weapon: firearm

In the early morning hours of June 19, 1995, Jamison murdered his friend, Arthur Kirkwood, 24, and stole his Oldsmobile Delta 88 in Memphis, Tennessee. The former bible college student then fled the state. While driving through Missouri, Jamison shot and killed a gas station attendant. He eluded a dragnet and moved on to Illinois. When his stolen car broke down, he shot a woman at a gas pump to steal her car. McLean County sheriff deputies spotted the stolen car and chased it. As they closed in, Jamison attempted to kill himself, but blinded himself instead. He was arrested.

Brian Nichols

Age/race-ethnicity: 51/Black

Victims: 4 dead, 1 injured

Place/number of locations: Atlanta, Georgia/4

Date/duration: March 11–12, 2005/28 hours

Weapon: stolen police handgun

Nichols overpowered a sheriff's deputy, stealing her gun and beating her into a coma. Nichols then changed into his trial clothes and entered the courtroom, where he walked toward Judge Rowland Barnes' chambers. He encountered Susan Christy, Gina Clarke Thomas, and David Allman, holding them at gunpoint. Sergeant Grantley White came in and was forced to handcuff the other three. Nichols fatally shot Judge Barnes and court reporter Julie Ann Brandau. While escaping, he shot and killed Sergeant Hoyt Teasley. During his escape attempt, he carjacked several vehicles. Later that day, U.S. Immigration and Customs Enforcement Agent David G. Wilhelm was shot dead in his home. His uniform, badge, gun, and truck were missing. Twenty-six hours later, Nichols was caught (with the help of a woman who had made him pancakes and read him the Bible).

Hank Earl Carr

Age/race-ethnicity: 30/Caucasian

Victims: 4 killed, 1 injured

Place/number of locations: Tampa, Florida/3

Date/duration: May 19, 1998/9 hours

Weapon: firearm

Ended in suicide

On the morning of May 19, around 10:30, Carr carried the young son of his girlfriend Bernice Bowen into a fire station. The boy had a gunshot wound to the head. Carr said it was an accident. He called himself Joseph Bennett and returned to the site of the shooting. The police followed. He threatened them with a rifle but fled. They caught up and arrested him. Carr successfully unlocked his handcuffs and disarmed one of the cops, shooting both in the face. Carjacking a pickup truck, Carr fled onto I-75 north. Florida State Trooper James Crooks pursued and ended up shot. Multiple police cars and a helicopter joined the chase. Carr entered a convenience store and took a hostage. Nearly 200 officers surrounded him. At 7:20 p.m., as the SWAT team forcibly entered, Carr released Kramer and killed himself. The boy he'd shot that morning also died.

Lovelle Mixon

Age/race-ethnicity: 26/Black

Victims: 4 dead

Place/number of locations: Oakland, California/2

Date/duration: March 21, 2009/4 hours

Weapon: firearms

Mixon had a gun, a parole violation, when police stopped him. He was also wanted on a no-bail arrest warrant. He shot and killed both officers. When SWAT team officers attempted to apprehend him 2 hours later, he killed two more. Finally, Mixon was killed in a barrage of gunfire.

Bertram Greenberg

Age/race-ethnicity: 38/Caucasian

Victims: 4 dead, 1 wounded

Place/number of locations: California, Arizona, and New Mexico/4

Date/duration: February 4–5, 1971/2 days

Weapon: hands, firearm

The LAPD Police issued an alert on February 5 after a 13-year-old girl was raped and killed the day before. Her body was found in a park. On that same day, two Arizona State Highway officers were killed when they stopped a man in a stolen car. Then came reports of a man and wife shot near the border between Arizona and New Mexico. The man was killed, his wife wounded. Officers in New Mexico identified the couple's stolen car. They chased, shot, and killed Greenburg.

James W. Hutchins

Age/race-ethnicity: 49/Caucasian

Victims: 3 dead

Place/number of locations: Rutherford County, North Carolina/2

Date/duration: May 31, 1979/1 hour

Weapon: firearm

Hutchins gunned down two Rutherford County deputy sheriffs when they arrived separately at his residence in response to a domestic disturbance call from his teenage daughter Charlotte. She had fled to a neighbor's house. After shooting the officers, Hutchins fled in his car. A North Carolina State Trooper, unaware of the killings, pulled him over for speeding. When Hutchins stopped, he killed the officer, then ran into the woods.

Evan David Smyth

Age/race-ethnicity: 40/Caucasian

Victims: 4 dead

Place/number of locations: Montgomery County, Maryland/3

Date/duration: September 14–18, 2003/4 days

Weapon: firearms

Smyth fatally shot Tristan Offiah in his car after stealing his drugs. The following day, the decomposing body of Phillip Walker was found in the trunk of his car. Police linked the crimes. A 911 call came from Shautise Gill at Smyth's residence. By the time police arrived, Gill had been beaten and strangled to death. There was a shotgun on the table and bone and brain matter on the wall. Investigators determined that the biological material was from Kay Carey, Smyth's girlfriend. All four victims were linked to Smyth via drug dealing, and he was arrested.

Robert E. Williams

Age/race-ethnicity: 41/Black

Victims: 3 dead, 2 injured

Place/number of locations: Nebraska, Iowa, Minnesota/3

Date/duration: August 11–12, 1997/2 days

Weapon: firearm

Williams got into a heated argument with a friend, Patricia McGarry. McGarry's neighbor intervened and Williams shot McGarry in the head, killing her. He then raped and shot her friend. The next day, deputies found Williams' abandoned car in Cherokee County, Iowa, where he'd entered a farmhouse. There, he'd raped and shot a woman before stealing her car. Driving to Minnesota, he killed another woman in order to change cars. When he returned to Lincoln, he was arrested.

Robert Charles

Age/race-ethnicity: 35/Black

Victims: 7 dead

Place/number of locations: New Orleans, Louisiana/6

Date/duration: July 23–27, 1900/4 days

Weapon: firearm

On July 23, police stopped Charles and a friend for trespassing. Charles shot at the officer, who returned fire. Both were injured and Charles escaped and went home. Police surrounded the house and Charles killed two and fled. The killing of a white officer launched riots throughout the city. On the 25th the police searched for Charles, as did gangs of white vigilantes. That night, Charles killed five more white men. He hid out until officers located and killed him. The enraged mob shot him hundreds more times and beat the body.

Juljan Mezowiec

Age/race-ethnicity: 49/Caucasian

Victims: 7 dead, 5 injured

Place/number of locations: Maciejów, Poland/5

Date/duration: October 21–22, 1928/2 days

Weapon: knife

Mezowiec attended a meeting at the local elementary school in Maciejów. He became so agitated with the mayor that police had to remove him. He grabbed a bayonet from the police supervisor and stabbed him to death, then killed the other officer present. He stabbed another man who confronted him before going to the farm of Lejba Małamet to kill him and his wife. After fleeing, he attacked Andrzej Kzera in the street and stabbed him in the heart. Mezowiec seriously injured five more and killed one before he ran into the woods to hide. He was caught there.

Mateo Banks

Age/race-ethnicity: 44/Hispanic

Victims: 8 dead

Place/number of locations: Buenos Aires, Argentina/5

Date/duration: April 18, 1922/1 day

Weapon: firearms

Banks, 44, was a prosperous rancher in Buenos Aires until his gambling addiction put him in debt to his brothers. Humiliated and desperate, he formed a plan to kill his siblings and their families, and frame two employees for it. On April 18, 1922, he carried it out, killing seven, plus one of the men. He sought help from a doctor, claiming that a pair of employees had slaughtered his family and that he'd shot the killer while the other got away. Investigators found the remains of the supposed fugitive and then determined that everyone had been shot with the same shotgun. They arrested Banks, who confessed.

Günter Hermann Ewen

Age/race-ethnicity: 36/Caucasian

Victims: 5 dead, 11 injured

Place/number of locations: Dillingen, Germany and Sierck-les-Bains, France/3

Date/duration: May 16, 1999/1 day

Weapon: firearms

Ended in suicide

Accused of burglary and falsely imprisoned, Ewen lost his business and home. Deep in debt, he also lost his girlfriend. He went on a suicidal spree, killing four people and wounding nine others at and around a disco in Dillingen, Germany, before escaping to Sierck-les-Bains, France, where he killed another person while trying to steal his car and wounded two more. Knowing the police were pursuing him, Ewen shot himself.

Barry Prudom

Age/race-ethnicity: 37/Caucasian

Victims: 3 dead, 2 wounded

Place/number of locations: England/4

Date/duration: June 17–28, 1982/11 days

Weapon: firearm

Ended in suicide

When officer David Haigh tried to serve a summons on a poacher, he was fatally shot. He had written the vehicle registration number, which was traced to a green Citroën that Prudom owned. The car was found in a cornfield, burned. On June 20, Prudom hitchhiked to Torksey, Lincolnshire, where he broke into a house to get money. Three days later, he broke into another home in Girton, shooting the couple who lived there. Sylvia Luckett survived, crawling to a neighbor's house. Prudom took the Lucketts' car and drove to Dalby Forest, North Yorkshire. When he was stopped the next day, Prudom shot the officer in the face and fled. On June 28, Police Sergeant David Winter and PC Mick Wood spotted a suspicious man and challenged him. Prudom shot Winter, killing him. For the next 8 days, Prudom evaded capture. When "The Phantom of the Forest" was finally cornered by a survivalist who'd trained him, he killed himself.

Robert Francis Mone and Thomas McCulloch

Age/race-ethnicity: 28 and 28/Caucasian

Victims: 3 dead, 3 wounded (1 killed earlier by Mone, 2 attempted murders by McCulloch)

Place/number of locations: Dundee, Scotland/3

Date/duration: November 30, 1976/several hours

Weapon: knives, axes, pitchfork, cleaver

In 1967, Mone had shot a teacher and raped a student in retaliation for being expelled from St. John's high school. Found to be schizophrenic, he was sent to a state psychiatric hospital. In 1976, he broke out with fellow inmate and lover, Thomas McCulloch (who had been declared an incurable psychopath). They murdered another inmate, a male nurse, and a police officer. They hacked one with a hatchet and sliced off the ears of the other. As they fled the grounds, they donned fake uniforms and flagged down a motorist. They also attracted a police officer, so they hacked both with hatchets and cleavers and stole the motorist's car. When they crashed, they hijacked a van, severely hacking two more people. When they got stuck in a field, they stole another car. After 3 hours of bloody rampage, they were arrested.

Jesse Imeson

Age/race-ethnicity: 22/Caucasian

Victims: 3 dead

Place/number of locations: Windsor and Mount Carmel, Ontario, Canada/2

Date/duration: July 18–22, 2007/4 days

Weapon: belt, firearm

After a gay sexual encounter that reportedly enraged him, Imeson strangled Carlos Rivera, a stranger that he had met at a gay bar. Imeson fled in his victim's car, stealing a rifle and ammunition. A day later, he broke into a farmhouse and killed an elderly couple in order to pilfer their money and food. A manhunt ensued for the next 12 days, cornering Imeson in the woods. He surrendered and pleaded guilty to all three murders.

Hans Vollenweider

Age/race-ethnicity: 31/Caucasian

Victims: 3 dead

Place/number of locations: Switzerland/3

Date/duration: June 14–23, 1939/9 days

Weapon: gun

In 1936, Vollenweider committed a bank robbery and was sentenced to 2.5 years in prison. After his sentence ended, he was considered to be dangerous, so he remained locked up. Escaping, he remained on the run for 9 days. In that time, he shot and killed a chauffeur, a postman, and a police officer. Recaptured, he was sentenced to die. He was executed by guillotine on October 18, 1940.

REFERENCES

Carrere, E. (2000). *The adversary: A true story of monstrous deception.* New York, NY: Picador.
Gibney, B. (1984). *The beauty queen killer.* New York, NY: Pinnacle.
Kellerman, J. (1999). *Savage spawn.* New York, NY: Ballantine.
Langman, P. (2014). *School shooters: Understanding high school, college, and adult perpetrators.* New York, NY: Rowman & Littlefield.

CHAPTER 5

Mental Illness

In Chapter 3, which included psychotic mission killers, we described the types of diagnoses commonly seen with severe mental illness in spree killers. We continue with cases of mental illness in this chapter, but these killers did not have clear missions. Most of these sprees were reactive rather than carefully planned. All involved lone killers. Only one was female. About 31% committed suicide, a figure that is possibly higher with potential suicide-by-cop incidents.

42 killers, 42 cases

Howard Unruh

Age/race-ethnicity: 28/Caucasian

Victims: 13 dead, 3 wounded

Place/number of locations: Camden, New Jersey/multiple locations on a city block

Date/duration: September 6, 1949/12 minutes, plus stand-off with police

Weapon: firearm

Unruh kept a list of grudges against his neighbors. He lived with his mother in Camden. Right after she left the house on September 6, Unruh vaulted a fence, cut through some back streets, and stepped into the road. For too long, he believed, people had been talking about him behind his back. He tried shooting a deliveryman in a bread truck, but the man escaped.

Unruh walked along 32nd Street. Entering a shoe repair shop, he aimed the gun at John Pilarchik, firing twice. Next door was Clark Hoover's barbershop. When Unruh entered, Hoover was cutting the hair of a 6-year-old boy. Unruh took aim and said, "I've got something for you, Clarkie." The first bullet hit the boy and the second one killed Hoover. Unruh next headed toward the tavern, but it was locked, so he shot two bullets into the door. He turned his attention to his primary targets, the Cohens, who ran the corner drugstore.

An insurance agent named James Hutton came out the door. Unruh asked him to move and when he didn't, he ended up dead. Unruh stepped inside and saw Maurice Cohen and his wife Rose run up the steps to their apartment. He followed them, watching Rose try to hide in a closet. He fired three times through the door, then opened it and shot her in the head. When he found Maurice's elderly mother calling police, he killed her as well. Cohen jumped out the window, but Unruh wounded him. He fell to the street, where Unruh finished him off and reloaded.

Nearby, Mrs. Harrie and her 16-year-old son, Armond, were outside. Mrs. Harrie went in and the shooter entered her house. Her son ran in and Unruh shot at them five times, wounding them. He now had hit nine people, killing seven.

Circling back, he walked down 32nd Street and encountered a motorist, Alvin Day, who had slowed down. Unruh leaned through the window of his car, killing him. He shot through the windshield of another car, killing the female driver and her mother, and wounding a 12-year-old boy. Next, he wounded Charlie Peterson.

Finally, Unruh entered the tailor's shop, but only his wife was there. She begged for her life, but Unruh killed her and left. His last victim was a 2-year-old who had looked out the window.

Running out of bullets, Unruh returned home. Police surrounded him. It took another five minutes, but finally Unruh surrendered.

To Camden County Prosecutor Mitchell Cohen, Unruh admitted that before going to sleep the previous night he'd made up his mind to go on this rampage to teach a lesson to people who'd said nasty things about him.

On the evening before, Unruh had been in Philadelphia at the 24-hour Family Theater, where he watched a double feature. When he came home, he'd discovered that someone had stolen his outside gate. That's when he'd decided to shoot people he disliked. On his list of grudges, he had recorded each person's imagined misdeeds. Then he had placed the word "retal," short for retaliation. He admitted he'd have killed many more if he'd had enough ammunition.

Unruh was sent to the New Jersey Hospital for the Insane, although the prosecutor claimed he had not been declared insane. After 2 months of personality and physiological tests, the diagnosis was paranoid schizophrenia. Unruh spent the remainder of his life in a unit for the criminally insane (Berger, 1949).

James J. Boyle

Age/race-ethnicity: 36/Caucasian

Victims: 5 dead, 2 wounded

Place/number of locations: Fort Wright, Connecticut/3

Date/duration: April 10, 1918/less than 1 hour

Weapon: firearm

Ended in suicide

Boyle, a 36-year-old Army sergeant, went on a shocking murder/suicide rampage in 1918. Army investigators believed that either of two physical setbacks might have contributed: an unspecified illness he'd suffered while fighting rebels in the Philippines, or a head injury.

Raised in a small Pennsylvania mining town, Boyle was born to Irish immigrants. While still a boy, he worked in the coalmines, as did his father. His mother stayed home to raise a brood that would eventually grow to eight, with James being the fourth oldest.

In 1898, at the age of 16, Boyle enlisted in the Army. He was honorably discharged as a private in January 1899, but he signed up several more times. His service during the Moro Rebellion qualified him as a Spanish-American War veteran.

In 1911, after his fourth enlistment he returned to his family in Allentown, PA. He took a job as a brakeman with the Central Railroad of New Jersey, suffering an accident that left him unconscious for 5 days.

When the United States entered the First World War in 1917, Boyle reenlisted. He reported to Fort Slocum, advancing to the position of first-class gunner, then sergeant. In 1918, he was assigned to the Coast Artillery Corps at Fort Wright on Fishers Island in Long Island Sound, seven miles from New London, CT.

On Sunday, April 7, Boyle went on a short furlough to say goodbye to his family and friends. He seemed to have contracted the Spanish flu. He wasn't his usual self and he complained about headaches. On April 9, Boyle rejoined his company at the fort, feeling weak and perspiring. The next day, he entered the barracks of 4th Company, his previous unit. From a holster hanging in a locker in the squad room, he grabbed a pistol and loaded it. Then Boyle went to the company office and shot Sergeants Fred Cook and Adolph Hoitomt, his closest friends. Cook died, but Hoitomt survived the bullet to his jaw.

After wrestling with Corporal Cochran, Boyle grabbed another pistol and loaded it. He went into the hall, where he killed Pvt. Tomacz Guzdek.

He went out to a back porch. Private Ernest M. Green jumped from the second-floor porch, fatally hitting his head on the steps. Either in the squad room or on the back porch, Boyle fatally shot 1st Lt. Jean Bechaud in the abdomen. Then in a lavatory in the barracks cellar, Boyle shot Pvt. Timothy Sullivan in the thigh.

Returning to the company office, Boyle fatally shot himself in the left side of his chest and in the right temple.

A board of four officers was convened to investigate. They concluded that Boyle was delirious when he went on his homicidal rampage. As a result, he was not responsible for his actions. "There is no question, it being established by the evidence, that he was insane at the time of the commission of the crimes in question," the report says, adding that

> his illness, while absent with leave, augmented by a fever from which it can be presumed he was suffering while ill … and also augmented perhaps by a reaction of his illness while in the Philippines, or by a reaction of [an] injury received in a railroad accident in 1912 when he was knocked unconscious for five days … caused him to become insane and to [commit] the crimes attributed to him. These crimes are not therefore caused as a result of his own misconduct.

The illness that hobbled Boyle appears to have been influenza. When he returned to Fort Wright, he had a fever, and the infection that caused it could have set him off (Venditta, 2018).

Sylvia Seegrist

Age/race-ethnicity: 25/Caucasian

Victims: 3 dead, 7 wounded

Place/number of locations: Springfield, Pennsylvania/3

Date/duration: October 30, 1985/10 minutes

Weapon: firearm

Shoppers at the Springfield Mall outside Philadelphia, Pennsylvania, were startled by the sound of gunfire in the parking lot. When a woman entered the mall, carrying a semiautomatic rifle and dressed in olive green military fatigues, a knit cap and black boots, many believed it was a Halloween prank.

However, Seegrist was angry at the pharmacist for not filling her prescription. Near a restaurant's entrance, a 2-year-old child lay dead and two children were wounded. The shooter aimed directly at shoppers who had failed to move fast enough and shot randomly inside several stores. She hit a 67-year-old man three times before making her way through the pedestrian area, randomly firing. Several people fell to the floor. After four minutes, graduate student John Laufer grabbed the shooter and sat her down. He returned with a security guard, who placed Seegrist under arrest.

At Seegrist's arraignment, which she attended barefoot, Seegrist indicated that she had expected to die. Finally, she asked, "Do you have a black box? That is my testimony."

Seegrist had a long record of mental illness, starting with a diagnosis of paranoid schizophrenia at age 15. Since her illness involved a developing hostility and aggression, she had alienated family and friends. She was hospitalized a dozen times and given drugs. Over the years, her delusions had worsened. Having enlisted in the Army, she'd been discharged from boot camp over her instability and threats of violence. During the weeks prior to the shooting, people who knew her said she was acting psychotic. Her mother had urged her to commit herself, but Seegrist had resisted.

Seegrist was found competent to stand trial, which began 7 months later. She was found guilty but mentally ill and given three consecutive life sentences for the murders, with 10 years each for the seven wounded. Sent to a psychiatric facility for evaluation, she was eventually moved to the state correctional institution at Muncy (Torok, Quinn & Fleck, 1985).

Dale Merle Nelson

Age/race-ethnicity: 31/Caucasian

Victims: 8 dead

Place/number of locations: Creston, Canada/3

Date/duration: September 4, 1970/24 hours

Weapon: fire extinguisher, knife, firearm

Nelson drove into Creston, purchased six beers and a bottle of vodka, and went to drink with friends. Prone to suicidal depression, he seemed even-tempered that morning. He left the tavern to retrieve his 7-mm caliber bolt-action rifle and drove back to Creston to purchase ammunition and more alcohol. He went to the King George Hotel bar, where he drank a lot more. Possibly, he also took a hallucinogenic.

Just after midnight, Nelson drove to the home of his relative, Shirley Wasyk. He beat her with a fire extinguisher, tied her hands behind her back, and left her on her bed, then gathered two of her children in a bedroom. He killed the youngest, Tracey, while 12-year-old Debbie escaped to a neighbor's house to call the police.

When law enforcement officers arrived, Nelson's truck was still parked outside. They found two bodies in the house. They went to Nelson's home to evacuate his wife and children. When they returned to the Wasyk home, they discovered that Tracey's body was missing. Shortly afterward, Isabelle St. Amand, a neighbor of the Wasyks, phoned the police to report a man at her home with a gun. Police responded, but four members of this family were dead from gunshots and their car and 8-year-old Cathy were missing

The authorities launched a manhunt. The missing vehicle was found stuck in a ditch. As they searched, they came across a bloody hammer. Soon, they discovered the dismembered remains of Tracey Wasyk. It wasn't long before they surrounded Nelson in a shack in the woods. He surrendered, admitting that he had killed Cathy, as well as the others. He blamed alcohol and LSD. When he talked about dismembering Tracey, he said he had tried to consume her organs. Despite his plea of criminal insanity, Nelson received a life sentence (Mellor, 2013).

Adam Lanza

Age/race-ethnicity: 20/Caucasian

Victims: 27 dead, 2 wounded

Place/number of locations: Newtown, Connecticut /2

Date/duration: December 14, 2012/less than 1 hour

Weapon: firearm

Ended in suicide

Lanza killed his mother on December 14, 2012, before going to Sandy Hook Elementary School in Newtown, Connecticut, to gun down staff members and students. He then shot himself, leaving no explanation. His severe mental illness, including obsessive-compulsive disorder and Asperger's, along with his obsession with mass murder, contributed to his rampage. His mother's decision to move across the country and possibly place him into a school might have triggered it, but he had clearly planned for it and probably had rehearsed it in his fantasy life.

Bryan Uyesugi

Age/race-ethnicity: 40/Asian

Victims: 7 dead

Place/number of locations: Hawaii/2

Date/duration: November 2, 1999/15–20 minutes

Weapon: firearm

Uyesugi was a quiet, reclusive man. On the morning of November 2, 1999, he went to work at the Xerox Corporation building prepared to kill people because he thought he was being set up to be fired. As he entered a second-floor office, he fatally shot a coworker. He went out to where he knew more coworkers were meeting. One by one, he picked them off, including his supervisor. As he walked away, he saw another man and fired at him, but missed. He then fled. Police surrounded him for 5 hours until he surrendered. He had two-dozen weapons at home. Four mental health experts evaluated him and three decided he had schizophrenia, but two argued that his illness had not precipitated the incident. Uyesugi had allegedly suffered from the delusion that one of his coworkers was an FBI agent and part of a conspiracy that had targeted him. He'd also had a serious head injury that had changed his personality. Despite his attempt to get an insanity acquittal, he was convicted.

Drew Ryan Maras

Age/race-ethnicity: 30/Caucasian

Victims: 3 dead

Place/number of locations: Maricopa County, Arizona/2

Date/duration: January 8, 2012/2 days

Weapon: firearm

On Jan 8, 2012, police were called to a burglary in Maricopa County off Highway 17. Sheriff's Deputy William Coleman and two other deputies arrived to investigate. They saw a minivan in the parking lot, and someone seemed to be asleep in it. Cohen tapped on the window and was met with semiautomatic rifle fire, which killed him. In the ensuing gunfight, another deputy shot the man in the minivan, Drew Maras. They wondered if he had been involved in the double homicide of a couple from New Hampshire 2 days earlier at a scenic overlook off Highway 17. The weapon was soon linked.

Maras was a former Marine, obsessed with natural disasters and the end of the world. A witness said that the couple had spoken to him at a local signing for his self-published book, *Open Your Eyes: To 2012 and*

Beyond. He had no history of violence, so apart from possible paranoia, the motive for the double homicide remains a mystery.

Marc Sappington

Age/race-ethnicity: 41/Black

Victims: 3 dead (1 killed the month before)

Place/number of locations: Kansas City, Kansas/3

Date/duration: April 7–10, 2001/3 days

Weapon: knife, firearm

Between April 7 and April 10, 2001, three young men in a Kansas City, Kansas, neighborhood were murdered, and a woman was kidnapped. Marc Sappington confessed to the crimes. He had stabbed Terry Green in his backyard. Afraid that someone had seen him, he placed the body into Green's car and drove it to an antiques mall parking lot in Kansas City. Green's body was found 3 days later, on April 10, the same day that Michael Weaver's body was discovered in the front seat of a car parked near his house. He had been stabbed repeatedly. Sappington moved on that same day to kill Fred Alton Brown with a shotgun. He cut off a piece of Brown's leg and tried to eat it. When he felt sick, he took the piece into his kitchen to fry it. He later said he was responding to voices in his head that ordered him to eat flesh and drink blood. Two days later, Sappington was arrested. He admitted to the murders. Diagnosed with schizophrenia, he added that he had taken PCP (phencyclidine). A jury found Sappington guilty of all charges.

Terry Strawn

Age/race-ethnicity: 58/Caucasian

Victims: 3 dead

Place/number of locations: Florida/2

Date/duration: December 19, 2018/1 hour

Weapon: firearm

Ended with suicide

Hillsborough County sheriff's deputy Terry Strawn fatally shot his wife, Theresa, and granddaughter, Londyn, in his home before heading to a second residence to kill his daughter, Courtney. Strawn then got on the Hillsborough County Sheriff's Office's radio channel to say how much he loved the sheriff's office but had "personal issues," felt that he had lost everything, and wanted to be with his family. He killed himself in front of his colleagues.

Steven Michael Stagner

Age/race-ethnicity: 42/Caucasian

Victims: 4 dead, 3 wounded

Place/number of locations: Rifle, Colorado/2

Date/duration: July 5, 2001/less than 1 hour

Weapon: firearm

On July 5, 2001, Stagner started drinking and threatened to go on a murder spree. Those who heard him just ignored him. A few hours later, he acted. Angry about the influx of Hispanics into the area, he shot a man at a pay phone and then went through a trailer park and shot more people. He left the park to reload and was placed under arrest. Found not guilty by reason of insanity (bipolar disorder and schizophrenia), he was sent to the Colorado Mental Health Institute.

William Workman

Age/race-ethnicity: 43/Caucasian

Victims: 7 dead

Place/number of locations: Palos Hills, Illinois/3

Date/duration: June 26, 1973/2 hours

Weapon: firearm

Workman, an alcoholic with a mental illness had been treated psychiatrically on five occasions but was discharged in 1972. His wife left him, but he continued to be abusive to her. Suffering from hallucinations, he was temporarily admitted to a psychiatric facility after threatening to kill his parents, family, and himself. When he got out, he purchased a rifle. On June 25, he entered the home of a friend and killed him and his parents. Moving on to where his own parents lived, he shot a girl who was playing outside. When her pregnant mother came out, Workman shot her as well. Inside his parents' home, he killed both. Police extracted him by using tear gas. In court, Workman said that "God's son" had to take matters into his own hands. He had once told his wife that he could do whatever God could do. He was found not competent to stand trial. Eventually deemed sane, Workman was convicted.

Cedrick Berryhill

Age/race-ethnicity: 16/Black

Victims: 4 dead

Place/number of locations: St. Roch, Louisiana/4

Date/duration: December 23–27, 2010/4 days

Weapon: firearm

With an IQ of 66 and a diagnosis of ADHD and schizophrenia, Berryhill was considered unable to understand a plea offer in connection with his series of robberies, rapes, and the fatal shooting of three men in three different locations within an hour. On December 27, Berryhill shot a man as he talked to his wife on the phone. In 2017, he was still found to be incompetent.

Isaac Zamora

Age/race-ethnicity: 28/Caucasian

Victims: 6 dead, 4 wounded

Place/number of locations: Alger, Washington/5

Date/duration: September 2, 2008/1 day

Weapon: knife, firearms

On Sept 2, 2008, Zamora emerged from the woods where he had been living for years to break into homes to steal drugs and weapons. Paranoid, he was certain that there was a conspiracy in the area. Someone who knew him notified his mother, who called the police. Over the years, she had tried in vain to get psychiatric help for him. The sheriff's deputy who responded ended up dead. By then, Zamora had already killed another man in his home. He went into an unfinished house, where he shot two construction workers and mutilated their bodies. Stealing a truck, he crashed it and shot two more people, one of whom died. He tried to shoot another man, but the gun jammed, so he stabbed him, declaring, "I know what you've been doing!" On the highway, Zamora shot at several drivers, killing one. Finally, he was pulled over. Zamora had been under state supervision and was considered a high-risk but non-violent offender. He had committed his crimes during a psychotic break, fueled by developing paranoia. A plea agreement stipulated that Zamora posed such a risk for future violence that he would be committed in a state hospital until such time as he could be moved to a prison.

Jiverly Antes Wong

Age/race-ethnicity: 41/Asian

Victims: 13 dead, 4 injured

Place/number of locations: Binghamton, New York/2

Date/duration: April 3, 2009/less than 1 hour

Weapon: firearms

Ended in suicide

At about 10:30 a.m., Wong used a vehicle registered to his father to barricade the rear door of the Binghamton American Civic Association building. He wore a bulletproof vest and carried a gun. He randomly fired at anyone in his path, hitting two receptionists and killing one. He entered a classroom for English as a Second Language and fired over and over, hitting the professors and 12 students. He took others hostage. When he heard alarms, he shot himself. Later, a two-page handwritten letter with photos of Wong holding a gun arrived at a Syracuse TV station that indicated that the reclusive Wong was suffering from paranoid delusions about police harassing him and visiting his home. He had recently lost a job and was depressed.

Teofilo Medina Jr.

Age/race-ethnicity: 41/Black

Victims: 4 dead

Place/number of locations: Orange County, Riverside County, California/4

Date/duration: October 18, 1984/2 weeks

Weapon: firearm

Less than 3 months after his release from prison, Medina began a robbery/murder spree. He stole a gun and killed four clerks at gas stations or drive-in dairies in Orange and Riverside Counties. Medina was tried and convicted for the three slayings that occurred in Orange County. His attorney argued unsuccessfully that his client was mentally ill and could not remember the murders. Medina claimed that as a youth he'd learned from a revelation that he was a "high priest." Psychiatric testimony from a staff psychiatrist at the prison where Medina was held indicated that he suffered from paranoid schizophrenia and was incompetent to assist in his defense. Another psychiatrist agreed with the diagnosis but said he was competent. Another mental health expert thought Medina was malingering. He went to trial and was found guilty.

Frank Kulak

Age/race-ethnicity: 41/Caucasian

Victims: 4 dead, 20 wounded

Place/number of locations: Chicago, Illinois/3

Date/duration: April 7–15, 1969/8 days

Weapon: bombs, firearm

A former Marine and decorated veteran of the Second World War and Vietnam, Kulak bombed a toy store, killing a woman and injuring others. On April 12, another bomb detonated and killed a man, while other bombing incidents injured many more people. Police developed leads on Kulak. He barricaded himself in his apartment on April 15, shooting at neighbors and bringing more than 100 police to his door. He killed two but eventually surrendered. Highly paranoid, Kulak was declared mentally incompetent to stand trial. Subsequent hearings continued to find him unfit to stand trial.

Gian Luigi Ferri

Age/race-ethnicity: 55/Hispanic

Victims: 8 dead, 6 wounded, and had a list of 30 intended

Place/number of locations: San Francisco, California/5

Date/duration: July 1, 1993/less than 1 hour

Weapon: firearms

Ended in suicide

Dressed in a business suit and carrying a briefcase, Ferri took the elevator at 101 California Street in San Francisco. Outside a glassed conference room, the failed real estate speculator opened fire, killing three people. He shot one more on that floor before moving to lower floors, killing and wounding people. Police officers arrived and shut down the elevators, trapping the gunman. When he saw officers coming up the stairs, he fled to an isolated area and shot himself to death with a single bullet. A 4-page rambling note was found on his body, in which he ranted in a paranoid tone about a flavor enhancer in food, the Food and Drug Administration, and the legal profession that had "raped" him. Twelve years earlier, he had consulted with the targeted firm and apparently held a longstanding grudge about their imagined part in his financial demise. "When you hire a consultant or an attorney," his note said,

> you don't hire for the purpose of getting raped and then having all your efforts toward legal recourse totally thwarted by a corrupt legal system of 'esquires'. Esquires in the dark ages romed [sic] the countryside to steel [sic] from the working people and give to the prince. Do attorney [sic] want us to call them esquires because their allegiance is to the monarchy?

Mark Storm

Age/race-ethnicity: 30/unknown

Victims: 5 dead

Place/number of locations: Wheeling, West Virginia/2

Date/duration: March 7, 1997/less than 1 hour

Weapon: firearm

Ended in suicide

On March 7, Storm checked himself out of a psychiatric ward. A riverboat pilot on leave, he'd been in the Ohio Valley Medical Center for 4 days for treatment for stress and a panic disorder. That night, he killed his wife and two daughters at home before driving two miles to his mother's house, where he fatally shot her and his brother. With one bullet left, he drove to his favorite fishing spot on the Ohio River and killed himself.

Joseph Martin Danks

Age/race-ethnicity: 26/Caucasian

Victims: 6 dead, 1 hurt

Place/number of locations: Los Angeles, California/6

Date/duration: January 6–20, 1987/13 days

Weapon: knife

In January 1987, six homeless men in a Los Angeles neighborhood fell prey to a random slayer. The second incident was 8 days after the first, but the third victim was just 3 hours later. Then 2 days passed before another died and one was hurt. He tried again on January 20, missing one man but killing another in an alley. Witnesses pursued the killer until the police arrested him. A drifter, Danks confessed to the stabbings. In a tape-recorded statement he said he disliked ''bums'' and ''dirty'' derelicts. During his trial, Danks stabbed his lawyer in the face and headed toward the jury box before he was stopped. He said he'd stabbed the transients while they slept and told jurors, "I would do it to you, too." Experts testified that he was delusional and paranoid, and that his IQ qualified as mentally retarded. He thought that celebrities excreted into his food, and he scrubbed his cell with a toothbrush six to 10 times a day.

Jeffrey Gerard Jones

Age/race-ethnicity: 22/Caucasian

Victims: 4 dead

Place/number of locations: Sacramento, California/4

Date/duration: January 21–22/February 18, 1985/25 days

Weapon: hammer

Jones was sent home from college for "abnormal behavior." Psychiatrists diagnosed him with paranoid schizophrenia and prescribed antipsychotic medication, but nothing seemed to help. He threatened his parents and robbed a disabled man. He was arrested and evaluated as not being dangerous. However, in January 1985, Jones slaughtered a man in a restroom at Sutter's Fort with a claw hammer. Hours later, he battered another man in a restroom at the University of California in Davis. The next day, he went to the same building to attack another man in a restroom. On February 18, Jones killed a fourth man at the UC-Davis physics-geology building. Jones was finally arrested. Apparently, he'd launched these attacks to try to get committed for treatment.

Michael Wayne Jackson

Age/race-ethnicity: 41/Caucasian

Victims: 3 dead

Place/number of locations: Indiana, Missouri, Kentucky/3

Date/duration: September 22–October 2, 1986/9 days

Weapon: firearm

Ended in suicide

Jackson's crime spree began when he shot and killed his federal probation officer. As he fled, he shot and killed a grocer in a robbery attempt. After a shootout with police, Jackson began a series of car thefts and abductions that took him to Missouri, where police linked him to the death of Earl Dallas Finn. For 10 days, Jackson remained at large. When police finally confronted the fugitive, he shot himself in an abandoned barn. Jackson had a 17-year history of mental problems.

Scott Harlan Thorpe

Age/race-ethnicity: 40/Caucasian

Victims: 3 dead, 2 wounded, 1 injured

Place/number of locations: Nevada City, California/2

Date/duration: January 10, 2001/1 hour

Weapon: firearm

Apparently unhappy with his healthcare, Thorpe went to the social services building in Nevada City and shot three people. His rampage caused a woman to jump from the window, breaking her leg. Thorpe traveled two miles to a restaurant near Grass Valley and shot the manager and cook. The manager died. Thorpe had believed they were poisoning him. He then went home, where he was arrested. He was found not guilty by reason of insanity and sent to a psychiatric hospital.

Nathan Nicholas Trupp

Age/race-ethnicity: 41/Caucasian

Victims: 5 dead

Place/number of locations: Albuquerque, New Mexico, Los Angeles, California/2

Date/duration: November 29–December 1, 1988/3 days

Weapon: firearm

Trupp believed that workers at a bagel shop were intentionally poisoning him. He had been hospitalized twice for hearing voices and having delusions about Nazis. On November 29, he went to the bagel shop and fatally shot three people. He then took a bus to Los Angeles to find "Highway to Heaven" star Michael Landon at Universal Studios. He took a tour of the grounds, looking for Landon. Not finding him, he asked to use a phone at the guardhouse. He was turned away, but came back and opened fire, killing two security guards. Police shot at Trupp, wounding him. Under arrest, he was declared not competent to stand trial. Considered psychotic, he was committed to a psychiatric hospital.

Arthur Paul Baird

Age/race-ethnicity: 40/Caucasian

Victims: 3 dead

Place/number of locations: Montgomery County, Indiana/2

Date/duration: September 6–7, 1985/14 hours

Weapon: hands, knife

Just before a shopping trip, Baird strangled his wife for no apparent reason. He remained home with the body, keeping busy until the following morning, when he drove to his parents' house. He fed the chickens and let his mother cut his hair before he stabbed her and then his father. He then stuffed his car full of their items and went home to watch baseball. The police arrested him there.

Rodrick Dantzler

Age/race-ethnicity: 34/Black

Victims: 7 dead, 2 wounded

Place/number of locations: Grand Rapids, Michigan/3

Date/duration: July 7, 2011/9 hours

Weapon: firearm

Ended in suicide

In a hand-written note to his mother, Dantzler, said "demons," depression, and failed relationships triggered his July 7, 2010 rampage that left seven people dead. He told her the medicine had failed. He shot and killed his wife, their daughter, and her parents in their home. His mother phoned the police. Drinking vodka and snorting cocaine, Dantzler entered the home of a former girlfriend, killing her, her sister, and her daughter. He wounded a female acquaintance that he saw on the street. Stealing a car, he drove to the home of strangers, taking them hostage. He used more cocaine, complaining that his wife had taken his kids. Eventually, he shot himself in the head. He had bipolar disorder and was not taking his medication.

Joseph Wesbecker

Age/race-ethnicity: 47/Caucasian

Victims: 7 dead, 15 wounded

Place/number of locations: Louisville, Kentucky/multiple locations in a building

Date/duration: September 14, 1989/20 minutes

Weapon: firearms

Ended in suicide

Wesbecker had worked for 20 years as a pressman at the Standard Gravure Printing Company when his supervisors placed him on a long-term disability leave for psychiatric problems. He was 47 and saw no way to get other employment. Also, his marriage had recently failed, and he was in debt from poor investments. Angry, he armed himself with an AK-47, an assault pistol, two semiautomatic Mac-11 pistols, a .38 revolver, a bayonet, and hundreds of rounds of ammunition. Then he went to the printing company, took the elevator to the business offices on the third floor and began to shoot anyone in his path. Wesbecker continued around the building, even going down to the basement to find victims. Finally, he shot himself. A psychiatrist whom Wesbecker had been seeing indicated that he suffered from bipolar disorder.

John Hyde

Age/race-ethnicity: 48/Caucasian

Victims: 5 dead

Place/number of locations: Albuquerque, New Mexico/3

Date/duration: August 18, 2005/18 hours

Weapon: firearm

In Albuquerque, Hyde went on a shooting rampage that left five people dead, including two police officers. He'd had a dispute with one victim at a transportation facility over his sick leave. He had called his case manager to make an appointment and made another call for help. Frustrated, he left a message about a list of people he wanted to kill. The hospital had also not returned his calls. He entered a motorcycle shop and shot two employees. Aware of his diagnosed schizophrenia, two officers looked for him at his home. Hyde shot both before jumping on his motorcycle and yelling, "Mexican Mafia rules!" After a chase, he was arrested. Found mentally incompetent to stand trial, Hyde was sent to a behavior health institute in Las Vegas. As of 2018, he was found still not competent.

Edward Allaway

Age/race-ethnicity: 37/Caucasian

Victims: 7 dead, 2 injured

Place/number of locations: Fullerton, California/2

Date/duration: July 12, 1976/10 minutes

Weapon: firearm

Allaway came to work at the campus library of the California State University at Fullerton, where he was a janitor. He brought a .22 caliber rifle. Entering the media center in the basement, he started shooting. He killed three. He proceeded upstairs and killed someone in the elevator before emerging on the ground floor to kill three faculty. He surrendered and was found not guilty by reason of insanity. He was diagnosed with paranoid schizophrenia.

Albert Keller

Age/race-ethnicity: 33/Caucasian

Victims: 3 dead, 1 wounded

Place/number of locations: Chicago, Illinois/3

Date/duration: July 27, 1976/15 minutes

Weapon: firearm

Ended in suicide

Keller created a list of 14 people he wanted to kill at his workplace, believing they had sabotaged his promotions. He shot four of them, killing three, before committing suicide.

Tristan van der Vlis

Age/race-ethnicity: 24/Caucasian

Victims: 6 dead, 17 wounded

Place/number of locations: Netherlands/various locations inside mall

Date/duration: April 9, 2011/20 minutes

Weapon: firearms

Ended in suicide

Diagnosed with paranoid schizophrenia, Tristan van der Vlis started shooting people in the Ridderhof Mall in the Netherlands for no clear reason. He killed a woman outside before he entered and shot more than 100 bullets randomly at shoppers before killing himself. In a note in his car, police discovered that he had left explosives in three other malls. These malls were evacuated.

Ernst August Wagner

Age/race-ethnicity: /Caucasian

Victims: 14 dead, 11 wounded

Place/number of locations: Degerloch, Germany/multiple

Date/duration: September 4, 1913/1 day

Weapon: knife, firearm

On September 4, 1913, Wagner fatally stabbed his wife and four children in Degerloch, Germany. He then drove to another town, where he set fires to four barns and walked through the streets. He shot 20 men, killing nine before villagers beat him unconscious. As a boy, he suffered from depression and suicidal thoughts. As an adult, he had developed paranoia. Forced into marriage, he felt that his wife was inferior to him. He tried and failed to kill himself. He kept having more children, which put a strain on him. His paranoia became oppressive, so he made plans to kill people he thought were ridiculing him. Upon his arrest, he asked to be decapitated. He was found not guilty by reason of insanity.

Walter Seifert

Age/race-ethnicity: 42/Caucasian

Victims: 10 dead, 22 injured

Place/number of locations: Cologne, West Germany/3

Date/duration: June 11, 1964/15 minutes

Weapon: flamethrower, mace, lance

Ended in suicide

On June 11, 1964, Seifert went to a local Catholic elementary school with a mace, lance, and homemade flamethrower. He approached a teacher outside and used the flamethrower on her and several girls. He then went to one of the four barracks, smashed his mace against the windows, and aimed his flamethrower at children in the classrooms, setting them on fire. He attacked anyone who ran from the burning building until he ran out of fuel. When teacher Gertrud Bollenrath stepped into the schoolyard, Seifert fatally stabbed her with his lance. As he approached the barracks door, two female teachers tried to keep him out, but he pushed and caused one to fall down a flight of stairs. Seifert followed and stabbed her in both legs and between her shoulders. Altogether, he killed eight students and two teachers, and injured 22 others. Seifert fled from the campus and swallowed insecticide. He died that evening.

Diagnosed with schizophrenia, Seifert had suffered from depression after his wife's death. Unemployed, he had tried unsuccessfully to get a military pension. Having nothing left, he went on his rampage.

David Malcolm Gray

Age/race-ethnicity: 33/Caucasian

Victims: 13 dead, 3 wounded

Place/number of locations: New Zealand/3

Date/duration: November 30, 1990/23 hours

Murder weapon: firearm

A massacre occurred on November 13, 1990, in the small seaside township of Aramoana, New Zealand. After a verbal dispute with a neighbor, Gray began indiscriminately shooting people in the township with a scoped semiautomatic rifle. After a house-by-house search the next day, police officers located Gray and shot him as he came out of a residence. Gray was an avid reader of warfare, weaponry, and survivalist literature who had amassed a cache of firearms and ammunition. Believed to have schizophrenia, his mental and physical state during the 6 months prior to the tragedy had deteriorated.

Nikola Radosavljevic

Age/race-ethnicity: 37/Caucasian

Victims: 9 dead, 3 wounded

Place/number of locations: Jabukovac, Serbia/7

Date/duration: July 27, 2007/1 day

Weapon: firearm

Nikola got into an argument with his wife and jumped into a well. After he was talked out of it, he got a rifle and walked through the streets and into several houses, shooting people. He let one woman live when she said she did not practice magic. He tried to kill himself but failed and was arrested. Treated the year before for paranoid psychosis, he was judged to be insane.

Lee Chi Hang

Age/race-ethnicity: 28/Asian

Victims: 6 dead, 37 injured

Place/number of locations: Hong Kong/4

Date/duration: June 3, 1982/a few hours

Weapon: knives, chisels

At around 1:30 p.m. Hang fatally stabbed his mother and sister in their apartment on the 12th floor of a building. Armed with two chisels and two knives, Hang ran downstairs, stabbing two women, and entered a kindergarten to slash and stab children, leaving 30 wounded and four dead. When officers arrived, Hang fled to the playground, where he stabbed a constable in the chest. Ignoring the injured policeman's orders to drop his weapons, Hang wounded two men, a woman, and a 14-year-old boy. The constable finally shot him in the left arm and stomach. Under arrest, he was found to be psychotic and sent to a psychiatric institution.

Mark Rowntree

Age/race-ethnicity: 19/Caucasian

Victims: 4 dead

Place/number of locations: Bingley, West Yorkshire, England/3

Date/duration: December 31, 1975–January 7, 1976/8 days

Weapon: knife

On December 31, 1975, Rowntree knocked on Grace Adamson's door and introduced himself as a police officer. Then he pulled a knife and fatally stabbed her. On January 3, he bought another knife and went up to a 16-year-old boy at a bus stop to stab him. The boy gave police a description before he died. Four days later, Rowntree visited Barbara Booth at her home and killed her and her 3-year-old son. Diagnosed with schizophrenia, he was placed in a secure hospital indefinitely.

Hermann Schwarz

Age/race-ethnicity: 25/Caucasian

Victims: 7 dead, 8 wounded

Place/Number of locations: Romanshorn, Switzerland/3

Date/duration: August 30, 1912/1 day

Weapon: firearm

When discharged from the Army due to mental trouble, Schwarz was angry. He barricaded himself in his room in the city of Romanshorn, and for 5 hours kept up steady gunfire from his window. He killed five men who tried to break down the door and wounded eight others. He escaped while the fire brigade was summoned. He encountered a police officer in the woods and shot him. Before he was captured, he killed another officer. He was found insane and ordered to be institutionalized for the rest of his life.

Giuseppe Leotta

Age/race-ethnicity: 32/Caucasian

Victims: 5 dead

Place/number of locations/Aci Castello, Sicily, Italy/4

Date/duration: May 1, 2003/less than 1 hour

Weapon: firearm

Ended in suicide

Leotta was concerned about his job prospects. On a temporary contract and upset that he had not been chosen to be the mayor's driver, he went to the Town Hall and entered several offices, shooting the mayor and four others, including a man who passed him on the stairs and a retiree on a park bench. He had a history of mental problems and had once attacked his brother with an ax. Later that day, he committed suicide in a church.

Mat Taram bin Sa'al (aka Utoh)

Age/race-ethnicity: 30/Asian

Victims: 11dead, 10 wounded

Place/number of locations: Bangi, Selangor, Malaysia /4

Date/duration: October 9–10, 1947/2 days

Weapon: knife

With his wife and three children, Utoh boarded the mail train from Singapore to Kuala Lumpur. At approximately 6 p.m., he entered the restaurant car, drew a knife, and attacked four British soldiers, an Indian, and a Malaysian. He killed three. When the train stopped, Utoh fled. Along the way, he killed seven people (three children) and wounded nine (four children). Thirty-six hours later, he arrived in his hometown on foot, where he was arrested. Utoh was deemed to have been psychotic at the time of the murders and was sent to a psychiatric facility.

Huang Wenyi

Age/race-ethnicity: 34/Asian

Victims: 6 dead

Place/number of locations: home and hospital in Foshan City, China/2

Date/duration: December 28, 2006/2 hours

Weapon: hammer

On December 28, 2006 in his home, Wenyi took a hammer to his wife, son, mother-in-law, sister-in-law, and a woman who worked in the pharmacy he owned. One hour later, Huang lured another sister-in-law into a garden at Foshan People's Hospital, where he killed her with the same hammer. Huang was deemed to be mentally ill at the time of the crimes.

Ronald Baquiran Bae

Age/race-ethnicity: 41/Asian

Victims: 8 dead, 12 wounded (plus one earlier victim)

Place/number of locations: Philippines/4+

Date/duration: January 4, 1983/30 minutes

Weapon: firearm

The spree began in the morning when Bae shot his neighbor's dog, then its owner. Bae walked toward a store, looking for a man named Berto Caimol. When he could not locate the man, he shot Caimol's three children. One died. Then he went into the street and shot more people. The carnage ended when responding policemen killed Bae. They arrested a man who had helped him to reload (under threat of death) and learned that Bae had killed another man. Police searched around Bae's house and unearthed the skeleton of a former associate. Bae reportedly had mental issues. He once had talked to a wall and said, "I am the devil." Some relatives thought he was demon-possessed. He was a heavy drinker and drug user, especially methamphetamines.

Gordon Cummins

Age/race-ethnicity: 28/Caucasian

Victims: 4 dead, 2 wounded

Place/number of locations: London, England/4

Date/duration: February 8–12, 1942/5 days

Weapon: hands, knife

Over 6 days in 1942, the "Black-out Ripper" exploited London's night-time black-out conditions during the war to murder four women and attempt to murder two others. He mutilated the bodies of three. Some he strangled, some he stabbed, or cut their throat. The third victim was mutilated with a razor blade, a knife, and a candlestick. Cummins, a married man, was finally arrested 2 days after the last murder. He was a pilot-in-training in the Royal Air Force. Tried, he was quickly convicted and sentenced to death. Although no mental health testimony was presented at his trial, he appeared to suffer from a compulsion to mutilate women postmortem.

REFERENCES

Berger, M. (1949, September 6). Veteran kills 12 in mad rampage in Camden street. *New York Times*, p. 1.

Mellor, L. (2013). *Rampage: Canadian mass murder and spree killing.* Toronto, ON: Dundurn.

Torok, T., Quinn, L., & Fleck, C. (1985, October 31). Suspect is described as explosive psychopath. *The Philadelphia Inquirer*, p. 1.

Venditta, D. (2018, December 29). A 100-year-old mystery: Why did Allentown soldier go berserk, killing 3 and himself? *Morning Call.* Retrieved from https://www.mcall.com/news/local/mc-nws-allentown-sergeant-boyle-deadly-rampage-20181210-story.html

CHAPTER 6

Robbery and Thrill

We include thrill with robbery, since these motivators were present together more times than not. When thrill is the primary motive, theft can be sporadic or an afterthought, especially the theft of a car or money. Sometimes we see desperation in this category, but more often the killings are senseless. The violence is often excessive and gratuitous, as most of the robberies could have been committed by intimidation without committing the murder. The use of force is recognized as excessive beyond what is necessary even in terms of witness elimination. It is the recognition of the excessive injury and use of multiple weapons that warrants our observation that thrill is often comorbid with robbery, and sometimes the offenders admitted it. In this category we also found more teams of two or more acting together, as well as the involvement of more females. None of the lone operators were female. The suicide rate for robbery/thrill killers is quite low compared to those motivated by anger or a mission. In this category, there were two suicides and one attempt.

Total: 78 cases, 121 killers (12 females, plus 2 that were not charged)

Teams: 33 cases, 76 killers

Lone operators: 45 cases, 45 killers

ROBBERY/THRILL: TEAMS

Jonathan and Reginald Carr

Age/race-ethnicity: 20 and 22/Black

Victims: 5 dead, 1 injured

Place/number of locations: Wichita, Kansas/3

Date/duration: December 8–12, 2000/6 days

Weapon: firearms

On December 14, 2000, the Carrs invaded a home and ordered the small gathering at an engagement party to remove their clothing. Over the course of 3 hours, they beat the three men and raped the two women. They also forced the victims to perform sex acts on each other. Holding them hostage, the young men took each person out, without clothes, to extract money from an ATM machine. They also stole the engagement ring and other items. Then after these atrocities were inflicted, the Carrs took the victims to a soccer field and forced them to kneel in the snow. They shot each one in the head and used the stolen truck to run over the bodies. One woman survived, thanks to a barrette in her hair that had deflected a bullet. She walked naked for over a mile until she found someone to help. Police arrested the brothers and learned that they were also responsible for two earlier cases the week before. On December 8, the brothers had robbed a man at gunpoint. Three days later, they'd fatally shot a librarian and cellist for the local orchestra. Jonathan, 20, and Reginald Carr, 22, had chosen people at random (although all were white), primarily to rob them, but had decided to have some sadistic fun. They were convicted and sentenced to death.

Alton Coleman and Debra Brown

Age/race-ethnicity: 28 and 21/Black

Victims: 8 dead, 1 injured

Place/number of locations: 6 states/multiple

Date/duration: May–July, 1984/2 months

Weapon: hands, firearms, ligatures

When Coleman got out on bail for a rape charge, he went on the run with his girlfriend Debra Brown. This ninth-grade dropout was also suspected of kidnapping a missing 9-year-old girl. After he was gone, her body was found, raped and strangled. Reports came of a black couple who lured children to their car, grabbing them to rape. The next crime occurred in Ohio, when a woman helped a couple who claimed they were without money or means. That night, she and her 10-year-old daughter were found strangled. Shortly afterward, a woman kidnapped from Gary, Indiana, was strangled and dumped near Detroit. Coleman and Brown moved quickly, returning to Ohio, where in Cincinnati, they attacked a couple to steal their car. On the way, they raped and strangled another young girl and shot an elderly man to death. An acquaintance of theirs brought their six-state spree to an end by alerting the police in Evanston, Illinois.

Lewis Eugene Gilbert and Eric Elliott

Age/race-ethnicity: 23 and 16/Caucasian

Victims: 4 dead

Place/number of locations: Ohio to Oklahoma/3

Date/duration: August 29–September 3, 1994/5 days

Weapon: firearm

On August 29, Gilbert and Elliot broke into the home of Ruth Loader near Port Washington, Ohio, tied her up, and put her in the trunk of her car. They took her to the woods and shot her before they drove to Missouri. Getting stuck, they entered a farmhouse and killed two people. Taking their car and a rifle, they went to Oklahoma, where they killed a man for his truck. This team was arrested in New Mexico.

Charles Roache and Christopher Lippard

Age/race-ethnicity: 25 and 20/Caucasian

Victims: 6 dead

Place/number of locations: North Carolina/3

Date/duration: September 29–30, 1999/2 days

Weapon: firearm

On the morning of September 29, Lippard and Chad Watt picked up Mark Stout and Charles Roache. Lippard damaged Watts' car, which upset him, so Roache and Stout beat him and threw him in the trunk. Lippard drove to a wooded area where Roache hit Watt with a shotgun and broke his neck. Then both men shot him and hid the body under a log. The next morning, Lippard stole a truck and picked up Roache. As they drove over one hundred miles away, they stole items from several vehicles. When they damaged the truck, they looked for a car to steal. Lippard entered the home of Earl and Cora Phillips and forced them to lie on the floor while he looked for items to steal. Roache came in and shot them. They stole the Phillips' truck but lost control. Returning, they killed the Phillips' son outside. Inside, they killed his wife and daughter.

David Pederson and Holly Ann Grigsby

Age/race-ethnicity: 31 and 24/Caucasian

Victims: 4 dead

Place/number of locations: Washington State, Oregon, and California/4

Date/duration: September 26–Oct 3, 2011/1 week

Weapon: knife, firearms

These two White supremacists killed Pederson's parents, allegedly for molestation, and executed a Black man because he was Black, and a young man whose name "sounded Jewish."

Anthony Thomas Wyatt and Michael Lovette

Age/race-ethnicity: 24 and 29/Caucasian

Victims: 4 dead

Place/number of locations: Vero Beach and Tampa, Florida/2

Date/duration: May 17–19, 1988

Weapon: firearm

On May 13, 1988, Wyatt and Lovette escaped from a prison work crew in North Carolina and went to Florida, landing in Vero Beach. Stealing a car, they found a .38 caliber handgun. On May 17, they went to a restaurant to commit a robbery. Wyatt ushered two of the employees into the bathroom and told the manager to open the time-delayed safe. Wyatt raped one employee before shooting all three. The team fled to Tampa, where they met a woman at a bar. They left with her, shot her, and stole her car.

Walter Kelbach and Myron Lance

Age/race-ethnicity: 28 and 25/Caucasian

Victims: 6 dead, 1 wounded

Place/number of locations: Salt Lake City, Utah/4

Date/duration: December 17, 1966/5 days

Weapon: knife, firearm

Cousins Kelbach and Lance went on a robbery-murder spree on December 17, 1966, in Salt Lake City. They forced a gas station attendant to undress and get into their car, where they assaulted him with a knife before killing him. They repeated this at another gas station. Two days later, they robbed and shot a taxi driver before they entered a bar. They shot one man in the head, robbed him, and then killed three more.

Henry Lee Burrell and Zakkawanda Zawumba Moss

Age/race-ethnicity: 36 and 35/Black

Victims: 6 dead

Place/number of locations: Park City, Tennessee/2

Date/duration: October 22, 2012

Weapon: feet, hands, firearms

Burrell assisted Warren Crutcher in his drug dealing business when they met in prison. Moss, a friend of Burrell's, joined them. Burrell and Moss decided that Crutcher was cheating them, so they decided to rob him. As they searched the two homes where he lived with two different women, they killed six people, including Crutcher.

Glenn Nash and Margo Freshwater

Age/race-ethnicity: 38 and 18/Caucasian

Victims: 3 dead

Place/number of locations: Tennessee, Florida, Mississippi/3

Date/duration: 1966/3 weeks

Weapon: firearm

In 1966, Nash, a married attorney, persuaded Freshwater to join him on a robbery spree that turned deadly. At a liquor store, Nash tied up Hillman Robbins Sr., stole $600 and shot Robbins in the head. Nash and Freshwater fled, killing a clerk in Florida and a cab driver in Mississippi.

Nash confessed to all the murders but was found to be incompetent to stand trial. In 1969, a Memphis jury convicted Freshwater of first-degree murder, even though the prosecution had stipulated that she had not shot Robbins. They decided that she was a willing accomplice.

Sammy Butler and Robert Lee Thompson

Age/race-ethnicity: 19 and 21/Black

Victims: 3 dead, 1 wounded

Place/number of locations: Houston, Texas/3

Date/duration: December 1996/24 hours

Weapon: firearms

Over the course of 2 months, Butler and Thompson went on a robbery spree in which three people were fatally shot in 24 hours during armed robberies in three of the eight targeted stores. Thompson said it was to punish racist storeowners, but he later attributed the spree to the "recklessness of youth."

Peter Lesko, Michael Travaglia, Ricky Rutherford (for Two)

Age/race-ethnicity: 19 and 19/Caucasian

Victims: 4 dead

Place/number of locations: Apollo, Delmont, Pittsburgh, Pennsylvania/4

Date/duration: December 26, 1979–January 2, 1980/1 week

Weapon: firearm

During the week after Christmas 1979, Travaglia and Lesko randomly killed four people in three western Pennsylvania towns. Lesko hooked up with Travaglia and they kidnapped a security guard and shot him. A woman picked them up hitchhiking and they took her hostage while they robbed a party store. Then they shot her. In the late evening of January 2, 1980, Lesko and Travaglia picked up a 15-year-old juvenile delinquent named Ricky Rutherford. The trio waited outside their hotel for someone to drive up. They brutalized the man before making him drive to the woods. There, they bound his legs and pushed him through a hole in an ice-covered pond. Dropping a large rock on the hole, they ensured his death. They used his car to go rob a convenience store and drive to Pittsburgh. They baited a patrol officer into chasing them. When they stopped to let him approach, they shot and killed him.

Martin Rutrell, Linzie Thompson, and Ben Chaney

Age/race-ethnicity: 15, 19, 16/Black

Victims: 4 dead, 2 wounded

Place/number of locations: North Carolina, Florida, South Carolina/3

Date/duration: April 25–May 20, 1970/25 days

Weapon: firearm

Rutrell and two accomplices, Thompson and Chaney, robbed and shot two White students on April 25, 1970. Both survived. On May 3 this gang robbed and murdered a White college student in Ft. Lauderdale. Eleven days later in Boca Raton, they carjacked two White females, shooting both women. Driving through South Carolina, they tried to rob a roadside fireworks stand. A clerk shot and killed Thompson. That day, the two surviving gang members were arrested.

Paul Ruiz and Earl Van Denton

Age/race-ethnicity: 29 and 28/Caucasian

Victims: 7 dead

Place/number of locations: Arkansas, Oklahoma and Louisiana

Date/duration: June–July, 1977/2 weeks

Weapon: firearms

In June–July 1977, Ruiz and Van Denton escaped from prison and went on a robbery/murder spree, killing seven in Alabama, Louisiana, and Oklahoma.

Michael Crenshaw and Kelvin Shelby Malone (Malone did two alone)

Age/race-ethnicity: 19 and 19/Caucasian

Victims: 4 dead

Place/number of locations: Missouri, Texas, California/4

Date/duration: March 18–21, 1981/3 days

Weapon: handguns

The beaten body of Myrtle Benham was found in an abandoned shack in the desert near Daggett, California. Four days later, Malone and Crenshaw were arrested in San Jose. In their possession were credit cards and jewelry from two other people. In a deal, Crenshaw testified that he and Malone were driving from Las Vegas when they stopped in at an Exxon station to rob the place. They raped and killed Bentham there. Then they killed another woman after robbing her. They stole a car from a man in Kansas City whom they later robbed and killed. Malone had also kidnapped and killed another man to steal his car. His body was never found.

Charles Noel Brown and Charles Edwin Kelley

Age/race-ethnicity: 28 and 20/Caucasian

Victims: 3 dead, 4 injured

Place/number of locations: Minnesota, Iowa/5

Date/duration: February 17–22, 1961/5 days

Weapon: firearms

In 1961, Brown met Kelley in Minneapolis. They went on a drunken two-state armed robbery spree, resulting in three deaths and several injured victims.

Ricky Javon Gray, Ray Joseph Dandridge, and Ashley Baskerville (one incident)

Age/race-ethnicity: 28, 28, and 21/Black

Victims: 8 dead, 1 injured

Place/number of locations: Pennsylvania/Virginia/4

Date/duration: December 31, 2005/1 week, plus an earlier murder

Weapon: knife, fire, hammer, duct tape

Following his release from prison, Ray Dandridge moved in with Ricky Gray. A week later, Gray's parents evicted Dandridge. Gray joined

Dandridge in Virginia. On December 31, they attacked Ryan Carey, leaving him in critical condition, but he survived. The next day, four members of the Bryan Harvey family were found dead in the basement of their burning house in Richmond, beaten, slashed, and bound with electrical cord and tape. Then a couple was robbed in a home invasion in Chesterfield County. Three days later, the police received a call from a resident who was concerned about Ashley Baskerville. The police entered the house where she lived with her mother and stepfather and found all three murdered. When Gray and Dandridge were arrested on January 7, they confessed, adding Ashley as a participant in the Harvey family murders and the Chesterfield robbery. She had posed as a victim as a part of the plan to rob her mother and stepfather, but "things just went wrong" and Gray had decided to kill Ashley and take her parents' car.

Thomas Eugene Braun and Leonard Maine

Age/race-ethnicity: 18 and 18/Caucasian

Victims: 4 dead, 1 injured

Place/number of locations: Washington, Oregon, California/3

Date/duration: August 18–23, 1967/5 days

Weapon: firearms

On August 17, 1967, Braun left his job in Ritzville, Washington, and picked up Maine. They had two pistols, a car, and no clear goal. In Seattle, on August 18, they stopped at a rooming house and pulled their guns on the landlady. She screamed and they ran. They used a different ruse the next day, kidnapping a woman and shooting her. Using her car, they drove to Oregon. On August 21, Samuel Ledgerwood saw them changing a flat tire and stopped to offer help. They shot him and took his car. Driving to California, they picked up a couple of hitchhikers. Raping the girl, they shot both, but one survived. Finally, they were arrested.

Ronald Raymond Woomer and Eugene Skaar

Age/race-ethnicity: 25, 40/Caucasian

Victims: 4 dead, 1 wounded

Place/number of locations: South Carolina/3

Date/duration: February 21–22, 1979/2 days

Weapon: firearms

Skaar killed himself, Woomer was arrested.

On February 21, 1979, Woomer and Skaar left West Virginia with a plan to steal rare coins from a collector in Cottageville. They stole his coins and fatally shot him. Then they drove to a neighboring community and broke into a home, looking for money and guns. They killed two residents. Later, they kidnapped two women from a convenience store on Pawleys Island. Both were raped and shot. One survived.

Jeffrey Joseph Daugherty and Bonnie Jean Heath

Age/race-ethnicity: 21 and 41/Caucasian

Victims: 6 dead, 1 wounded

Place/number of locations: Florida, Alabama, Pennsylvania/6

Date/duration: February 19–March 11, 1976/20 days

Weapon: firearm, knife

On a trip from Michigan to Florida with his girlfriend, Daugherty killed six people, mostly for small sums of cash. Heath, who did not do the shooting, made a plea deal to testify against Heath in exchange for a reduced charge.

Freddie Lee Glenn and Michael Corbett

Age/race-ethnicity: 18 and 20/Black

Victims: 3 dead

Place/number of locations: Colorado Spring, Colorado/3

Date/duration: June 19–July 1, 1975/12 days

Weapon: knife, bayonet, firearm

The killings began on June 19, 1975, when they kidnapped a soldier and shot him. Eight days later, they met another soldier at Prospect Lake, ostensibly to sell him some marijuana. Corbett stabbed him with a bayonet. Their last victim was Karen Grammar, who was waiting for her boyfriend outside a Red Lobster restaurant. They kidnapped and raped her, stabbed her multiple times, and slit her throat.

Daniel Eugene Remeta, Mark Walter, and Lisa Dunn; James Hunter (for four shootings; possibly did one)

Age/race-ethnicity: 27, 18, 18, and 33/Caucasian

Victims: 5 dead, 3 wounded

Place/number of locations: Kansas/Arkansas/Florida/6

Date/duration: February 8–13, 1985/5 days

Weapon: firearm

Dunn and Walter bailed Remeta, Dunn's boyfriend, out of jail in Michigan and went on a trip to Florida. On February 8, Remata shot a clerk in a convenience store in Ocala, Florida, to take $52. He repeated this act 2 days later in Texas, but this clerk survived. On February 11, in Mulberry, Arkansas, Remeta shot a grocery store clerk 10 times to pocket $556. They picked up a hitchhiker, James Hunter. On February 13, Remeta gunned down a man at a restaurant in northwest Kansas. Undersheriff Ben Albright pulled their car over. Remeta got out and shot him, but he survived. At about 4:15 p.m., Remeta forced two men to get in the back of their truck. They drove for six miles before he made them get out and lie in the road. He shot them execution-style in the back of the head. Cops chased the truck into a farmyard, where a shootout killed Walter and injured Dunn and Remata. Hunter fled but was captured. He claimed he'd tried to stop them, which contradicted the surviving officer's account.

Marvallous Keene, Laura Taylor, DeMarcus Smith, and Heather Matthews

Age/race-ethnicity: 19, 16, 17, and 20/3 Black, 1 Caucasian

Victims: 6 dead, 2 wounded

Place/number of locations: Dayton, Ohio/5

Date/duration: December 23–26, 1992/3 days

Weapon: firearms

For 3 days around Christmas in 1992, the "Downtown Posse" went on a robbery and thrill-killing spree that left four people seriously injured and six dead. Laura Taylor, the only White member, was the youngest, at 16. DeMarcus Smith and Heather Matthews joined Marvallous Keene, their self-proclaimed leader. First, they killed Joseph Wilkerson in his apartment and robbed the place of pawnable goods. Next, Smith shot a woman at a payphone to take her shoes and jacket. The third victim was a man in a car they wanted to steal. Over the next 2 days they killed three more, two of whom were witnesses.

Robert Wesley Knighton, Lawrence Britton, and Ruth Renee Williams

Age/race-ethnicity: 48, 17, and _ /Caucasian

Victims: 4 dead

Place/number of locations: Missouri/2

Date/duration: January 6–8, 1990/3 days

Weapon: firearms

Knighton befriended Britton in a halfway house in Missouri. With Williams, Knighton's girlfriend, they stole a van and drove to Clinton where Knighton shot two people to grab money and weapons. They ran out of gas near a farmhouse. Entering, they killed the two residents.

Allen Nicklasson, Dennis Skillicorn, and Tim DeGraffenreid

Age/race-ethnicity: 32, 34, and 17/Caucasian

Victims: 3 dead

Place/number of locations: Missouri, Arizona/2

Date/duration: August 24–26, 1994/2 days

Weapon: firearms

Skillicorn, Nicklasson, and DeGraffenreid went out to score drugs when their car broke down. After they burglarized a home, they broke down again. Richard Drummond stopped to help. They kidnapped him and shot him. Skillicorn and Nicklasson fled to Arizona, where their car got stuck in some sand. They killed the person who offered assistance, along with his wife.

Raymond Deleon Martinez (two incidents with accomplices for two)

Age/race-ethnicity: 37/Hispanic

Victims: 5 dead, 1 injured

Place/number of locations: Texas/5

Date/duration: July 11–15, 1983/4 days

Weapon: firearms

In Texas on July 11, 1983, Martinez and two accomplices robbed a bar in Houston at gunpoint, killing a man. The next day, Martinez robbed another bar, assaulting a patron. On July 13, with his accomplices, he robbed another bar and killed the owner. Two days later, he fatally shot his sister and her boyfriend before killing a prostitute.

Joseph L. Taborsky and Arthur Culombe

Age/race-ethnicity: 32 and 33/Caucasian

Victims: 6 dead

Place/number of locations: Connecticut/5

Date/duration: December 15, 1956–January 26, 1957/6 weeks

Weapon: firearm

In December 1956 in Connecticut, Taborsky and Columbe went on a 6-week "mad dog" armed robbery spree that ended with six people killed.

George York and James Latham

Age/race-ethnicity: 18 and 19/Caucasian

Victims: 7 dead

Place/number of locations: Louisiana, Florida, Tennessee, Illinois, Kansas/7

Date/duration: May 29–June 10, 1961/12 days

Weapon: firearm

York and Latham met in the Army at Fort Hood. They decided to go AWOL. They beat or killed several people to steal vehicles or money.

When arrested for possessing a stolen car, they bragged about killing people. They claimed that being placed in a mixed-race unit in the Army had angered them. Convicted, they were the last offenders to be executed in Kansas.

James Briley, Linwood Briley, and Duncan Meekins

Age/race-ethnicity: 22, 24, and 16/Black

Victims: 11 dead (plus 1 earlier)

Place/number of locations: Richmond, Virginia/numerous

Date/duration: March 12–October 19, 1979/7 months

Weapon: firearm, baseball bat, knives, scissors

Linwood Briley killed a neighbor when he was 16. Eight years later, he helped his brother, J. B., and Meekins terrorize a Richmond neighborhood for 7 months. They chose random homes to enter and rob, often hurting or killing people.

Shane Glen Harrison and Esther Beckley

Age/race-ethnicity: 26 and 41/Caucasian

Victims: 5 dead

Place/number of locations: New Mexico/2

Date/duration: March 3, 1996/2 hours

Weapon: firearms

Harrison and Beckley killed three employees of a Hollywood Video store during an armed robbery, kidnapping the grandparents of one employee. They took both to the Sandia Mountains and executed them.

Douglas Eric Gretzler and William Steelman

Age/race-ethnicity: 22 and 28/Caucasian

Victims: 17 dead

Place/number of locations: Arizona/4+

Date/duration: October 28–November 6, 1973/10 days

Weapon: firearm

These two drifters met, shared a penchant for mayhem, and decided to start killing together. Steelman was mentally ill. Their spree began when they entered a trailer in Mesa, Arizona, and shot a couple. Then they traveled to Tucson and killed a young man, leaving his body in the desert before returning to the city to murder another couple in their apartment. As they left and drove into the desert, they found a man in a sleeping bag and killed him as well. In Phoenix, they grabbed two more young men, stripped and killed them, leaving their bodies in California. On November 6, this spree-killing team hit again, but this time with nine victims all at once. They went to a house where an 18-year-old girl was baby-sitting Walter and Joanne Parkins' two children. The sitter's parents had dropped by, along with her brother and fiancé, and then the Parkins came home. The killers shot them all. Two days later, the killers were apprehended.

Chad Alan Lee and David Hunt

Age/race-ethnicity: 19 and 14/Caucasian

Victims: 3 dead

Place/number of locations: Maricopa County, Arizona/3

Date/duration: April 6–27, 1992/3 weeks

Weapon: firearm and knife

Lee and Hunt kidnapped a female delivery person to assault, rob, and murder. Their next victim was a cab driver. Then they abducted and killed a convenience store clerk.

Viktor Sayenko and Igor Suprunyuk

Age/race-ethnicity: 19 and 19/Caucasian

Victims: 21 dead, 8 injured

Place/number of locations: Dnepropetrovsk, Ukraine/numerous

Date/duration: June 25–July 16, 2007/3 weeks

Weapon: hammer, steel bar

On June 25, 2007, these two began torturing and killing people randomly for fun, making video recordings as they went to post on the Internet. Some victims had their eyes gouged out while alive. As the killers pawned items they'd stolen, they were arrested and charged with 21 murders and eight attempted murders. They had come from wealthy homes and the father of one was a lawyer. Allegedly, they had planned to sell the murder videos to get rich. Their goal had been 40.

Charmaine Phillips and Peter Grundling

Age/race-ethnicity: 19 and 35/Caucasian

Victims: 4 dead

Place/number of locations: Johannesburg and Durban, South Africa/4

Date/duration: June 1983/2 weeks

Weapon: firearms

This thrill-killing couple murdered four people in Johannesburg and Durban. Charmaine, 19, confessed to being the trigger person in one.

LONE OPERATORS

William Edward Cook Jr.

Age/race-ethnicity: 21/Caucasian

Victims: 6 dead

Place/number of locations: Missouri, California/2

Date/duration: 1950/2 weeks

Weapon: firearm

As 1950 drew to a close, ex-convict William "Cockeyed" Cook, in his black leather jacket and "hard luck" tattoos, carjacked a family near Joplin. When a police car went by, he panicked and shot them all, then drove around with their corpses before depositing them in an abandoned mineshaft. He forced a salesman to drive him to California, where he killed the man. He kidnapped several other people but was arrested in California. Cook was convicted in Missouri of the murder of the family, but California got him for his sixth victim, and executed him.

Raymond Lee Stewart

Age/race-ethnicity: 29/Black

Victims: 6 dead

Place/number of locations: Rockford, Illinois and Beloit, Wisconsin/4

Date/duration: Jan. 27, 1981/7 days

Weapon: firearm

Stewart went on a weeklong spree of armed robbery that ended in six people dead in two states.

Frank Carter

Age/race-ethnicity: 45/Caucasian

Victims: 2–4 (or more) dead

Place/number of locations: Omaha, Nebraska and Council Bluffs, Iowa/multiple

Date/duration: February 1926/2 weeks

Weapon: firearms

Carter killed three men in their homes by shooting through windows before Omaha recommended a blackout. Then a man was shot during the day. More shootings occurred until Carter was caught. Tried for only two deaths, he claimed he had killed 43.

Gary Lee Sampson

Age/race-ethnicity: 41/Caucasian

Victims: 3 dead, 1 attempt

Place/number of locations: New Hampshire, Massachusetts/3

Date/duration: July 24–30, 2001/6 days

Weapon: knife, hands

In 2001, Sampson engaged in a crime spree that included a series of bank robberies in North Carolina, two carjackings in Massachusetts, and a deadly home invasion in New Hampshire. He used a knife to threaten the drivers, forcing them to secluded areas before stabbing them to death. In New Hampshire, he strangled a caretaker to grab a new vehicle. When Sampson tried a third carjacking, the driver escaped. Sampson turned himself in.

Nicholas Troy Sheley

Age/race-ethnicity: 28/Caucasian

Victims: 8 dead

Place/number of locations: Illinois, Missouri/4

Date/duration: June 23–30, 2008/1 week

Weapon: firearm, hammer

Sheley's spree began when he killed 93-year-old Russell Reed in Sterling, Illinois, while looking for money. On June 28, Sheley murdered a man at a car wash to steal his truck. That night, Sheley drove to Rock Falls, Illinois, and murdered a family of four in their apartment, supposedly because he thought the man was having an affair with his wife. He fled to Festus, Missouri, where he committed two more murders.

Fred E. McManus

Age/race-ethnicity: 18/Caucasian

Victims: 5

Place/number of locations: New York, Illinois, Minnesota/3

Date/duration: March 27–30, 1953/4 days

Weapon: firearms

The spree began when McManus, a Marine, drove into Rochester, New York, with his girlfriend, 16-year-old Diane Weggeland. They were looking for a state where they could legally marry, but they had no money. McManus kidnapped a college student and shot him to death, taking his money. Rolling into Keeneyville, Illinois, on March 28, he bungled a robbery at a local market, so he killed the two owners. A day later, in Dubuque, Iowa, McManus robbed another couple of their car. Stopping at Spring Valley, Minnesota, on March 30, he held up a restaurant, killing a waitress and the owner's wife. Returning to Dubuque, the young lovers were stopped by police. Since Weggeland had not killed anyone, she was judged innocent, although she knew what McManus was doing and had not tried to get help.

John Sterling Gardner

Age/race-ethnicity: 24/Caucasian

Victims: 3 dead

Place/number of locations: North Carolina/2

Date/duration: December 17/23, 1972/6 days

Weapon: shotgun

Just before Christmas in 1972, Gardiner killed a man in a home invasion burglary. Five days later, he murdered two people in an armed robbery of a restaurant.

William Duane Elledge

Age/race-ethnicity: 23/Caucasian

Victims: 3 dead

Place/number of locations: Hollywood, Jacksonville, Florida/3

Date/duration: August 1974/2 days

Weapon: hands, firearm

In 1974, in Florida, Elledge strangled a waitress during a rape and fatally shot the other two during robberies shortly thereafter.

Dennis Wayne Eaton

Age/race-ethnicity: 32/Caucasian

Victims: 4 dead

Place/number of locations: Shenandoah County, Virginia/4

Date/duration: February 20, 1989/2 days

Weapon: firearms

On February 20, 1989, while under the influence of drugs and alcohol, Eaton shot and killed Walter Custer, Jr., near the mobile home they shared. Later,

Eaton went to his neighbor's home, killing and robbing him. Eaton joined his girlfriend, Judy Ann McDonald and they fled to avoid Eaton's court appearance. That evening, Virginia State Master Trooper Jerry L. Hines pulled them over. Eaton shot him and fled. Another officer pursued them on a high-speed chase. Judy, the driver, crashed. Eaton shot her in the left temple and then fired a shot into his own head. He survived to stand trial.

Eric Royce Leonard

Age/race-ethnicity: 22/Caucasian

Victims: 6 dead

Place/number of locations: Sacramento, California/2

Date/duration: February, 1991/1 week

Weapon: firearm

Leonard robbed a Quik Stop convenience store in February 1991 and fatally shot two clerks and a customer. A week later, he robbed a Round Table Pizza restaurant six blocks away and killed three employees. Three months later, Leonard, who lived half a block away, was arrested after police found the murder weapon at the home of his father, who told officers Leonard had confessed.

Stanley Tookie Williams III

Age/race-ethnicity: 25/Black

Victims: 4 dead

Place/number of locations: Los Angeles, California/2

Date/duration: February 28–March 11, 1979/11 days

Weapon: firearms

Starting at the end of February, 1979, during an eleven-day robbery spree, Crips gang founder Stanley Williams fatally shot four people in two places, killing one and then three.

Robert Excell White

Age/race-ethnicity: 36/Caucasian

Victims: 3 dead, 1 wounded

Place/number of locations: Waco and Princeton, Texas/2

Date/duration: May 9–10, 1974/2 days

Weapon: firearm, knife

White killed a 73-year-old man and two 18-year-old boys. The day before, he'd been drinking in Waco with an acquaintance, who'd sharpened a knife for him. White took the knife, stabbed the man, and stole several guns.

Jesse Jones

Age/race-ethnicity: 19/Black

Victims: 4 dead, 1 injured

Place/number of locations: Spartanburg County, South Carolina/2

Date/duration: February 14/23, 1942/9 days

Weapon: ax

On February 14, 1942, Maggie Peters called for help. When authorities responded, they found her in a rocking chair in a dazed condition. She said a Black man had attacked her, apparently believing she and her two siblings kept money in the house. Her brother and sister had been murdered with an ax. Nine days later, police found James Hughes' pickup truck along a road with a bloody ax in the back. They went to his house and discovered him and his wife slaughtered with an ax. Under arrest, Jones admitted to all four murders and one attempted murder.

Stephen Correy Bryant

Age/race-ethnicity: 23/Caucasian

Victims: 3 dead, 1 injured

Place/number of locations: South Carolina/4

Date/duration: October 5–15, 2004/8 days

Weapon: firearms

Bryant began a crime spree with a first-degree burglary on October 5 and continued to rob and burglarize for over a week. He entered isolated rural homes to look for vulnerable people. He would appear midday with the ruse of looking for someone or needing help. He killed three men and severely injured another. In one place, he scrawled a message on the wall: "victim number four in two weeks, catch me if you can." On another wall, he wrote, "Catch," partially written in blood. He lit candles around one body. He seemed motivated more by thrill than self-enrichment.

Jose Gilberto Rodriguez

Age/race-ethnicity: 46/Hispanic

Victims: 3 dead, 1 wounded

Place/number of locations: Harris County, Texas/3

Date/duration: July 12–16, 2018/4 days

Weapon: firearm

In July 2018, Rodriquez killed three people in 4 days. His crimes began in northwest Harris County. Pamela Johnson, 62, was found dead in her home, with items missing. Two more bodies were discovered at two mattress stores. On July 16, during the early morning hours, police responded to a call about a shooting at a gas station. A METROLift driver was shot and robbed, but he survived. Rodriquez was arrested.

Paul Beasley Johnson

Age/race-ethnicity: 32/Caucasian

Victims: 3 dead

Place/number of locations: Polk County, Florida/2 (3 separate incidents)

Date/duration: January 8–9, 1981/5 hours

Weapon: firearm

Johnson killed a cab driver to take his money. He torched the car and asked a couple for a ride. He killed the man, but the woman got away. The police went to the location and Johnson fired on them, killing one, before he was arrested.

John C. Young

Age/race-ethnicity: 17/Black

Victims: 3 dead, 3 injured

Place/number of locations: Macon, Georgia/2

Date/duration: December 7, 1974/1 day

Weapon: hands, feet

Young went on a 1-day rampage, viciously attacking six white elderly residents in their homes before stealing items. Three survived and described him. Three died after being severely beaten, kicked, and stomped to death.

William Howard Putman

Age/race-ethnicity: 37/Caucasian

Victims: 3 dead

Place/number of locations: Georgia/2

Date/duration: July 10, 1980/5 hours

Weapon: firearm

On July 10, Putman robbed and shot a man three times at a truck stop. At a rest area later that night, thirty miles north, he killed a man who had four sleeping children in his car. He tried to kidnap the woman, but she resisted, so he shot her, too. He fled but was soon arrested.

Wilber Martinez-Guzman

Age/race-ethnicity: 19/Hispanic

Victims: 4 dead

Place/number of locations: Reno, Nevada/3

Date/duration: January 10–15, 2019/6 days

Weapon: firearm

During home invasion robberies, Guzman committed four murders, including a couple that had once employed him.

Tyrone Lamont Baker (with a girlfriend who did not kill)

Age/race-ethnicity: 19/Black

Victims: 3 dead

Place/number of locations: Kansas/two

Date/duration: December 3–4, 1989/2 days

Weapon: firearm

Baker told his girlfriend he wanted to go on a robbery spree. Both were homeless, so they broke into the upscale home of widow Ida Dougherty, 72, to rob her and take over her house. Baker killed her in the kitchen. He dumped the body and returned to the house. The next morning, three friends of the victim, Lester and Nancy Haley and Verne Horne came to check on her. Baker took them hostage and forced them to go with him to another county. He bound them to trees in the woods. Horne escaped, but Baker killed the Haleys. The police caught Baker the next day.

Gary Alan Walker

Age/race-ethnicity: 30/Caucasian

Victims: 5 dead

Place/number of locations: Kentucky, Oklahoma/5

Date/duration: May 6–25, 1984/19 days

Weapon: hands

On May 6, Walker was hitchhiking. Eddie Cash picked him up. Later, Walker went to Cash's home to burglarize it, killing him. Two days later, Walker got a ride with Margaret Bell and forced her to drive him to three states until he killed her in Kentucky. On May 14, he raped, robbed, and murdered Jane Hilburn. He stole her car and headed for Tulsa, where he encountered a woman whose car had run out of gas. He raped, robbed, and killed her, taking her car to Oklahoma. There he abducted another woman, robbed her, and strangled her. Police arrested him 5 days later.

Leslie Torres

Age/race-ethnicity: 17/Hispanic

Victims: 5 dead, 6 injured

Place/number of locations: East Harlem, New York/5

Date/duration: January 1–7, 1988/7 days

Weapon: firearm

Torres had a crack cocaine addiction. In 6 hours, he robbed four people, killing one. The next day, he held up three stores, shooting four people, killing two. In his next robbery incident, he shot three people, fatally wounding one. Five days later, he shot two more people during a robbery, killing one. Police caught him during a foot-chase and placed him under arrest.

David Bullock

Age/race-ethnicity: 22/Caucasian

Victims: 6 dead

Place/number of locations: Manhattan, New York/6

Date/duration: December 4–January 4, 1982/1 month

Weapon: firearm

After Bullock shot and killed 42-year-old James Weber in Central Park, he told a prostitute about it. She refused to believe him, so he shot her in the head. On December 15, Bullock took Stephen Hassell home for sex, then killed him for amusement. Bullock killed his fourth victim on December 22. The following day, he shot and killed his roommate, dumping his body in the Harlem River. On January 4, Bullock needed cash, so he killed a man during a robbery.

Michael Hampton Sonner

Age/race-ethnicity: 25/Caucasian

Victims: 3 dead

Place/number of locations: Texas, Nevada/2

Date/duration: November 26, 1993/5 days

Weapon: firearm

On November 16, 1993, Sonner escaped from a North Carolina jail and stole a car. During his cross-country spree, he killed a clerk and customer at the Landergin Truck Stop outside Vega, Texas. On November 30, he stole $22 worth of gas from a truck stop outside Lovelock, Nevada. A state trooper pulled Sonner over on I-80. Sonner shot him point blank in the head and fled. A police dragnet caught him the next day.

Richard N. Clarey

Age/race-ethnicity: 23/Caucasian

Victims: 3 dead

Place/number of locations: Michigan/2

Date/duration: April 15–17, 1984/3 days

Weapon: firearm

On April 15, Clarey killed 35-year-old Robert Baranski in Kalamazoo, dumping his body in Lake Michigan and stealing Baranski's car. He only made it to New Buffalo before running the car into a ditch. When two men offered assistance, Clarey killed them and stole their car. He fled to Indiana, where he was arrested. During prison interviews with a psychiatrist, he claimed to have killed between 100 and 150 people.

Allen Leroy Anderson

Age/race-ethnicity: 33/Caucasian

Victims: 8 dead

Place/number of locations: Wisconsin, Minnesota, Virginia, Florida, Iowa, Washington, and California/numerous places

Date/duration: August–October, 19762.5 months

Weapon: firearm and a blunt instrument

Anderson fled from a halfway house in Seattle in a stolen car. Then he stole a revolver. He shot several people in August and September so he could rob them, stealing cars along the way. Police tracked him down through the stolen vehicles.

Dean Philip Carter

Age/race-ethnicity: 29/biracial Caucasian-Eskimo

Victims: 5 dead, 2 injured

Place/number of locations: California/4

Date/duration: April 10–14, 1984/4 days

Weapon: hands

Carter was working as a freelance cameraman when he moved to California. A confirmed burglar, he killed two roommates and three other women to rob them of money, their cars, and their personal items. On May 15, he was arrested.

Marion Albert Pruett

Age/race-ethnicity: 31/Caucasian

Victims: 5 or 6 dead

Place/number of locations: New Mexico, Mississippi, Arkansas, Colorado/4

Date/duration: March 2–October 12, 1981/7 months

Weapon: hammer, firearm

Placed into Federal Witness Protection, Pruett started a crime spree that involved kidnapping, robbery, and murder, including the murder of his common-law wife. Pruett admitted he had robbed her in order to support a $4,000 a week cocaine habit.

Patrick Tracy Burris

Age/race-ethnicity: 41/Caucasian

Victims: 5 dead, 1 wounded

Place/number of locations: Cherokee County, South Carolina/4

Date/duration: June 27–July 3, 2009/6 days

Weapon: firearm

Over a span of 6 days, Burris shot and killed five people before police killed him in a shootout. At the time of his death, he had a criminal record running to more than 25 pages. He was an experienced burglar.

Dennis Manford Whitney

Age/race-ethnicity: 17/Caucasian

Victims: 7 dead

Place/number of locations: California/Arizona/Florida/6

Date/duration: February–March 1960

Weapon: firearm

When Whitney committed his first murder, he said, "I did one and I thought I just might as well go on. I planned to kill maybe a dozen or so. I was fed up. I was broke. I thought I'd better get some money somehow." Eight days later, he murdered two men in Arizona to steal a car. On February 29, Whitney murdered two men at two gas stations. On March 3, he shot someone in another gas station holdup, but his victim survived to give police a description. That day, he abducted a woman and shot her.

Syvasky Lafayette Poyner

Age/race-ethnicity: 28/Black

Victims: 5 dead

Place/number of locations: Virginia/5

Date/duration: January–February, 1984/11 days

Weapon: firearm

Poyner's fatal robbery spree left five women dead from gunshot wounds to the head. He entered shops and stole cars. One woman he raped. During his confession, he admitted that he chose only women as victims because they were afraid of guns.

Nikko Jenkins

Age/race-ethnicity: 27/Black

Victims: 4 dead

Place/number of locations: Spring Lake Park, Nebraska/3

Date/duration: August 11–30, 2013/3 weeks

Weapon: firearm

Early on August 11, 2013, a patrol officer discovered two bodies in a white Ford pickup truck parked near a city swimming pool. Both had been shot in the head, their pockets turned inside out. Jenkins had left prison 2 weeks before. He killed again on August 19, shooting a man in his garage. Jenkins' final victim was discovered on August 21, lying in the road with bullet wounds. Her SUV was found abandoned 12 miles away, partially burned. When Jenkins was arrested, he faked a mental illness.

Mickey David Thomas

Age/race-ethnicity: 29/Black

Victims: 3 dead

Place/number of locations: Oklahoma, Arkansas/2

Date/duration: June 12–14, 2004/3 days

Weapon: firearm

Thomas murdered Geraldine Jones during a home invasion robbery in Broken Bow, Oklahoma. He fled to Arkansas and murdered two women during a robbery at a Monument store. Thomas then stole a car and was apprehended after a police chase.

James Allen Paul

Age/race-ethnicity: 37/Caucasian

Victims: 3 dead

Place/number of locations: New Jersey, Connecticut, Vermont/3

Date/duration: May 15–22, 1984/8 days

Weapon: firearm

A woman found dead in Readington Township, New Jersey, had lived at a local motel, where she had met James Paul. He lured another woman in Connecticut with the promise of employment before shooting her. He moved on to Vermont, killing a woman there before police caught up with him.

Gilbert Eugenio Archibeque

Age/race-ethnicity: 29/Hispanic

Victims: 5 dead

Place/number of locations: Colorado Springs, Colorado/2

Date/duration: May 17, 1986/2 hours

Weapon: firearm

Ended in suicide

Archibeque killed three people in a bar before going to a nearby convenience store to fatally shoot two others. When police came to arrest him, he killed himself.

Gregory McMaster

Age/race-ethnicity: 21/Caucasian

Victims: 4 dead

Place/number of locations: Quebec, Ontario, Manitoba, Canada and MN in US/4

Date/duration: July 27–August 2, 1978/5 days

Weapon: firearm

Arrested for drug possession and awaiting sentencing, McMaster crossed into Canada instead with his girlfriend. She took his money and fled. Then his car broke down. Angry and without resources, he thumbed rides, killing to steal a truck and then money. His final victim was a patrol officer.

Joseph Schwab

Age/race-ethnicity: 26/Caucasian

Victims: 5 dead

Place/number of locations: Australia/2

Date/duration: June 9–14, 1987/5 days

Weapon: firearm

Dubbed the Kimberly Killer for the area where he murdered tourists, Schwab killed a father and son, and then a group of three.

Anthony Paul Arkwright

Age/race-ethnicity: 21/Caucasian

Victims: 4 dead

Place/number of locations: England/4

Date/duration: August 26–29, 1988/56 hours

Weapon: knife, ax

After being fired, Arkwright went on a drinking spree. Aspiring to be like Jack the Ripper, he found his grandfather and stabbed him in the neck, dragged him into a shed, and hit him with an ax. He gave the housekeeper the same treatment. Soon, he was ready again, so he donned a "Prince of Darkness" mask to enter a home to kill the resident. He stabbed a man more than 250 times, gutting him like the Ripper's final victim. He then went after another neighbor, stabbing him over 70 times. He gouged out the man's eyes and placed unlit cigarettes in the empty sockets. He was soon arrested. Since his fantasies did not qualify as a mental illness, he was considered a thrill killer.

Phillip Smith

Age/race-ethnicity: 28/Caucasian

Victims: 3 dead

Place/number of locations: Birmingham, England/3

Date/duration: November 8–11, 2000/4 days

Weapon: hands, blunt instrument

In 4 days, Smith murdered three women who were strangers. He left a pub with one, killing her in his apartment. He met the second one in the same pub but killed her in another town. He killed his third victim while she was on her way to work. His motive appeared to have been thrill.

Junaid Nawaz lal Nawaz

Age/race-ethnicity: 29/Caucasian

Victims: 5 dead, 3 injured

Place/number of locations: United Arab Emirates (UAE)/5

Date/duration: June 21–July 2, 2000/14 days

Weapon: pesticide

Nawaz was arrested in July 2001 for poisoning five taxi drivers in the suburbs of Abu Dhabi and Al Ain. After his arrest, he said he had poisoned eight taxi drivers to rob them. Nawaz used a strong pesticide diluted in soft drinks. After robbing his victims, he left them to die in their cars from the heat.

Sohrab Aslam Khan

Age/race-ethnicity: 42/Caucasian

Victims: 13 dead

Place/number of locations: Pakistan/13

Date/duration: Nov 13–Dec 9, 1986/3 weeks

Weapon: firearm

Khan stalked most of his victims before killing them, but sometimes he killed if he didn't like how someone treated him. He left his ID on his fourteenth victim, leading to his arrest. He appeared to have killed just for the thrill.

José María Jarabo

Age/race-ethnicity: 35/Caucasian

Victims: 4 dead, plus an unborn baby

Place/number of locations: Spain/2

Date/duration: July 19, 1958/2 days

Weapon: firearms, knife, iron

Jarabo helped his British girlfriend Beryl Martin sell a ring. When she wanted it back, he killed the two businessmen who had purchased it, along with a servant. He used a ruse to get into the home of one to wait, killing the cleaning women with an iron and knife. He then shot the man who had the ring, but it was nowhere to be found in his home. A pregnant woman came in, and he killed her as well. The next day, Jarabo went to the store to kill the second man. When he took his bloodstained suit to a cleaner, police arrested him.

Olaf Dater

Age/race-ethnicity: 31/Caucasian

Victims: 5 dead, 1 injured

Place/number of locations: Bremerhaven, Germany/6

Date/duration: June 5–14, 2001/9 days

Weapon: hands, towels, body

Dater was fired from the geriatric nursing service. In debt, he chose elderly women who knew him as a nurse to suffocate with the weight of his obese body so he could rob them. He posed them as natural deaths, which fooled doctors until the sixth victim survived and turned Dater in.

Asanda Baninzi

Age/race-ethnicity: 18/Unk

Victims: 14 dead

Place/number of locations: Cape Town, Western Cape, South Africa/numerous

Date/duration: June–August, 2001/3 months

Weapon: firearm

Baninzi admitted to killing 14 people in a carjacking spree, motivated by a desire to "get money in order to live, and to buy Mandrax and other drugs."

Sylvester MofoKeng

Age/race-ethnicity: 23/Caucasian

Victims: 12+ dead

Place/number of locations: Johannesburg, South Africa/multiple

Date/duration: April–June 1995

Weapon: firearm

Besides 12 murders, MofoKeng also broke into houses to rob people. His criminal record included sentences for theft, robbery, vandalism, unlawful possession of arms and ammunition, escaping from prison, attempted murder, and murder. He killed for thrill.

CHAPTER 7

Movement in Tight Locations

Spree murders that cross into the category of mass murder are those that involve movement in tight locations (MTL) and a brief time period, from a few minutes to no more than a few hours. In this category, the offender's movement is nearly always on foot. Selecting victims requires the killer to move from one distinct and often isolated location to another. It's not as simple as going room to room in a residence, and no sprees with these criteria are included in this category. The movement for this type of spree requires the killer to make a deliberate effort to locate targets.

These cases include traveling from one building to another within a complex of buildings, to multiple floors within a building, or from one neighborhood residence to other residences in the same or nearby neighborhoods. The individual murder locations might be distant enough from each other that future victims are unaware of the pending danger because they can neither see nor hear the killings taking place. The killings might begin outside, with the killer entering and engaging victims inside. Movement is usually more mobile than is typically observed in mass murders, where it is often confined to a single floor. The MTL spree killer generally moves from place to place without revisiting locations where he or she has already been.

Some cases are targeted, some are both targeted and random, and quite a few are simply random. Among the latter are those killers that assault a symbolic target, such as a workplace, public function, or school campus. Anger is generally a motivator, but because the locations are so tight, we collected the following cases into a distinct category. They are different from the Mixed Multicide incidents described in the next chapter, because this category contains cases with labeling ambiguity (mass or spree) rather than cases that have distinct crime components. Those MTL incidents that clearly involved mental illness are in Chapter 5.

Because they occur quickly, the cases in this category offer little utility for law enforcement. We include only the basic details for three subcategories: Targeted, targeted and random/opportunistic, and random/opportunistic. It is rare to find teams in this category, or females, but suicide or attempted suicide occurred in nearly 44%. Like desperation sprees, these killers seem to know that there's no way out.

Category Totals: 48 cases, 52 killers

Targeted: 19 cases, 20 killers

Targeted and Random-Opportunistic: 14 cases, 15 killers

Random-Opportunistic: 15 cases, 17 killers

MOVEMENT IN TIGHT LOCATIONS: TARGETED

Edward L. Lutes

Age/race-ethnicity: 42/Caucasian

Victims: 5 dead, 2 injured

Place/number of locations: Seaside Heights to Barnegat Township, New Jersey/3

Date/duration: April 9, 2002/2 hours

Weapon: firearm

Ended in suicide

Lutes, a police officer, went into the homes of two neighbors, killing five with his police issue MP5. Lutes then drove 20 miles to shoot Seaside Heights Police Chief James Costello. He hit the man twice in the leg and once in the wrist as he was leaving to respond to the report of the shootings. Costello survived, but Lutes killed himself.

Willie Woods

Age/race-ethnicity: 42/Black

Victims: 4 dead

Place/number of locations: Los Angeles, California/4

Date/duration: July 19, 1995/1 hour

Weapon: firearm

Woods thought he was being unfairly singled out at Piper Technical Center in Los Angeles. He brought a gun to work. After a negative performance evaluation, the repairman hunted down and shot two supervisors in their work cubicles. He went down into the building's basement, where he killed two other employees in separate locations. Security arrested him.

Curtis Windom

Age/race-ethnicity: 26/Black

Victims: 3 dead, 1 wounded

Place/number of locations: Winter Garden, Florida/3

Date/duration: February 7, 1992/1 hour

Weapon: firearm

Windom grew angry when he learned that an acquaintance who owed him money had won at a dog track but had not repaid him. He purchased a gun and used it to execute the man. He then went to his girlfriend's place and shot her, believing she had become a drug informant. As he fled, he wounded a man outside. Then he saw his girlfriend's mother at a stop sign and killed her.

Billie Wayne Coble

Age/race-ethnicity: 41/Caucasian

Victims: 3 dead, 1 wounded

Place/number of locations: McLennon County, Texas/3

Date/duration: August 29, 1989/4 hours

Weapon: firearm, knife

Upset over a divorce, Coble tied up his estranged wife's daughters before walking across the street to her parents' house. There, he killed her father. Going to the home of her brother, a police sergeant, Coble ambushed him in his garage. He then returned to where his wife lived to wait for her. When she did not return, he went back to her parents' house and shot her mother. When his wife came home, he forced her to go with him to a remote location, where he stabbed her in the chest. She survived. Police pursued Cobble and arrested him.

Eugene Molter

Age/race-ethnicity: 68/Caucasian

Victims: 3 dead

Place/number of locations: San Diego, California/3

Date/duration: April 4, 2001/1 hour

Weapon: firearm

Ended in suicide

Molter shot and killed three people at a senior citizens apartment complex because he was angry that he was about to be evicted. First, he fatally shot the couple who managed the facility. Then he went to the 16th floor and shot the man who'd lived directly above him, whom he disliked. When police arrived, Molter committed suicide.

Jason Oric Williams

Age/race-ethnicity: 23/Caucasian

Victims: 4 dead, 3 wounded

Place/number of locations: Mobile County, Alabama/2

Date/duration: February 15, 1992/1 hour

Weapon: firearm

Following a night of ingesting alcohol and drugs, Williams went to the home of a family that had taken him in when his ex-wife kicked him out 2 weeks earlier. He grabbed a .22-caliber rifle and shot all three, killing one. Williams went to a neighbor's home and killed the woman who answered the door. He entered and killed her husband and son. He shot the surviving child in the hand.

John W. Mabrie

Age/race-ethnicity: 70/Caucasian

Victims: 4 dead

Place/number of locations: Toms River, New Jersey/3

Date/duration: February 21, 2002/30 minutes

Weapon: firearm

Mabie locked his wife in the basement of their home and walked to his mother-in-law's house nearby, where he used a .38-caliber pistol to shoot and kill Natalie Gingerelli, his 22-year-old granddaughter. Forcing his mother-in-law to go with him, he walked to a nearby home and used her as a "Trojan horse" to gain entry. Inside, he shot 42-year-old Susan Kerian. Mabie returned to his house to get more ammunition before walking to another home to shoot Thomas Luyster and his fiancée, Suzanne Lavecchia. Paranoid and reclusive, he apparently thought these people had been noisy neighbors.

Douglas Dean

Age/race-ethnicity: 19/Caucasian

Victims: 5 dead

Place/number of locations: Wilson, Wisconsin/2

Date/duration: July 18–19, 1971/2 hours

Weapon: firearm

At approximately 12:15 p.m. on July 19, 1971, the pastor of St. George's Church found Dean sitting on the back stairs with a blank expression. The pastor called the sheriff's department, who transported Dean to a hospital. While attempting to find his mother, police discovered that she was dead from a gunshot wound. A block away, four members of Dean's girlfriend's family were also dead. Dean claimed that he had been under the influence of LSD when he killed them. However, he was aware that his girlfriend's family estate was worth $100,000. He and she both needed money, since he did not have a job and she was attending a university. He'd told acquaintances that he wanted to shoot his mother and his girlfriend's mother.

Hastings Arthur Wise

Age/race-ethnicity: 43/Black

Victims: 4 dead, 3 wounded

Place/number of locations: Aiken, South Carolina/4

Date/duration: September 15, 1997/1 hour

Weapon: firearm

Attempted suicide

Angry that he had been fired from the plant where he worked, Wise returned to get revenge. He shot the guard outside, then went to shoot the plant's personnel director. Killing two more, he located his final victim in the quality control area – a woman whom Wise believed had taken a job he should have had. After the murders, Wise drank insecticide poison in order to commit suicide, but it only made him ill. In November 2005, Wise was executed by lethal injection.

Robert T. Cordell

Age/race-ethnicity: 42/Caucasian

Victims: 3 dead

Place/number of locations: Hamilton County, Ohio/2

Date/duration: April 2, 2002/1 hour

Weapon: hands, firearm

Cordell strangled his former sister-in-law in the house they shared after she accused him of stealing medicine from her. Also angry with his neighbor for a petty grievance, Cordell went over and shot him and his wife.

Douglas Williams

Age/race-ethnicity: 48/Caucasian

Victims: 6 dead, 8 wounded or injured

Place/number of locations: Meridian, Mississippi/3

Date/duration: July 8, 2003/15 minutes

Weapon: firearm

Ended in suicide

Williams had to attend a mandatory ethics and diversity class, due to racist threats. Shortly after the meeting started, he went out and retrieved a shotgun from his truck. Returning, he shot people in the room and went looking for employees who'd reported him. Williams walked through the plant and shot five other people, killing three before turning the shotgun on himself.

Michael McDermott

Age/race-ethnicity: 42/Caucasian

Victims: 7 dead

Place/number of locations: Wakefield, Massachusetts/3

Date/duration: December 26, 2000/10 minutes

Weapon: firearms

McDermott was angry that the IRS had garnished his wages and believed that the human resources and accounting departments were complicit. Targeting them, he killed two employees in the reception area and three in a hallway. He shot the hinges off a locked door at the accounting office and killed two more.

Wesley Neal Higdon

Age/race-ethnicity: 25/Caucasian

Victims: 5 dead, 1 wounded

Place/number of locations: Henderson, Kentucky/3

Date/duration: June 25, 2008/30 minutes

Weapon: firearm

Ended in suicide

After an argument with his supervisor, Higdon was escorted out of the Atlantis Plastics Factory. He retrieved a .45 pistol from his car and shot his supervisor outside the building. Higdon then entered the building and found four coworkers in the break room. He killed them all. Going onto the factory floor, he shot a man in the back of the head before killing himself.

Guilherme Taucci Monteiro and Henrique de Castro

Age: 17 and 25/Hispanic

Victims: 8 dead, 9 wounded

Place/number of locations: Sao Paulo, Brazil/2

Date/duration: March 12, 2019/1 hour

Weapon: firearm, knives, axes, crossbow

Ended in a murder-suicide pact

Monteiro and de Castro, former students at Raul Brasil school, shot and killed the owner of a rental car business (Monteiro's uncle) before driving a car they stole from the business to the nearby school less than 500 meters away to launch their main attack. They killed five students, a teacher, and a school administrator, and wounded nine others. Monteiro used a .38 handgun while de Castro used a crossbow. Both had bombs and axes. After going down hallways and into the schoolyard, they failed to force their way into a room at the back of the school where many students were hiding. There, Monteiro shot de Castro in the head and then killed himself. It appeared to be a copycat of the 1999 incident at Columbine. Montiero's mother said that her son had been bullied at the school, so he'd dropped out. His uncle had fired him from the car rental business, where he'd washed cars. Monteiro seemed to have planned this attack for a year.

Valery Fabricant

Age/race-ethnicity: 52/Caucasian

Victims: 4 dead, 1 wounded

Place/number of locations: Montreal, Quebec, Canada/5

Date/duration: August 24, 1992/less than 1 hour

Weapon: .38 caliber revolver

Fabricant was a professor at Concordia University in Montreal. Hired at the university in 1980, his behavioral disruptions had launched numerous complaints. When he failed to get tenure, he identified several colleagues that he believed were responsible. On August 24, 1992, Fabricant brought three guns to campus. On the ninth floor of the Henry F. Hall building, he killed one man in his own office, then crossed the hall and fatally wounded another. He went to the department chair's office, shooting the secretary, who survived. Fabricant moved to the other side of the building and shot another man, who would die the next month. He ended his spree by shooting a man who tried to reason with him. A security guard managed to get his gun from him.

Robert Daniel Vecino

Age/race-ethnicity: 57/Hispanic

Victims: 5 dead, 2 injured

Place/number of locations: Necochea, Argentina/2

Date/duration: July 2016/10–15 minutes

Weapon: machete

Ended in suicide

In his house in Necochea, Argentina, Vecino got into an argument with his wife. Enraged, he picked up a machete and killed her and their two adult daughters. His adult son got away, but Vecino pursued and overpowered him, slicing his throat. A neighbor tried to intervene and was killed for his efforts. Vecino also attacked two police officers before running away to hang himself.

Simone Pianetti

Age/race-ethnicity: 56/Caucasian

Victims: 7 dead

Place/number of locations: Camerata Cornello, Lombardy, Italy/multiple

Date/duration: July 13, 1914/1 hour

Weapon: firearm

Unsuccessful in several businesses and believing that a number of the townspeople were responsible for his businesses failing, Pianetti went on a rampage in town, killing seven people. He fled into the mountains and was never found.

Li Hsing-Ju

Age/race-ethnicity: 29/Asian

Victims: 10 dead, 4 injured

Place/number of locations: Nantou City, Taiwan/3

Date/duration: September 21, 1959/Unk

Weapon: semiautomatic rifles

Ended with suicide

Hsing-Ju was in love with Lu Lu-sheng, who'd become engaged to his rival. She tried to introduce him to another girl, which only enraged him. The night before Lu was to get married, Hsing-Ju broke into her family's house and fatally shot her father, three siblings, and fiancé. He dragged Lu outside and critically wounded her. When neighbors came to investigate, he killed one and wounded the other. He then entered an apartment building nearby to slaughter the girl he'd met, along with her family. He wounded two and killed four. When police arrived, he killed himself.

Guo Zhongmin

Age/race-ethnicity: 36/Asian

Victims: 13 dead

Place/number of locations: Yangxiaoxiang, Huludao, China/3

Date/duration: February 18, 2003/1.5 hours

Weapon: knife, stick

Ended in suicide

Zhongmin lashed out at neighbors after a dispute over land. With a knife and stick, he bludgeoned and stabbed 13 people in three different homes. Fleeing, he committed suicide in the mountains.

MOVEMENT IN TIGHT LOCATIONS: TARGETED AND RANDOM-OPPORTUNISTIC

Edwin James Grace

Age/race-ethnicity: 33/Caucasian

Victims: 6 dead, 6 wounded

Place/number of locations: Cherry Hill, New Jersey/multiple

Date/duration: June 1972/7 minutes

Weapon: firearm

Ended in suicide

Angry at an employment agency for not hiring him as a security guard, Grace entered the building where the agency was located and walked from one office to another. Waiving away women, he fired more than 100 bullets, shooting 12 men, six of whom died. Grace shot himself behind the ear, dying 2 weeks later.

Richard Farley

Age/race-ethnicity: 35/Caucasian

Victims: 7 dead, 4 wounded

Place/number of locations: Sunnyvale, California/multiple

Date/duration: February 16, 1988/5 hours

Weapon: firearms, knife, and flammable liquid

Over a period of 4 years, Farley wrote more than 200 love letters to Laura Black, his coworker. To send a clear message of her disinterest, she returned a letter, unopened. Farley became more persistent, so she filed a sexual harassment suit that got him fired. When Laura filed for a restraining order in February 1988, Farley took an assault rifle, two shotguns, a knife, and flammable liquid to his former workplace. He strode toward Laura's office, shooting other employees along the way before wounding her. The police managed to stop him and save Laura's life, but seven people died. Farley claimed that he'd intended only to kill himself to make Laura feel guilty, but things had gotten out of hand.

Albert L. Petrosky

Age/race-ethnicity: 36/Caucasian

Victims: 3 dead

Place/number of locations: Denver, Colorado/2

Date/duration: April 28, 1995/1 hour

Weapon: firearms

Petrosky walked into an Albertson's Grocery Store in Denver and shot his estranged wife and the store manager. Armed with a .50-caliber sniper rifle, an SKS Chinese semiautomatic assault rifle, a .32 revolver, and a 9-mm semiautomatic pistol, Petrosky went out to the shopping center parking lot, where he exchanged fire with a federal IRS agent passing by and killed Sgt. Timothy Mossbrucker of the Jefferson County Sheriff's Department. "50-cal Al" had used all four weapons. After his conviction, he hanged himself in his cell.

Juan Lopez

Age/race-ethnicity: 32/Hispanic

Victims: 3 dead

Place/number of locations: Chicago, Illinois/2

Date/duration: November 19, 2018/ less than half an hour

Weapon: firearm

Ended in suicide

Dr. Tamara O'Neal had called off her engagement to Juan Lopez. He wanted his ring back, so he showed up at the hospital where she worked. She saw him in the parking lot and called for help. When Lopez confronted her, they argued. Lopez shot her. As a squad car pulled up, Lopez turned his gun on police, striking the vehicle before he ran into the hospital. There, he shot and killed a resident in the pharmacy program and struck an officer in the neck, killing him. He tried and failed to get into the pharmacy before he was shot in the abdomen. He then killed himself.

Timothy Hendron

Age/race-ethnicity: 51/Caucasian

Victims: 3 dead, 5 wounded

Place/number of locations: St. Louis, Missouri/2

Date/duration: January 7, 2000/2 hours

Weapon: firearm

Ended in suicide

Hendron felt discriminated against by people in his company for trying to start a union. Angry, he shot two coworkers in the parking lot before entering the plant. He fired at 23 people, wounding five and killing one more. Hendron eventually committed suicide in one of the offices.

Charles Lee Thornton

Age/race-ethnicity: 48/Black

Victims: 5 dead, 2 wounded

Place/number of locations: Kirkwood, Missouri/2

Date/duration: February 7, 2008/20 minutes

Weapon: firearm

Thornton could no longer contain his anger at the city council. He parked across the street from the city hall building, approached a police officer, and shot him. Stealing the man's weapon, Thornton made his way to the city council chambers meeting room. He shot another officer before killing the council members whom he believed had wronged him. Responding officers killed him.

Muhammed Ahmang al-Nazari

Age/race-ethnicity: 48/Arab

Victims: 6 dead, 14 wounded

Place/number of locations: Yemen/4

Date/duration: March 30, 1997/2 hours

Weapon: firearm

Al-Nazari was angry. He shot the headmistress of the school where he'd worked, a bus driver, and a cafeteria employee. Then he went from one classroom to the next, shooting at students and teachers. He went to a neighboring school to continue shooting before he was wounded and arrested. He said he'd reacted to being fired from his job as a bus driver. There were also rumors that he suspected the headmistress and her husband of raping his daughter.

Duong Van Môn

Age/race-ethnicity: 35/Asian

Victims: 12 dead, 6 wounded

Place/number of locations: Krông Pắk District, Vietnam/4

Date/duration: August 8, 1998/4 hours

Weapon: knives

Attempted suicide

Môn, a member of the Nùng minority, was a poor rice farmer who suffered from a mental illness. When his mother died, he was severely in debt, so he could not afford the lengthy funeral feast. On the third day, when his guests complained, he grabbed two large knives. Starting at his house, he attacked and chased people around the village. Afterward, he tried to commit suicide by swallowing insecticide, but villagers forced him to vomit so he would face judgment.

Marciano Contaoe

Age/race-ethnicity: 32/Asian

Victims: 9 dead, 3 wounded

Place/locations: Manila, Philippines/2

Date/duration: May 27, 1988/several hours

Weapon: firearms

Contaoe got into a fight while drinking with neighbors. He shot six, killing five. He went home and fetched an M-16 rifle. Barging into a neighbor's house, he killed four more and wounded two children.

Domingo Salazar

Age/race-ethnicity: 42/Asian

Victims: 16 dead, 1 wounded

Place/number of locations: Roxas, Palawan, Philippines/6

Date/duration: October 11, 1965/several hours

Weapon: spear, bolo knife

Suspicious that his wife was pregnant with another man's child, Salazar went on a rampage to defend his honor and punish his enemies. He killed his wife, nephew, and his wife's pregnant sister. Salazar then went to the village, entering four houses and killing everyone he found. When a teacher at the local school barricaded the door, Salazar rang a bell to gather villagers to kill him. They refused. The police arrived and arrested him.

Danilo Guades

Age/race-ethnicity: 51/Asian

Victims: 10 dead, 17 injured

Place/number of locations: Calbayog, Philippines/6

Date/duration: June 2, 2007/1 hour

Weapon: bolo knife

A mentally unstable man, Guades was paranoid and alcoholic. Having quarreled with a man at a wake, he went to the man's home with a 22-inch knife, killing him and his family. Only the wife escaped. Guades went into a neighboring home, injuring two and killing six. He visited three more locations, wounding and killing, before he was chased away. He took his final victim on the road before turning himself in. Police later disclosed that Guades told them he committed the crime to "strengthen his amulet."

Liu Yongbaio and Wang Mouming

Age/race-ethnicity: Yongbaio – 30, Wang Mouming – 41 /Asian

Victims: 4 dead

Place/number of locations: Zhili, Huzhou, China/2

Date/duration: November 29, 1995/1 hour

Weapon: Club and hammer

On November 29, 1995, Liu entered a guesthouse in Huzhou, China, with another man, Wang, to commit robbery. When the targeted victim fought back, they beat him to death. To conceal their crime, they located and murdered the couple who ran the guesthouse and their 13-year-old grandson. Twenty-two years passed before these crimes were solved with DNA. Yongbaio had written the details into a bestselling novel, *The Guilty Secret*, which features a writer who gets away with murder.

Yang Qingpei

Age/race-ethnicity: 28 /Asian

Victims: 19 dead

Place/number of locations: China/7

Date/duration: September 29, 2016/2 hours

Weapon: knife

In a remote village in China, Qingpei killed his parents during an argument over money. To cover it up, he went into the homes of six neighboring families and killed 17 more, including children. Caught, he was sentenced to death.

Elias Francisco

Age/race-ethnicity: 45/Hispanic

Victims: 5 dead, 2+ injured

Place/number of locations: Casais da Espinheira, Portugal/3

Date/duration: July 30, 1956/1 hour

Weapon: firearm

Francisco had been arguing with relatives for several days regarding a land purchase. He picked up a shotgun and killed his wife, brother-in-law, cousin, and nephew. Afterward, Francisco ran through the streets, firing randomly. He killed one person and wounded several others. Police located him hiding in a well.

MOVEMENT IN TIGHT LOCATIONS: RANDOM-OPPORTUNISTIC

William D. Baker

Age/race-ethnicity: 66/Black

Victims: 4 dead, 4 wounded

Place, number of locations: DuPage County, Illinois/4

Date, duration: February 5, 2001/15 minutes

Weapon: firearms

Ended in suicide

The day before Baker was to report to prison for felony grand theft, he loaded four guns into a golf bag and went to the Navistar International factory. Forcing a guard to let him in, he began firing randomly into offices. He had not worked at this place for 6 years, so he knew none of them.

Aaron Alexis

Age/race-ethnicity: 34/Black

Victims: 12 dead, 8 injured or wounded

Place/number of locations: Washington, DC/5

Date/duration: September 16, 2013/1.5 hours

Weapon: firearms

Alexis entered the Washington Navy Yard with a valid pass. He carried a disassembled shotgun in a shoulder bag. In Building 197, he went to the fourth floor and assembled the shotgun inside a bathroom. He emerged and crossed a hallway into the building's 4 West area to start shooting. In a few minutes, Alexis killed eight people. He went to the third floor, where he fatally shot two more people and wounded one. At the front entrance on the first floor, he killed a security officer and took his Beretta 92FS 9mm pistol. Alexis used it to kill another man. Two officers and two NCIS agents entered the cubicle area where Alexis was hiding. He opened fire, hitting one, but they managed to shoot and kill him.

Pete Carl Rogovich

Age/race-ethnicity: 26/Caucasian

Victims: 4 dead

Place/number of locations: Phoenix, Arizona/4

Date/duration: March 15, 1992/9 hours

Weapon: firearm

Rogovich shot and killed the clerk at a Super Stop Food Mart. He told a maintenance man that he was upset with his girlfriend for breaking up with him. Three hours later, Rogovich fired at a couple in their car, then killed a woman in a laundry room and another in her driveway at a mobile home community. He invaded one home and shot the female resident. When police caught him in a stolen car, Rogovich said, "I just snapped. I was so angry. I just couldn't stop. I was full of anger."

Snochia Moseley

Age/race-ethnicity: 26/Black

Victims: 3 dead, 3 wounded

Place/number of locations: Aberdeen, Maryland/2

Date/duration: September 20, 2018/a few minutes

Weapon: firearm

Ended in suicide

Moseley was a temporary employee at the Rite Aid distribution center, where she was hired for the holiday rush. At one point that morning, she was involved in a disagreement over cutting in line. She left the center and went home to get a hood and Glock 9-mm handgun. She returned and started firing outside before she entered the building, pulled the hood over her head, and kept shooting. In all, she fired 13 rounds, including two at herself. Two years earlier, she'd been diagnosed with a mental illness.

Allen Fryer, David Fryer, James Fryer

Age/race-ethnicity: 29, 24, and 21/Caucasian

Victims: 4 dead

Place/number of locations: Gitchie Manitou State Park, Iowa/2

Date/duration: November 17, 1973/10 minutes

Weapon: firearm

Five teenagers went to the Gitchie Manitou State Preserve to get high and sing around a campfire. Nearby, three brothers, frustrated from a day of unsuccessful poaching, overheard them. They killed one at the campfire and wounded another, leading the others up to where their van was parked. There, they placed the 13-year-old girl into a truck and shot the other three kids. After driving around with the girl, they let her go. She was able to lead police to where they lived in South Dakota. They were all placed under arrest, tried, and convicted.

DeWayne Craddock

Age/Race-ethnicity: 40/Black

Victims: 12 dead, 4 wounded

Place/number of locations: Virginia Beach, Virginia/4+

Date/duration: May 31, 2019/less than 2 hours

Weapon: firearm

Craddock entered Building 2 of the city's Municipal Center near the end of the workday and shot indiscriminately at people on all three floors. One victim was found inside a vehicle. Craddock was a certified professional engineer with Virginia Beach city. Someone described him as disgruntled. Four officers confronted him in a long gun battle, fatally wounding him.

Sibusiso Madubela

Age/race-ethnicity: 28/Black

Victims: 8 dead, 1 wounded

Place/number of locations: Bloemfontein, Free State, South Africa/multiple

Date/duration: September 16, 1999/Unk

Weapon: firearm

A black army officer in a South African army base, Madubela, killed seven white soldiers and a female South African National Defense Force employee. He moved from building to building at the Tempe military base, randomly shooting at white soldiers with an R4 semiautomatic rifle. A wounded soldier killed him. Allegedly, Madubela had been angry that his pay that month had been cancelled because he left the base without permission to attend his father's funeral.

Frank Vitkovic

Age/race-ethnicity: 22/Caucasian

Victims: 8 dead, 5 wounded or injured

Place/number of locations: Melbourne, Australia/multiple in building

Date/duration: December 8, 1987/6 minutes

Weapon: firearm

Ended in suicide

Vitkovic, a former law student at Samaritan Catholic College, walked into a building on Melbourne's Queen Street with a sawed-off M1 carbine. He entered the fifth-floor offices of the *Australia Post*, pulled out the gun and fired at fleeing workers, killing a young woman. Vitkovic went from floor to floor, shooting at people in the elevators or offices. On the 12th floor, an officer wrestled his gun away. He broke a window and jumped to his death. He'd studied other mass murders and had left a note to his parents: "Today is going to be the day. The anger in my head has got too much for me. I've got to get rid of my violent impulses. The time has come to die. There is no other way out."

Yang Jia

Age/race-ethnicity: 28/Asian

Victims: 6 dead, 4 wounded

Place/number of locations: China/5

Date/duration: July 1, 2008/1 hour

Weapon: knife

Yang carried gasoline bottles, a knife, a pair of gloves, tear-gas spray, and a gas mask into the police station. He set the gasoline ablaze and stabbed a security guard before he attacked four unarmed police officers on the first floor. He then rushed up the stairs and stabbed five other officers on four different floors.

Yang Mingxin

Age/race-ethnicity: 39/Asian

Victims: 9 dead, 3 injured

Place/number of locations: Shaanxi Province, China/unknown

Date/duration: July 23/1998/less than 1 hour

Weapon: ax

Suicide attempt

In a dispute over 10 geese, Mingxin grabbed an ax and went through his village, hacking people, including a 4-month-old girl.

Robert Steinhauser

Age/race-ethnicity: 19/Caucasian

Victims: 16 dead, 1 wounded

Place/number of locations: Erfurt, Germany/multiple

Date/duration: April 26, 2002/15–20 minutes

Weapon: firearms

Ended in suicide

Steinhauser had been expelled from the secondary school for truancy and forgery. He was depressed over his limited opportunities, so he donned a black ninja outfit and returned to the school. He went from one classroom to another, shooting teachers, administrators, and students. Police soon arrived and Steinhauser fatally shot one. A teacher who knew him confronted him and challenged him to shoot. Steinhauser reportedly said, "That's enough for today." The teacher pushed him into a room and locked him in. Steinhauser killed himself.

Pierre Lebrun

Age/race-ethnicity: 40/Caucasian

Victims: 4 killed/1 wounded

Place/number of locations: Ottawa, Ontario/4

Date/duration: April 6, 1999/less than 1 hour

Weapon: firearm

Ended in suicide

Frustrated with people at his workplace, Lebrun came into the OC Transpo garage with a rifle. He fired at two coworkers but missed. They ran, leaving another employee to take a fatal shot. Lebrun kept walking until he found another victim. Then he entered the office and killed a woman. A witness yelled, "He's nuts," and was next to die. A worker used the public address system to warn everyone to get out. Lebrun had 36 more rounds, but his intended victims were gone. He set a fire and shot out several computer terminals. When a police tactical team arrived, Lebrun killed himself.

Michael Ryan

Age/race-ethnicity: 27/Caucasian

Victims: 16 dead, 15 wounded

Place/number of locations: Hungerford, England/multiple locations over 2 miles

Date/duration: August 19, 1987/several hours

Weapon: firearm

Ended in suicide

Ryan, a gun-loving, hypersensitive young man, took an AK-47 assault rifle and several other weapons on a shooting spree in Hungerford, England, killing 16 and wounding as many before retreating to his former school to turn the gun on himself. He began that day in the woods, killing a woman who ran from him, then drove home to shoot the family dog and grab ammunition. When his car failed to start, he set fire to his house and began a 2-mile walk through the streets of Hungerford, shooting acquaintances, strangers, and his mother. Police set up blockades and inadvertently sent motorists directly into the killer's path. Some were killed. Ryan entered one home and shot an elderly man to death. Finally, he went into the John O'Gaunt School. Surrounded by police, he shot himself in the head. Some said he might have been mentally ill, but aside from his rampage, there was no evidence of it.

Ramesh Sharma

Age/race-ethnicity: 28/Indian

Victims: 14 dead, 9 wounded

Place/number of locations: Mandsaur, India/7

Date/duration: July 23, 1982/1 hour

Weapon: firearm

At 7:30 in the evening, Sharma was on guard duty at the Pashupatinath temple. Armed with a rifle, he entered an adjacent teashop and killed the shop owner's nephew. He went to another shop and shot the owner, wounding him. He then killed a woman and her son. Searching for the wounded man who'd fled into the temple, he killed him. Outside, he killed a police officer and then went back into the temple. He killed the priest and wounded a number of worshippers. He then went into town and killed several people in the streets. He was stopped around 8:20 p.m., in a gun battle with police.

Lazaro Obwara

Age/race-ethnicity: 55/Black

Victims: 12 dead

Place/number of locations: Kampala, Uganda/different rooms in the hospital

Date/duration: July 28, 1950/unknown but brief

Weapon: knife

The Mulago Hospital massacre occurred on July 28, 1950. After visiting his dying son at the hospital, Obwara ran down the ward and stabbed a woman and 11 children with a knife, all of whom died.

CHAPTER 8

Mixed Multicides

Some killers might be categorized as a specific type of multicidal offender but might actually fit two (or more) classifications. We're concerned in this chapter only with those who have participated in a spree (at least three deaths, two locations) as a component of their crimes. They might be serial killers who go on a spree, or they might be mass murderers who took victims just before or soon after the primary carnage. The spree places them into this book, but the mix of other types of multicide creates a distinct subcategory. There might be utility for law enforcement if there are clear targets or a mission that becomes known before it is finished. For example, a spree/mass murderer like Brenton Tarrant, described in Chapter 3, became visible at once through his posted manifesto, live-streamed video, and signature targets. Calls to police and their awareness of his mission got him pulled over before he could reach a third location. A spree that might have ended many more lives was terminated in just over half an hour.

In this category we have the following three subtypes: spree/mass crossover, spree/serial crossover, and spree/mass/serial crossover. Their motives vary. In the first subcategory, 72% were suicidal versus none in the second category and one of the three cases in the third category.

Overall for category: 25 cases, 26 killers

Spree/Mass Crossover (spree that included a mass murder): 11 cases, 11 killers

Spree/Serial Crossover (spree that included unrelated murders): 11 cases 12 killers

Spree/Mass/Serial Crossover: 3 cases, 3 killers

SPREE/MASS CROSSOVER (SPREE THAT INCLUDED A MASS MURDER)

Charles Whitman

Age/race-ethnicity: 25/Caucasian

Victims: 15 dead (plus unborn child), 32 wounded

Place/number of locations: Austin, Texas/3

Date/duration: July 31–August 1, 1966/14 hours

Weapon: firearms, machete, hatchet

Ended in suicide-by-cop

On the last day of July 1966, Charles Whitman killed his mother and wife in separate incidents before driving the next morning to the University of Texas at Austin's clock tower. In his car was a footlocker full of supplies and survival gear, and in the trunk a virtual arsenal. Whitman used a wheeled dolly to haul his heavy load into a service elevator to get to the observation deck on the 30th floor. He killed a female greeter, fired at a family, killing two, and set up on the observation deck at the top. As people walked across the open area below, Whitman picked them off until police officers got to him that afternoon and killed him. He'd been shooting about an hour and a half.

Two years earlier, Whitman had talked about feeling that he might explode. He mentioned to friends that he had ideas about shooting people from the tower. That year, Whitman was honorably discharged from the Marines, so he took on a job and a heavy load of courses. To keep up, he took amphetamines. Four months before the massacre, Whitman described to the university's staff psychiatrist his fantasy of going up on the tower and shooting people. When he finally did, he wrote a note to explain his actions, requesting an autopsy to see if there was a disorder that explained his homicidal thoughts (Levin & Fox, 1985).

Seung-Hui Cho

Age/race-ethnicity: 23/Asian

Victims: 32 dead, 17 wounded, 6 injured

Place/number of locations: Blacksburg, Virginia/3

Date/duration: April 16, 2007/3 hours

Weapon: firearms

Ended in suicide

In April 2007, Cho shot two students in a campus dorm at Virginia Tech University. He then went to a post office to mail a package of photos and videotapes. Two and a half hours after the first shooting, he took a 9-mm handgun, a 22-caliber handgun, and hundreds of rounds of ammunition into a classroom building. Chaining the main doors closed, he entered several classrooms, shooting whoever was there. After 10 minutes, he shot himself. He'd killed 32 and wounded 17 more. Other students were injured when they jumped out the classroom windows. Two days later, NBC News received a package of materials from Cho that included photos of him posing with guns and a rambling video about his hatred for wealthy or successful students. He had no specific targets, but he'd apparently hoped to become the world's most famous mass murderer. He had suffered from a severe anxiety disorder and social immaturity. Despite treatment in high school, he'd remained angry (Report, 2008).

Andrew Kehoe

Age/race-ethnicity: 55/Caucasian

Victims: 44 dead, 58 (or 61) wounded or injured

Place/number of locations: Bath, Michigan/2

Date/duration: May 18, 1927/1 hour

Weapon: explosives, firearm

Ended in suicide

The Bath Consolidated School opened in 1922, bringing children from the general area together under one roof. This new building raised the local taxes but kept the children safer and standardized their education. Kehoe, a farmer, was angry, because he had a lot of land for taxation assessment, so he tried to thwart over-spending by taking a seat on the school board. Then his wife got sick, further depleting his funds. Frustrated, he devised a payback scheme. He pretended to help with electrical work at the new school to cover for the fact that he was planting explosives. He also put explosives in his house and barn. On May 18, Kehoe killed his wife, along with two horses. He detonated bombs there on his farm to draw the fire crew from town, so he could set off the explosives at the school to their most devastating effect. In town, Kehoe killed the school superintendent and himself with his shrapnel-laden truck.

Nikolay Lazukin

Age/race-ethnicity: 27/Caucasian

Victims: 5 dead

Place/number of locations: Salem, Oregon/2

Date/duration: May 22, 2012/2 hours

Weapon: firearm, baseball bat

Ended in suicide

Lazukin beat to death a stranger before driving home to fatally shoot his wife and three young daughters. He set the house on fire and shot himself in the head. No one was aware of any domestic problems or mental illness that would explain the sudden massacre.

Jeff Weise

Age/race-ethnicity: 16/Native American

Victims: 9 dead, 5 wounded

Place/number of locations: Red Lake, Minnesota/2

Date/duration: March 21, 2005/2 hours

Weapon: firearms

Ended in suicide

Depressed and suicidal over being bullied and living on a poverty-stricken reservation, Weise killed his grandfather and his grandfather's girlfriend before driving his grandfather's police car to his school, where he shot and killed a security guard. Inside, he fired randomly, killing six more. When police shot at him, he killed himself. It came out later that his father had committed suicide when Weise was a child.

Anders Behring Breivik

Age/race-ethnicity: 40/Caucasian

Victims: 77 dead, 319 wounded or injured

Place/number of locations: Oslo, Norway, and Utoya/2, and locations on the island

Date/duration: July 22, 2011/3 hours

Weapon: fertilizer bomb, firearms

Although some psychiatric reports questioned his sanity, Breivik insisted that killing 77 people on July 22, 2011 and wounding hundreds more had been carefully planned and morally justified. He'd used a bomb to kill eight and injure more than two hundred in Oslo before going to a youth camp at the island of Utoya, 25 miles away, to shoot more, killing 69 (mostly teenagers) and injuring over 100. The far-right fanatic claimed the attacks were "necessary" and that the victims had betrayed Norway by embracing immigration. Hours before, Breivik had e-mailed a 1,500-page manifesto, entitled *2083 – A European Declaration of Independence.* He despised multiculturalism and Muslim immigration. He wrote that he is a "savior of Christianity," and claimed to be part of an order called the Knights Templar.

Martin Bryant

Age/race-ethnicity: 28/Caucasian

Victims: 35 dead, 18 wounded

Place/number of locations: Port Arthur, Australia/numerous

Date/duration: April 28–29, 1996/1 day

Weapon: firearms

On April 28, 1996, Bryant killed the two owners of Seascape Cottage in Australia, then took two semiautomatic rifles to a tourist area in Port Arthur, where he shot and killed 20 people. Fifteen were wounded. He then walked around shooting more, got into his car to drive a few hundred yards, killed more people, stole a car, killed more, took a hostage, and went back to the cottages, where he shot several people who were driving by. Then he killed the hostage. The police held him under siege overnight. When the building went up in flames, Bryant ran out. His total in less than a day had been 35 dead, 18 wounded. He survived but was considered to have a mental illness.

Nordine Amrani

Age/race-ethnicity: 33/Caucasian

Victims: 6 dead, 125 wounded (intended many more)

Place/number of locations: Liege, Belgium/2

Date/duration: December 13, 2011/a few hours

Weapon: firearm, grenade

Ended in suicide

Due in court to answer a criminal summons about molesting a young girl, Amrani went on a spree. He killed his neighbor's cleaning woman in his apartment and drove to a public area to launch three grenades, killing five and injuring 125.

Stephanus Swart

Age/race-ethnicity: 37/Caucasian

Victims: 8 dead, 3 wounded, 1 intended

Place/number of locations: Charlestown, KwaZulu-Natal, South Africa/4

Date/duration: May 6, 1927/a few hours

Weapon: firearms

Ended in suicide

Swart fired a shot at his neighbor, set his car on fire and wrote a 28-page suicide statement before police arrived with an arrest warrant. He holed up and said he would kill anyone who approached. When they closed in, Swart killed five officers and wounded another. He grabbed a revolver and a horse. Taking off, he told a neighbor he was going to town to kill some people. On the way, he killed two men who had testified against him about a crime for which he'd served a sentence. He also fatally shot his ex-wife. When police caught up, Swart shot himself.

Lubomir Harman

Age/race-ethnicity: 48/Caucasian

Victims: 7 dead, 17 wounded

Place/number of locations: Bratislava, Slovakia/4–5

Date/duration: August 30, 2010/1 hour

Weapons: firearms

Ended in suicide

The spree began at 9:40 a.m. when Harman entered a neighbor's apartment and murdered all five occupants. Going to the first floor, he killed another member of the same family. Harman exited the building and walked toward a shopping center, shooting randomly at cars and people. When police caught up, Harman wounded one, so they drew back to await a special tactical team. This team cornered Harman and wounded him, so he committed suicide.

Patrick Okot Odoch

Age/race-ethnicity: 20s/Black

Victims: 10 dead, 4 wounded

Place/number of locations: Uganda/2

Date/duration: March 9, 2013/several hours

Weapon: firearm

Fleeing from a failed rape attempt 3 days before his spree, Odoch came to his post at the 23rd Air Defense Regiment with an AK-47 assault rifle and 30 rounds of ammunition. He went to a bar in Pakele at 12:12 a.m. and opened fire, killing Onesmus Odule, his wife Florence, the bar owner, four soldiers, and two civilians. Odoch fled toward Gogonya, killing one more. After an extensive manhunt that lasted 10 days, Odoch was captured.

SPREE/SERIAL CROSSOVER (SPREE THAT INCLUDED UNRELATED MURDERS)

Andrew Cunanan

Age/race-ethnicity: 27/biracial: Caucasian-Asian

Victims: 5 dead

Place/number of locations: Minnesota, Illinois, New Jersey, Florida/5

Date/duration: spree: April 27–May 9, 13, 1997 and July 15/2.5 months

Weapon: hammer, screwdriver, hacksaw, firearm

Ended in suicide

Cunanan had suffered some setbacks in his personal life. On April 25, he went to Minnesota to rekindle a relationship with a former lover, whom he found involved with one of his former friends. He viciously killed both in separate incidents before stealing a Jeep and going to Chicago. There, he brutalized and murdered a 72-year-old developer. Cunanan remained in the man's house for a few days and then stole his car. He killed a man in New Jersey to switch vehicles, stealing his truck and driving to Florida. Two and a half months after his first murder, Cunanan fatally shot fashion designer Gianni Versace on July 15. Eight days later, cornered, Cunanan killed himself. Known to be a fantastical liar and a narcissist who expected to be catered to, Cunanan appeared to be enraged that life was not working as he'd expected.

Paul John Knowles

Age/race-ethnicity: 28/Caucasian

Victims: possible 20–35 dead

Place/number of locations: multiple across the United States

Date/duration: July 26, 1974–November 21, 1974/4 months

Weapon: hands, knife

In early 1974, Knowles was serving time at Raiford Prison in Florida when he began corresponding with Angela Covic. They got engaged and she paid for legal counsel that got him released. However, a psychic warned her about him, so when he arrived in California, she sent him packing. He claimed to have murdered three people that night (not verified) out of anger. Arrested in the area for stabbing a bartender, he escaped and started killing. He broke into the home of a 65-year-old woman, bound and gagged her, then ransacked her home for money and valuables. She choked on her dentures. On the street, Knowles killed two young girls he knew, as well as several hitchhikers. On August 2, Knowles strangled another woman in her apartment. Near the end of August, Knowles showed up in Georgia and killed another woman in her home. He met a man in a bar in Ohio, whom he killed for his car. In a campground, he killed an elderly couple and stole their credit cards. He kept going like this until police tried to arrest him on November 17 in Florida. He killed the officer and another man. Cornered by an armed civilian, Knowles gave up. He tried to take an officer's gun and was killed. Knowles claimed to be responsible for 35 murders, but only 20 were confirmed.

Joseph Christopher

Age/race-ethnicity: 25/Caucasian

Victims: 13 dead

Place/number of locations: Buffalo and Manhattan, New York/multiple in two areas

Date/duration: September 22–December 30, 1980/2 months

Weapon: firearm, screwdriver, hammer

On September 22, 1980, a 14-year-old African American boy was shot in Buffalo, New York. There were two similar murders the following day, with a fourth incident in nearby Niagara Falls. Witnesses had seen a young white man with dark hair running away. He carried a bag large enough for a gun. An investigation produced a dropped .22-caliber shell casing. Thus, this unknown perpetrator was dubbed "the .22-Caliber Killer." Switching weapons, he emerged again to kill several more times. He used a screwdriver on one man and a hammer on another. Several weeks passed. Then another series began, this time in Manhattan. In just a few hours, a knife-wielding man attacked five black males and one Hispanic man, killing four. Then two more black men were stabbed to death back in Buffalo.

Investigators were stymied until a soldier at Fort Benning in Georgia named Joseph Christopher admitted to a nurse that he'd killed some black people in New York. Forensic evidence was found among his possessions and when he confessed to law enforcement, he said, "It was something I had to do." Christopher was convicted of several of the murders and sentenced to life in prison. Although his behavior seemed racially triggered, all he would say was that "something came over" him.

John Muhammad and Lee Boyd Malvo

Age/race-ethnicity: 41 and 17/Black

Victims: 17 dead, 10 wounded (in spree: 10 dead, 3 wounded)

Place/number of locations: Maryland and Virginia/multiple

Date/duration: February 16, 2002–October 23, 2002/8 months

Weapon: firearm

This string of random shootings occurred in 2002 in Maryland and Virginia, claiming 13 victims over a span of 3 weeks, 10 of whom died. The perpetrators demanded $10 million to stop killing before being found in their car along I-95 on October 24. Ballistics linked them to all 13 shootings and to six shootings in other states, three of them fatal. Malvo admitted to being the triggerman, making him eligible to be tried as an adult. He said the shootings were planned, with one of them serving as the shooter, the other as a lookout. John Muhammad was an angry man with plenty of issues, not the least of which was an affinity with anti-U.S. terrorist groups. Supposedly, anger at his ex-wife had triggered the spree.

Randy Greenawalt (with Gary Tison for the spree)

Age/race-ethnicity: 47/Caucasian

Victims: 6 dead in spree, 3 more dead earlier

Place/number of locations: Arizona, Colorado/2

Date/duration: July 30–August 11, 1978/10 days

Weapon: firearms

During the summer of 1978, Randy Greenawalt shared a cell at Arizona State Prison with Gary Tison. Greenawalt was in for killing a truck driver and had confessed to two other murders. This serial killer went on a spree when Tison's sons broke them both out. They escaped in Donald Tison's 1969 Lincoln Continental. When a tire blew near the California border, a man stopped to assist and paid with his life, along with that of his wife, son, and niece. The fugitives took their car. They allegedly murdered another couple in Colorado to steal their van before they ran a police roadblock. Greenawalt was caught, but Tison escaped into the Arizona desert, where he died of exposure.

Todd West

Age/race-ethnicity: 24/Black

Victims: 7 dead, 1 wounded

Place/number of locations: Elizabeth, New Jersey; Allentown, Pennsylvania/8

Date/duration: May 18, June 25, July 5, 2017/first spree: 20 hours/second spree: 45 minutes

Weapon: firearm

West killed seven people in New Jersey and Pennsylvania. In May 2017, he killed his cousin in Easton, Pennsylvania. In June, he killed three men in Elizabeth, New Jersey in three separate locations. In July, with two friends in the car, he randomly killed three people between Easton and

Allentown, Pennsylvania. He wounded a fourth person in the Elizabeth killings.

Michael Silka

Age/race-ethnicity: 25/Caucasian

Victims: 9 dead, plus an unborn child, 1 wounded

Place/number of locations: Manley Hot Springs, Alaska/3

Date/duration: April–June 1984/just over a month

Weapon: firearms

On April 29, 1984, police questioned Silka about fresh blood and a snow-covered mound at his cabin. He said it was from skinning a moose. But his neighbor had been missing since the day before and witnesses had seen them together. Troopers returned to the cabin on May 8, but Silka was gone. He was next seen on May 14 in Manley Hot Springs, a small mining town near Fairbanks. Silka told the villagers that he planned to settle in the area. On May 17, seven villagers went to the boat landing and disappeared. Locals contacted Alaska State Troopers, giving them Silka's license plate number, and the police learned he was wanted for the murder of his neighbor. At the boat landing, Troopers found blood and spent cartridge casings. When they located Silka, he shot at them, hitting two, The troopers returned fire and killed him. Five of the bodies were recovered from the river. Silka's motive remains unclear, although it was possibly robbery.

Chester Comer

Age/race-ethnicity: 27/Caucasian

Victims: 3 dead (killed 2 others, non-spree)

Place/number of locations: Oklahoma/2

Date/duration: November 19–23, 1935/5 days

Weapon: firearm

Comer had murdered two wives in separate incidents before he went on his robbery and killing spree. On November 19, Comer was hitchhiking and got a ride with a man that he killed to steal his car. Comer abandoned the car and began hitchhiking. On November 23, Piedmont farmer L.A. Simpson and his 14-year-old son picked him up. They drove about 10 miles before Comer shot both to death and dumped their bodies by the roadside. Police chased him and killed him in a shootout.

Christopher Dwayne Peterson

Age/race-ethnicity: 21/Black

Victims: 4 dead, 2 wounded (2 other murders occurred 2 months earlier)

Place/number of locations: Indiana/3

Date/duration: October 30 and December 13–18, 1990/5 days for spree

Weapon: firearm

On October 30, 1990, Peterson shot Lawrence Mill to death in his car in front of the American Legion Post in Griffith, Indiana. Two and a half hours later, he shot Rhonda Hammersley at a gas station. Peterson's spree began on December 13, when he robbed and killed four people in 5 days and wounded two.

Eric Edgar Cooke

Age/race-ethnicity: 28–32/Caucasian

Victims: 8 dead, 14 injured

Place/number of locations: Perth, Australia/numerous

Date/duration: 1959–63/4 years

Weapon: knives, scissors, ax, firearms, cord

Referred to as "the Night Caller," Cooke ran amok in the city of Perth for 4 years. The victim of child abuse by an alcoholic father and bullied at school, he had become an angry adult. He often reacted to perceived rejection with violence. He tried the military but was quickly discharged over his criminal record. Marrying at the age of 22, he had seven children. When he was 28, he started attacking people and stealing cars. His spree involved bludgeoning, stabbing, hit-and-run, and shooting. The incidents seemed entirely random. When captured, he confessed to eight murders and 14 attempted murders. He tried an insanity defense based on schizophrenia, but this was rejected. After he was convicted, Cooke became the last man hanged in Western Australia.

Tiago Henrique Gomes da Rocha

Age/race-ethnicity: 26/Hispanic

Victims: 37 dead

Place/number of locations: Goiânia, state of Goiás, Brazil/numerous

Date/duration: November 2011–August 2014/2 years, 9 months

Weapon: hands, knife, firearm

By the time da Rocha was arrested in 2014, the former security guard had randomly murdered 37 people (he claimed 39). In some cases, he killed two people on the same day or on successive days. In a 2-week period before he was caught, da Rocha killed seven people, similar to a mission-oriented spree killer. He generally targeted the homeless, homosexuals, and women. He often approached his targets on a motorcycle to shoot them, although his earliest murders had involved strangling or stabbing. After his arrest, da Rocha offered the unlikely excuse that, having been sexually abused when he was an infant, he'd developed uncontrollable murderous impulses.

SPREE/MASS/SERIAL CROSSOVER

William Unek

Age/race-ethnicity: 25 and 28/Caucasian

Victims: 57 dead, 30 injured (two separate sprees)

Place/number of locations: Mahagi, Belgian Congo and British Tanganyika Territory/multiple

Date/duration: January 1, 1954 and February 1957/1.5 hours and 12 hours

Weapon: ax, knife, firearm

Unek, a police constable in the Belgian Congo, went on two murder sprees 3 years apart. His first rampage occurred near Mahagi on January 1, 1954, where he killed 21 people and wounded many others with an ax before escaping. He assumed a new identity and got a job in British Tanganyika Territory. In 1957, he had a dispute with his boss. Armed with a police rifle, a knife, and an ax, he broke into homes and shot anyone he saw. Over the course of 12 hours, Unek fatally shot 10 men, eight women, and eight children; murdered five men with the ax;

stabbed another one; burned two women and a child by trapping them in their house and setting it on fire; and strangled a 15-year-old girl. Among the dead was his wife, whom he killed in their hut before setting it on fire. After 9 days of pursuit by police, Unek was captured.

Anatoly Onoprienko

Age/race-ethnicity: 54/Caucasian

Victims: 52 dead

Place/number of locations: Ukraine/multiple

Date/duration: 1989–96/7 years

Weapon: firearms, ax, hammer, fire

An offender in the Ukraine, Onoprienko invaded homes to slaughter whole families, sometimes forcing them together to blast them with a shotgun. His motive appears to have been robbery, but his killings were more extreme than merely eliminating witnesses. Called "the Terminator," he often slaughtered whole families. Some were shot, some bludgeoned to death, a few were attacked with an ax, and four were burned to death. He was a serial killer, but at times, he was also a mass murderer and a spree killer. He said he had killed in response to voices commanding him to, although this excuse fell flat at his trial. His first incident, in the company of an accomplice in 1989, involved killing a family of 10 after a botched robbery. That same year, he then killed a family of five. In an 8-day period in1995, Onoprienko shot two families of four each in their homes; the second mass murder included the killing of a male pedestrian at another location. Four days later, he killed four people in three incidents on the same day. Eleven days after that, he killed a family of five, along with two potential witnesses nearby. And on it went until March, when he killed a family of four and set their home on fire. He moved in with relatives, one of whom discovered his stash of items linked to the murders and told police. Finally, Onoprienko was arrested.

Tore Hedin

Age/race-ethnicity: 25/Caucasian

Victims: 9 dead

Place/number of locations: Saxtorp/Hurva, Sweden/2

Date/duration: August 21–22, 1952/several hours

Weapon: ax, fire

Ended in suicide

On 28 November 1951, Hedin robbed and murdered his friend, John Allan Nilsson, after a poker game. To cover his tracks, he burned down the building. As the local police representative, he took part in the investigation, deflecting it away from himself. On August 21, 1952, Hedin went on a killing spree in reaction to being dumped by his girlfriend, Ulla Östberg. He killed his parents and set the house on fire. Thirty minutes later, he arrived at the retirement home where his ex-girlfriend worked. With an ax, he killed her and a friend before setting a fire that killed five residents. He wrote a suicide note and drove to a cabin. Police arrived too late. In the note, Hedin said he had killed his parents to prevent their humiliation when they learned what he'd done. Then he'd drowned himself.

REFERENCES

Levin, J., & Fox, J. A. (1985). *Mass murder: America's growing menace.* New York, NY: Plenum Press.

Report of the Virginia Tech Review Panel. (2008). Retrieved from http://www.governor.virginia.gov/TempContent/techPanelReport.cfm

CHAPTER 9

Spree Analytics

We have collected a database of 359 cases of spree killing involving 419 individuals from 43 countries in order to group them by type and to identify through motives and circumstances those cases for which law enforcement can develop an effective action plan. Within the scope of this approach, we group these offenders into five primary categories (Anger/Revenge, Mission, Desperation, Mental Illness, and Robbery/Thrill) and four secondary categories (Movement in Tight Locations, Mixed Multicides, Intended Spree, and Unique Circumstances), although we did not include the latter two in our calculations. The statistical analysis covered seven categories in total. Three primary and two secondary categories yielded further division into subcategories. We call each inclusion in a category a case rather than an incident, because each spree covers two or more incidents. Some cases feature a lone offender, while others involve teams. In a few cases, some team members did not participate in all of the killings (and occasionally a team member became a victim).

This chapter offers data analytics on key items such as past criminal record, state of mind, sex, age, race, weapons, substance use, military or law enforcement background, and spree duration. We applied them to the overall total of spree cases, but each item could be further broken down inside a given category. In some cases, such as with suicide percentages or prevalence of female killers, we discussed the finer distinctions in the chapters devoted to specific categories.

Some cases could have been placed into more than one category, such as an Anger/Revenge-Targeted spree undertaken by a psychotic individual in tight locations. That individual would be in three potential categories. Where mental state or motive was a significant factor, we usually chose the category that seemed the best fit. A more comprehensive analysis would allow for placing these cases into more than one category, but that was outside the scope of this work.

The analyzed items are listed below, with accompanying charts (created by Kaelee Rupell.) Those categories that appear most useful to law enforcement receive the most attention. Tables 9.1 and 9.2 show overall numbers and percentages for the primary and secondary categories.

TABLE 9.1 Primary Category Totals/Percentages

Category	Number of Cases	Percentage
Anger/Revenge	110	30.6%
Mission	31	8.6%
Desperation	25	7%
Mental Illness	42	12%
Robbery/Thrill	78	21.7%
MTL	48	13.3%
Mixed	25	6.8%

TABLE 9.2 Primary Category and Subcategory Totals/Percentages

Category	Number of Cases	Percentage
Anger/Revenge: Targeted	67	18.7%
Anger/Revenge: Targeted and Random-Opportunistic	33	9.2%
Anger/Revenge: Random-Opportunistic	10	2.8%
Mission: Psychotic	13	3.6%
Mission: Nonpsychotic	18	5%
Desperation	25	7%
Mental Illness	42	12%
Robbery/Thrill: Teams	33	9.2%
Robbery/Thrill: Lone Operator	45	12.6%
MTL: Targeted	19	5.3%
MTL: Targeted and Random-Opportunistic	14	3.9%
MTL: Random-Opportunistic	15	4%
Mixed Multicide: Spree/Mass	11	3%
Mixed Multicide: Spree/Serial	11	3%
Mixed Multicide: Mass/Spree/Serial	3	.8%

The Anger/Revenge category was further divided into three subcategories: Targeted; Targeted and Random-Opportunistic; and Random-Opportunistic. Mission-driven killers might be Psychotic or Nonpsychotic (including terroristic sprees). Desperation was fairly straightforward, with a clear motivator that precluded planning and did not divide well into subcategories, but we saw a distinction between Team and Lone Operators for the Robbery/Thrill category. Of note is the prevalence of females on these teams.

The secondary categories are useful mostly for discussing the complexities of spree murder. Some killers who fit the spree definition commit their crimes so close in time or location that they are often categorized as mass murderers. Movement in Tight Locations (MTL) is among the most difficult to include in the spree category, accounting for 13%, but there were clearly at least two locations in these cases, with deaths at each, so we opted to create this category. Some MTL cases have targeted victims and others are random or opportunistic. About 7% of spree killers operate as both mass and spree, or both spree and serial, so a discussion of crossover crimes (Mixed Multicide) is justified. Also of interest are those cases in which an offender fails to kill three people in two locations but clearly intended to. This category is difficult to define, but we provided illustrative cases, because some came close to being included in a primary category and they offer useful data. The final secondary category, Unique Circumstances, includes cases with unusual features that have spree-like qualities but that are sufficiently different from typical cases to warrant a separate chapter. We did not count them as spree killers for analysis.

Of the seven categories analyzed, the motive we saw most frequently was Anger/Revenge (30.7%). The cases with clear targets (Targeted) (61% of this category, 18.7% of cases overall) and an extended timeline have the most to offer a study like this. However, some that began as Targeted devolved into Random-Opportunistic, so we had a mixed subcategory (30% of this category, 9% of overall cases). As mentioned before, we use 'opportunistic' to indicate that people became victims because of where they were, not who they were. 'Random' means that anyone along the path of a spree killer can be a target; they're just in the wrong place at the wrong time. About 9% of cases in the Anger/Revenge category were completely random or opportunistic. (We hyphenate Opportunistic-Random to simplify reference to these subcategories).

The age range was 14 to 73, with both extremes from cases in the United States. The highest percentage were 25–34 (33%), followed by 35–44 (25%) and 18–24 (24%). Although we thought that spree killers in countries outside the United States would trend toward older individuals, instead they similarly distributed from adolescence to mid-60s. Most spree killers in this collection were in their 20s and 30s. In the Anger/Revenge-Targeted category, for example, there were three teenagers, nine in their 40s, six in their 50s, three in their 60s, and one aged 73. The rest (68%) were distributed evenly between their 20s and 30s. When Random-Opportunistic sprees were added, the age trended younger, with the highest percentage (34%) in the 20s. Comparing the United States against 18 other countries in which Anger/Revenge sprees occurred, the percentage of killers in their 20s and 30s surpassed other age groups. Older killers were not more prevalent. This result might differ in other categories, but since those categories have less utility for law enforcement, we did not make further analysis. The age range is consistent with mass murder. Overall, law enforcement can expect to face off most often with killers from the mid-twenties to the mid-forties.

The next most prevalent motive was Robbery/Thrill (21.7%). We included thrill with robbery, since these two motivators often intertwined, but thrill as a sole primary motivator was infrequent. Mental illness showed up in other categories and sometimes it was suggested (or malingered) during a court proceeding, but we included only the clearest cases in the Mental Illness category. If the killers had a clear albeit delusional mission, they went into the subcategory of Mission: Psychotic. The prevalence of mental illness thus accounted for 15% of the overall cases. It's likely that the prevalence is higher, since the disposition of a case does not necessarily show the accuracy of diagnosis, and since some killers who committed suicide could have had undiagnosed disorders, especially clinical depression.

Initially, we were going to analyze the number of locations, but this proved impractical, because variable distance between locations made it difficult to judge how this category mattered. To accompany this book, we will set up a separate chart online, where researchers can make their own decisions about which aspect of this study is important.

A spree's duration is important. We considered setting a minimum time in which law enforcement could reasonably respond, but we found a few in which factors like a manifesto or a witness report assisted with a quick response. Those sprees that had clear targets, motivators, and an extended time period, like that of Christopher Dorner or Dwight Lamon Jones, provide the best opportunity for an effective law enforcement response. We discuss this more fully in Chapter 12.

Precipitating events were part of the motive, and motive assisted us with delineating the categories, except for MTL and Mixed Multicides. Most of the MTL cases would fit into one of the primary five. However, due to their short duration, these cases would not be useful for law enforcement.

We had thought about including an analysis for evidence of planning, but it proved difficult to acquire information from a representative sampling of cases. Since this factor is more interesting to criminologists than to law enforcement, we left it out.

One of us (Ramsland) is keenly interested in how many of these cases ended in suicide. Sometimes they were the overt expressions of a suicidal mental state, but at other times, suicide seemed the only way out for the killer in question. We discuss it further below, although it's a sufficiently complex topic to become a separate paper.

This book is just a start. At first, we were going to describe and analyze selective cases from a smaller database of 125. However, as we added countries and saw more variation, we kept collecting. We searched newspapers archives, Internet news sources, legal websites, open-source databases, our own prior work, the work of colleagues, criminological databases, and books devoted to homicide or multicidal killers. We were unable to acquire full background data on some cases, but we strove to gather the most comprehensive information possible. Our full data lists were summarized for this book, but we worked off of hundreds of pages of information.

Among the traits and behaviors of identified spree killers, we selected a list of key items for analysis, listed below. The tables, charts, and graphs demonstrate numbers and/or percentages.

Based on 359 cases, the totals for each category break down according to Table 9.1.

Subcategories show a finer sense of what the totals mean.

Anger/Revenge-based sprees are most prevalent, followed by Robbery/Thrill. For motive, Desperation is lowest on this list. Examining the subcategories provides greater perspective on the prevalence of the most urgent cases. Anger/Revenge -Targeted remains the highest, but an anger-based opportunistic-random spree proves to be rare. Lone operators in Robbery/Thrill outpace teams with the same motives, while desperation-driven sprees move up, relative to other subcategories (see Figure 9.1).

The category with the largest percentage (61%) is the one that can be most useful to law enforcement. Among the 30% of Anger/Revenge killers who initially targeted victims but then murdered random or opportunistic victims, some cases show the potential for intervention, although

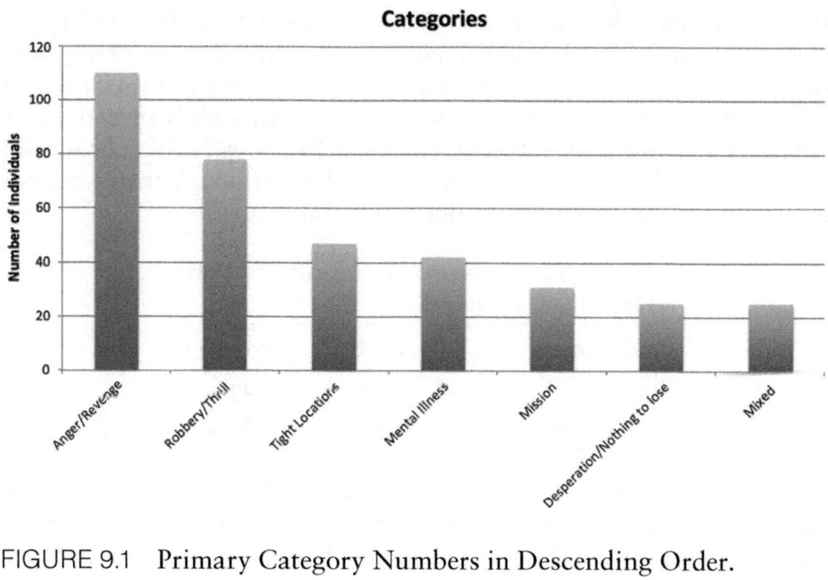

FIGURE 9.1 Primary Category Numbers in Descending Order.

randomness increases difficulty. The 9% of anger-motivated random killers offers no intervention utility short of outright luck (see Table 9.3).

TABLE 9.3 Anger/Revenge Subcategory Percentages

Subcategory	Number	Percentage
Targeted	67	61%
Targeted and Random-Opportunistic	33	30%
Random-Opportunistic	10	9%

Mission killers, at 8.6% of the total, also offer opportunities for risk evaluation and potential intervention, especially Mission: Nonpsychotic killers (42% of this category) who post warnings, manifestos, or clear targets on social media. People who know the offender generally know the content of their threats, obsessions, and delusions, which enhances the potential for leads in a spree with an extended time period. For example, a racially motivated killer who has grumbled about killing members of a hated race and has expressed anger about where these people tend to meet has offered breadcrumbs for tracking him down (see Table 9.4).

TABLE 9.4 Mission Subcategory Percentages

Subcategory	Number	Percentage
Psychotic	13	42%
Nonpsychotic	18	58%

The second highest percentage of sprees – Robbery/Thrill – is useful for understanding motives and movements but has little utility for law enforcement's immediate response, unless the spree is carried out in a way that shows repetition and predictability (e.g., always robbing convenience stores). About 42% operate in teams, usually of two. More females participated in sprees in the team Robbery/Thrill subcategory than in any other subcategory of spree killers, although they were not leaders and some were just tag-alongs (see Table 9.5).

TABLE 9.5 Robbery/Thrill Teams vs. Lone Operator Percentages

Subcategory	Number	Percentage
Teams	33	42%
Lone Operators	45	58%

As with mass murder, MTL cases generally happen too fast for law enforcement to respond effectively to save victims, unless officers are already nearby, such as on a military base. These spree killers are often called mass murderers. About 13% of sprees fall into this category, divided into the same subcategories as Anger/Revenge: Targeted, Targeted and Random-Opportunistic, and Random-Opportunistic.

In some cases, Desperation combines with MTL, making it impossible for law enforcement to respond quickly. There's little planning and the person generally acts quickly. For example, when Dr. Tamara O'Neal called off her engagement to Juan Lopez, he arrived in the parking lot of her workplace, ready to get revenge. She saw him and called for help. She told a companion that she was afraid and that person retreated to the hospital to call 911. But Lopez was enraged. He confronted her, they argued, and he demanded that she return the engagement ring. We don't know her response, because he shot her. As a squad car pulled up, Lopez turned his Glock semiautomatic handgun at it, striking the vehicle multiple times before he ran into the hospital. Once inside, he kept firing at pursuing officers. He also fired at a resident in the hospital's pharmacy, who was on an elevator when its doors opened. Officer Samuel Jimenez was struck in the neck, just above the bulletproof vest he was wearing, and soon died. When police shot Lopez in the abdomen, he killed himself. Lopez was angry, desperate, and willing to shoot at police. Possibly he'd expected to kill himself or be killed by them (see Table 9.6).

TABLE 9.6 MTL Subcategory Percentages

Subcategory	Number	Percentage
Targeted	19	40%
Targeted and Random-Opportunistic	14	29%
Random-Opportunistic	15	31%

Only the spree part of cases of mass or serial murder matters in this category, which accounts for just under 7% of the cases we gathered. When sprees occur, they seem to occur equally between mass and serial, although in rare cases, we see all three types of multicide (see Table 9.7).

TABLE 9.7 Mixed Multicides Subcategory Percentages

Subcategory	Number	Percentage
Mass/Spree	11	44%
Serial/Spree	11	44%
Mass/Serial/Spree	3	12%

As in other multicidal categories, males outnumber females. In spree incidents, we find very few females operating on their own. They're more likely to be found on teams, like Caril Ann Fugate with Charles Starkweather, but never as the mastermind or ringleader. There were no spree teams (yet) comprised only of females. Some female participants might be considered compliant accomplices, except in the case of a thrill-based spree. Often they're quite young (Fugate was 14). Laurie Wasserman Dann was the only female of 12 cases in the "Intended Spree" category.

Overall, about 5% of spree killers are female, with just five operating on their own (including one intended spree). Two were in the Anger/Revenge category, five were in the Mission category, one was Mentally Ill, 12 participated in Robbery/Thrill sprees, and one was in the MTL category, in a short-lived spree that seemed spontaneous and motivated by anger (see Figure 9.2).

Almost 65% of spree killers are Caucasian. The stereotype of the angry middle-aged white male spree killer seems justified. African-Americans come up second, but at 17%, they're not a close second. Forty-nine nationalities were represented, with the highest percentage (59%) being American and Chinese (3.2%). Canadian and German constitution were equal at 2.6%, with 10 spree killers each (see Table 9.8).

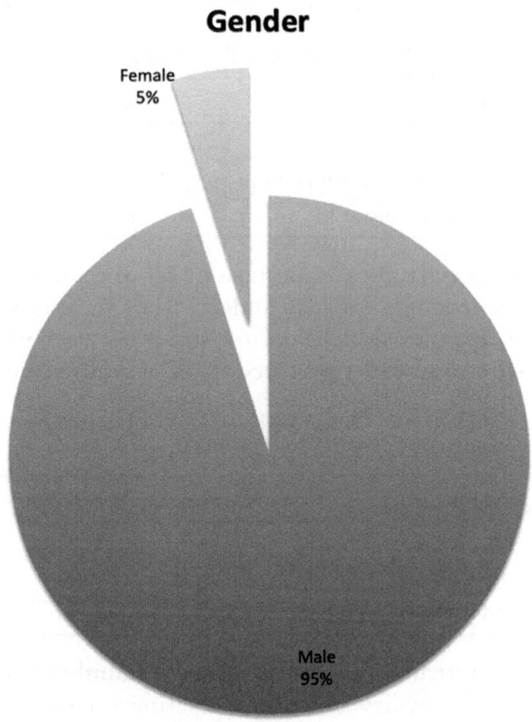

FIGURE 9.2 Male vs. Female Percentages.

TABLE 9.8 Race-Ethnicity Percentages

Race-Ethnicity	Number	Percentage
Caucasian	269	64.4%
African-American	72	17%
Asian	38	9.1%
Hispanic	15	3.6%
African	5	1.2%
Algerian	2	.5%
African-American and Caucasian	1	.2%
Arabic	1	.2%
Indian	1	.2%
Latin-American	1	.2%
Moroccan	1	.2%
Unknown	13	3.1%

The weapon of choice for spree killers is a firearm, usually a handgun (75%). Those who used a gun plus other weapons, such as a knife, came next, at 12%. "Blades" included knifes, machetes, and axes, seen more often in international sprees. Only about 2% bludgeoned their victims (usually with hammers) and 1% choked or asphyxiated them. The final 2% involved miscellaneous methods, like bombs, a mace, or pesticides (see Figure 9.3).

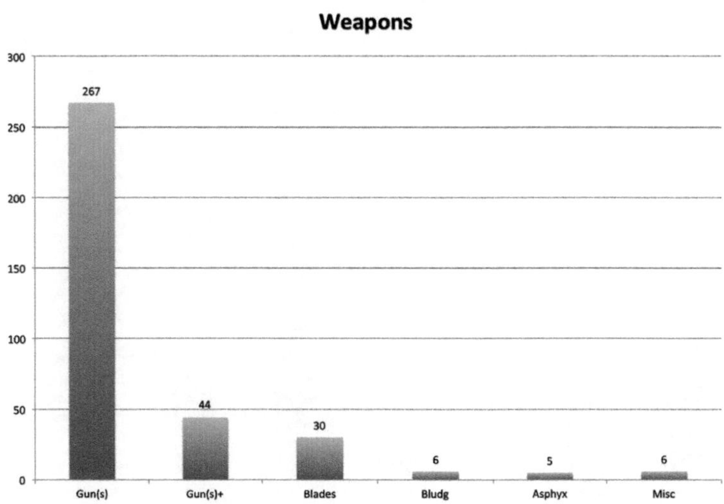

FIGURE 9.3 Weapon Type Percentages.

Most sprees (40%) involved a duration of 1 to 3 days, followed by 18% that lasted less than 2 hours. When we consider those that lasted 1–7 days, we get 52%, and about 18% lasted more than a week. So, around 70% lasted long enough (more than 1 day) for law enforcement to develop and deploy a plan of action. In the Anger/Revenge-Targeted subcategory (the one most likely to be linked through investigation to future targets), 22 cases (33%) lasted more than one day. In the Anger/Revenge: Targeted and Random-Opportunistic subcategory, 12 cases (36%) lasted a day or longer, and 20% did so in the Random-Opportunistic subcategory (see Figure 9.4).

The majority of spree killers were arrested, usually dying in prison or by execution, although some died in shootouts with police. Suicide and attempted suicide accounted for a significant number of deaths in several categories. We counted only suicides or attempted suicides during the spree and not those that occurred later in prison. Of 419 killers, we had 99 suicides and attempts, for 23.6%. Following is the breakdown of percentages within each primary category (see Table 9.9).

For subcategories, in the Anger/Revenge: Targeted subcategory, more than 37% killed themselves (including a double suicide in Japan). This figure declined for Targeted and Random-Opportunistic (27%) and for Random-Opportunistic (20%) in the Anger/Revenge category. In the Mission category, only four sprees ended in suicide. One was in the Psychotic subcategory (.7%) and three were in the Nonpsychotic subcategory (16.6%). Desperation had the highest percentage when

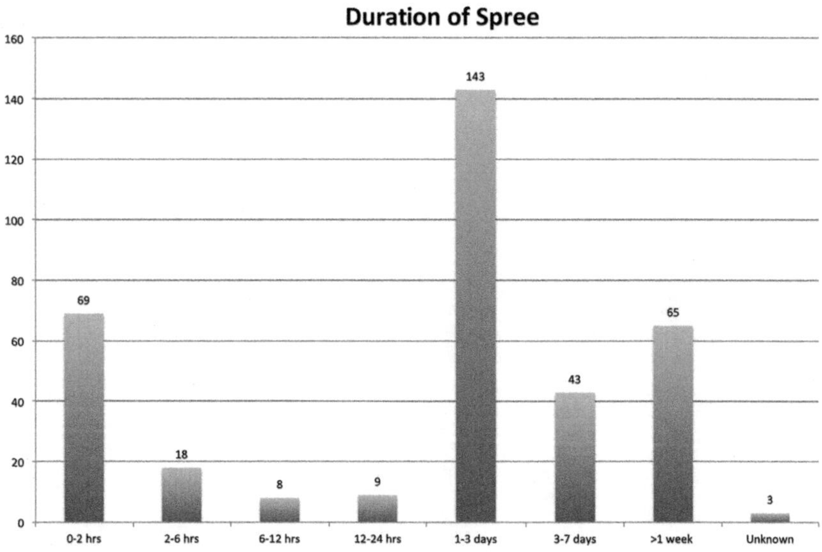

FIGURE 9.4 Spree Duration Percentages.

TABLE 9.9 Suicide Percentages

Category	Number	Attempts	Percentage for category
Anger/Revenge	36	0	32.7%
Mission	4	0	12.9%
Desperation	8	4	48%
Mental Illness	13	1	33%
Robbery/Thrill	2	1	3.8%
Movement in Tight Locations	17	4	43.7%
Mixed Types	9	0	36%

the attempted suicides were added. Nearly one out of two committed suicide, or tried to. Given the reactive nature of the spree and the "nothing-to-lose" mentality, this is expected. One in three killed themselves in the Mental Illness category, while only one person in each of the Robbery/Thrill subcategories committed suicide, with one attempt. With MTL, often driven by anger or desperation, we had 17 suicides and four attempts (43.7% overall). The MTL: Targeted subcategory had the highest number, with eight suicides and one attempt out of 19 cases. In the Mixed Multicide category, it is no surprise that the mix of spree with mass murder resulted in eight suicides out of 11 cases (72%), since many mass murderers are suicidal, while the mix of serial and spree had none. The rare category of Spree/Mass/Serial had one suicide among the three cases.

If a spree killer died in a shoot-out, it wasn't possible to tell if this was an intended suicide-by-cop or just the result of a police effort. In one case, the killer did have a suicide note in his pocket, but most were not quite this clear. Sometimes, the situation obviously had no escape route. For example, disgruntled engineer DeWayne Craddock shot people in May 2019 on all three floors of a city municipal center in Virginia Beach before police engaged him in a lengthy gun battle in which he died. There had been no way out in a place so close to police resources, so the incident seems likely to have been a suicide-by-cop. Other shoot-out incidents are similar, so the suicide rate could be higher. As it stands, 23.6% of spree killers ended, or tried to end, their own lives. If we remove the anomalous Robbery/Thrill category, the percentage rises to 31.5%. Of the Intended Spree category (not an exhaustive collection of cases), five of the 12 (41.6%) killed themselves.

In about 9% of cases, we could not identify the precipitating factor that initiated the spree, but significant losses appear to be a primary motivator (relationship, money, employment) at almost 30%, followed by motives related to a mission or hate (15%) and mental illness (12%), including delusions about being the agent of some higher power. Among Robbery/Thrill sprees, prior crimes were influential. Less than 1% of sprees involved stated terrorism. About 1.4% sought fame (see Table 9.10).

TABLE 9.10 Precipitating Event Percentages

Precipitating Factor	Percentage
Significant Loss or Failure	29.6%
Mission or Hate	15.6%
Mental Illness	12%

As noted above, it is difficult to determine when a killer was mentally ill, since this label covers many conditions. We were mostly interested in the kinds of psychotic disorders that contributed to a spree, such as a delusional mission or reactive schizophrenia. Many of the Robbery/Thrill cases show antisocial personality disorder and even psychopathy, but we do not count these conditions as mental illness. Depression could be a contributor to suicidal sprees, as could undiagnosed conditions. For law enforcement, it's important to know (1) whether they believe they're dealing with a psychotic individual, (2) whether the individual is currently in a psychotic break condition, and (3) how best to handle such an individual to prevent further loss of life. Police trainings generally cover these concerns (see Figure 9.5).

We were surprised to discover the low percentage of spree killers (6%) who had a history of substance abuse, especially among those who were mentally ill. For our purposes, the substance abuse had to

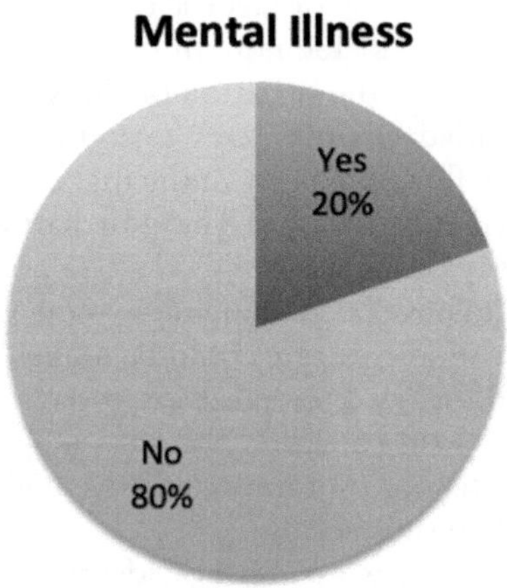

FIGURE 9.5 Mental Illness Prevalence.

be a contributory factor to the spree, so it's likely that substance use is more prevalent. Cases in which drugs or alcohol played a significant role were not difficult to identify. A Robbery/Thrill spree could have been triggered by the need for drugs, and alcohol often enhanced an Anger/Revenge spree, perhaps decreasing inhibition, exaggerating an offense, or triggering sudden rage (see Figure 9.6).

Spree killers generally do not have criminal records, except for those who went on Robbery/Thrill sprees. About 15% had been previously incarcerated, with a few killers going on a spree after they had broken out of prison (see Figure 9.7).

Only about 2% of spree killers had a law enforcement background, like Christopher Dorner, who targeted people that he believed had ruined his career. On the chart that follows, Figure 9.9, the percentage is higher for those with a military background. Still, given the number of killers using guns (75%), one might think they had the kind of training that comes with these careers. In addition, PTSD can contribute to violence, especially reactive or anger-based violence. But the numbers speak for themselves. Spree killers tend to have neither law enforcement nor military background (see Figures 9.8, 9.9, and 9.10).

Most of our cases occurred in the United States, but we acquired numbers from other countries as well. We ended up with 43 in total. It can be difficult to acquire records in some countries. In Germany, for

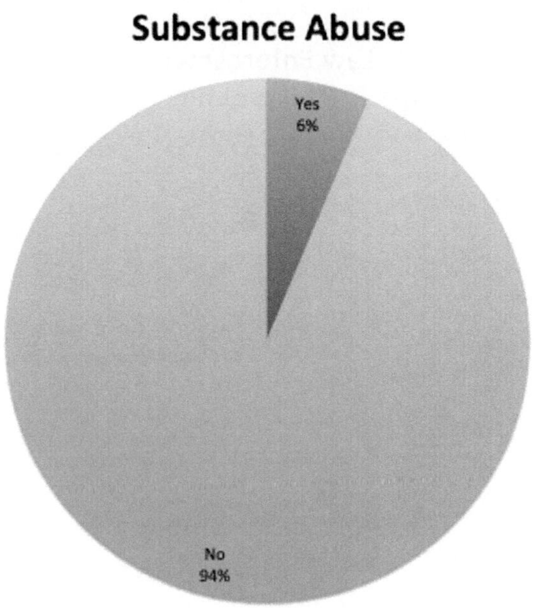

FIGURE 9.6 Substance Abuse Percentages.

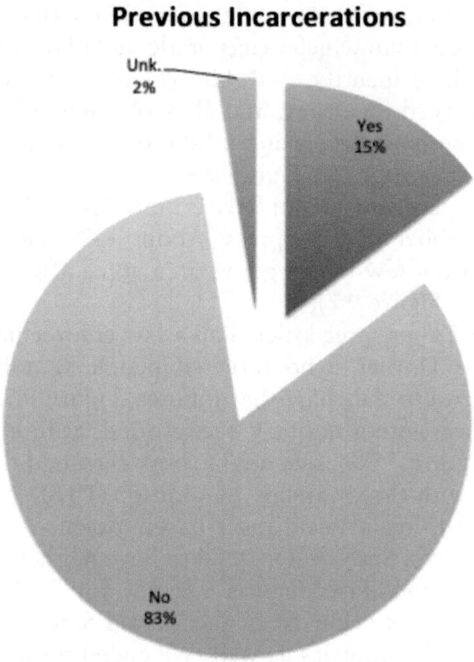

FIGURE 9.7 Previous Incarceration Percentages.

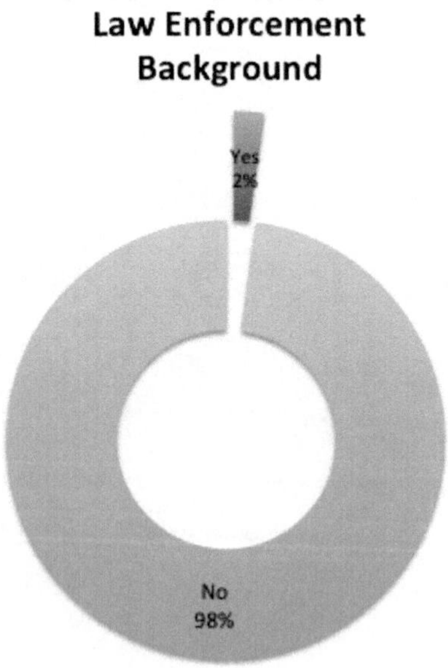

FIGURE 9.8 Law Enforcement Background Percentages.

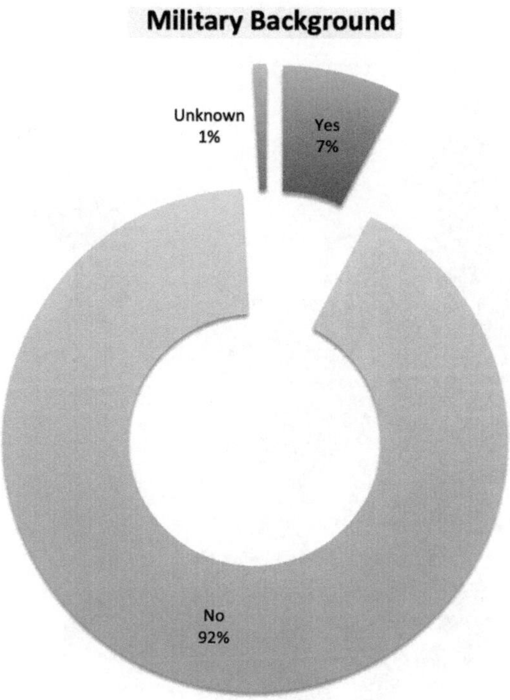

FIGURE 9.9 Military Background Percentages.

example, we found that some multicide cases covered in the news or police records omitted the offender's name. With digging, we were usually able to find it, along with other biographical data. However, as with other criminal incidents, the quality of the data depends on the quality of the investigative and recording mechanisms.

For weapon choice, firearms predominate. Of 22 countries in the Anger/Revenge: Targeted subcategory, firearms or firearms with other weapons were used in all but one (Wales), where the spree killer used a knife. Not all cases in some of these countries involved a firearm, however. Of nine countries in the Mission category, weapons besides firearms were involved in only two: Japan and England. Of seven countries outside the United States in the Desperation category, the case in Scotland involved a knife, ax, and cleaver, but cases in all other countries involved firearms. In the Mental Illness category, sprees in two of the 10 countries involved no firearm (China and England). In Germany, one killer had a firearm and one used a lance, mace, and flamethrower. The spree killers in England in this category used knives and the one in China wielded a hammer.

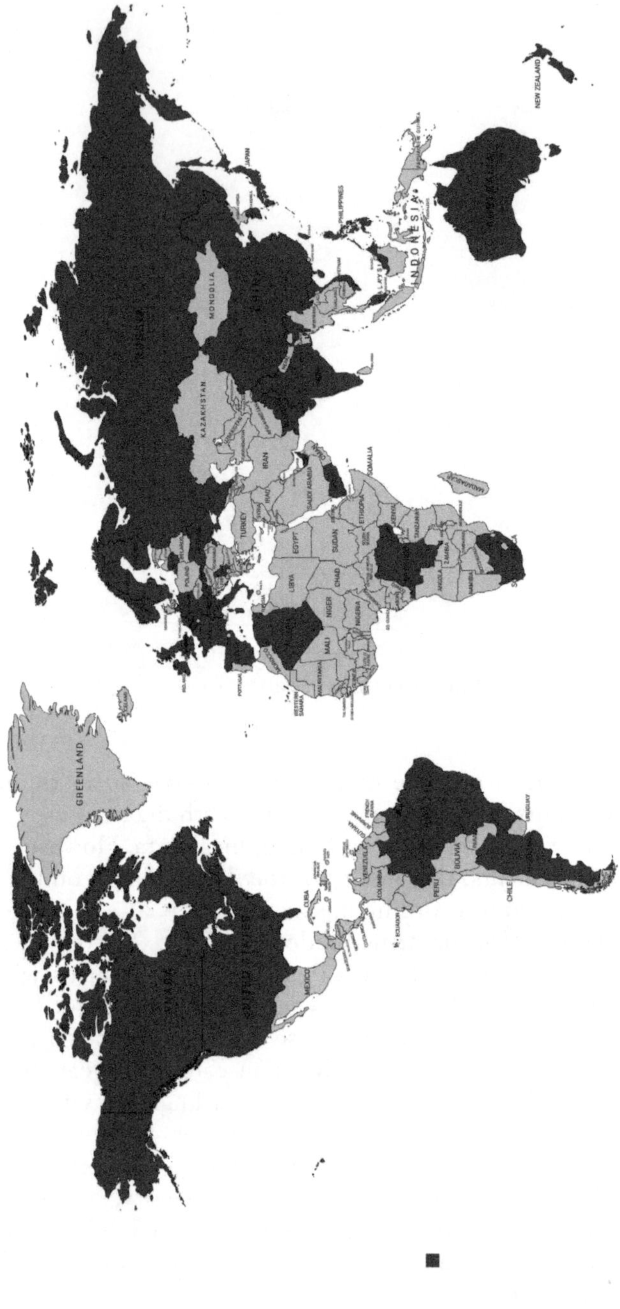

FIGURE 9.10 A World Map of Represented Countries.

Two countries outside the United States were represented for the Robbery/Thrill: Team subcategory. A firearm was used in South Africa, but a hammer and steel bar were used in the Ukraine. Lone Operators in the Robbery/Thrill category showed up in seven other countries, with a firearm used in five of eight cases. Pesticide was used in one country (the only time it was mentioned as a weapon).

In MTL: Targeted sprees, four of six cases involved firearms or firearms with other weapons, and a bladed implement was used in two. For the Targeted and Random-Opportunistic subcategory, knives were used in as many cases as firearms. For the Random-Opportunistic subcategory, of the seven countries counted, a firearm was involved in five, a knife or ax in three.

In the Mixed Multicide category, firearms or firearms plus other weapons were involved in all six other countries outside the United States for Spree/Mass incidents. Firearms were used in both Spree/Serial in countries outside the United States. All three cases in the Spree/Mass/Serial subcategory were international, with two involving firearms. In Sweden in this subcategory, an ax and fire were the weapons of choice.

* * * * *

The following two chapters cover cases in which a killer intended but failed to complete a spree, as well as a collection of odd cases with spree-like qualities. Chapter 12 uses the analytics from this chapter to form strategies for law enforcement.

CHAPTER 10

Intended Spree

Although the criteria for being a spree killer requires at least three murders at two or more locations, several people who intended their acts to result in multiple murders failed to kill the minimum or kill at two locations, and thus did not qualify for this database. Nevertheless, some deserve mention, because their serious intent was evident. These cases are not included in the total count or in the analytics in Chapter 9, and this chapter is more illustrative than exhaustive. We wanted to show some examples, and a few have unique twists.

Joseph Delling

Age/race-ethnicity: 21/Caucasian

Victims: 2 dead, 1 injured

Place/number of locations: Tucson, Arizona; Boise, Idaho/3

Date/duration: March 20–April 2007/1 month

Weapon: firearm

Delling was mentally ill when he set out on a month-long bike trip in 2007 that took him 6,500 miles through seven states and resulted in two murders and one attempted murder, with four more target individuals on his list. He would have qualified as a Mission: Psychotic spree killer, and the police did have time to warn other potential targets after linking his victims and learning about his delusions.

Suffering from paranoid schizophrenia, Delling believed that former classmates at Timberland High School in Boise, Idaho, were stealing his power. In a preemptive strike, he hoped to end their lives before they could end his.

On March 1, he set out from Idaho on his bicycle, arriving in Tucson, Arizona. On March 20, he lured Jacob Thomson from his home and shot him in the head, arm, and shoulder. Thompson survived, calling police. Getting on a plane, Delling flew back to Idaho to ambush David Boss 11 days later at his apartment near the University of Idaho. Delling then rented a car and killed Bradley Morse as he left his job, dumping his body in a pond. Police caught up to him, ending his spree before he could kill anyone else.

In court, there was testimony from Delling's brother and mother to the effect that Delling believed his targets were "stealing his powers." Delling apologized but said the crimes would not have happened if other people hadn't been "using me as Jesus or something like this, trying to sacrifice me to give people eternal life." He insisted he'd acted in self-defense.

The trial court found that Delling suffered from a mental illness so intense that his delusions had compelled him to murder his former friends. However, in Idaho, he was unable to mount the type of insanity defense he would need for mitigation. If he'd been able to form intent (which he had), he was out of luck (Boone, 2009).

Laurie Wasserman Dann

Age/race-ethnicity: 30/Caucasian

Victims: 1 dead, 6 injured, more intended

Place/number of locations: Highland Park and Winnetka, Illinois/11 locations

Date/duration: May 20, 1988/1 day

Weapon: poison, fire, firearms

Ended in suicide

In 1988, Dann set out to kill people, but she was erratic and unpolished in her strategy. Most of her targeted victims survived. Otherwise, she would have been classified as a mentally ill spree killer.

Dann had married in 1992, but the marriage had ended after 4 years. During the divorce proceedings, someone entered the home of her estranged husband and stabbed him with an ice pick. He survived. He believed but could not prove that Dann had been his assailant. He thought she was dangerous.

Despite her mental deterioration, Dann was able to purchase three handguns. Then she started her rampage. First, she made threatening calls to several acquaintances to warn them they were about to die. Then, she drove to two fraternities and six homes where she'd worked, delivering gifts of food that she'd laced with arsenic. She also sent tainted packages to her ex-husband and her psychiatrist.

At her next two stops, Dann set fires before she drove to Hubbard Woods Elementary School in Winnetka, Illinois. Armed with a .357 Magnum, she entered the school, shot and missed a boy, and then went into a classroom. She shot six kids, killing her sole victim, an 8-year-old boy. Then she moved on as people scrambled to get the wounded children to a hospital.

Finally, Dann forced her way inside a house. She shot and wounded a man, then went to a room on the second floor and locked herself in. With a .32 revolver, she shot herself through the mouth. Dann left no explanation, but she was angry and had no coping skills (Egginton, 1991).

Anthony Garcia

Age/race-ethnicity: 35 and 40 in separate incidents)/Hispanic

Victims: 4 dead, 3 more intended

Place/number of locations: Omaha, Nebraska/2

Date/duration: March 13, 2008 and May 12, 2013/2 incidents 5 years apart

Weapon: knife, gun

Garcia might have qualified as an "Anger/Revenge-Targeted" spree killer if he had achieved his objectives in 2008. During the first of two incidents separated by 5 years, he killed two people, but intended at least one other at another location. Since he missed the opportunity, there was time for police to investigate him, based on tips, before he killed again in 2013. Given his frame of mind and what is known about the assessment of risk for future danger, it was likely that he would try again. He did.

The first incident involved the murder of a woman who supervised the 11-year-old son of Dr. William Hunter after school. Garcia came looking for Hunter. Not finding him home, he stabbed this woman and Hunter's child. The knives were left in their necks. Hunter found them that afternoon when he arrived from work. A neighbor had seen a silver Honda SUV driving slowly in the area with out-of-state plates. There were no other leads, but tips were called in about a disgruntled med student, Anthony Garcia.

Five years later, Dr. Roger Brumback and his wife, Mary, were murdered inside their home, shot and stabbed. Since both had received wounds to the right side of the neck, this double homicide appeared to be linked to the murders in Dr. Hunter's home.

Hunter and Brumback had both worked at the Department of Pathology at Omaha's Creighton University School of Medicine. Going through the list of people who had worked there since 2000, detectives recalled the tips about a disgruntled medical resident with dreams of becoming a brain surgeon who'd been fired for incompetence.

Garcia had botched an autopsy. He'd also tried setting up another student to fail an exam. Teachers had written negative evaluations, finding Garcia to be a poor candidate for the medical field. Hunter and Brumback had also blocked him from getting his medical license in other states. Cellphone records showed that he'd been in the area during the Brumback murders and had looked up their address on the Internet. He drove a silver Honda CRV with Louisiana plates. A search of Garcia's home turned up a note reminding him to wear Band-Aids on his fingers (presumably to prevent leaving fingerprints) and to park away from the house. Other notes listed things like, "Invade rich house, torture, murder, rich children, gun, knife, kidnap family." Soaking in liquid in the sink were the poor performance reviews written by a Dr. Bewtra, Garcia's former teacher, and signed by Hunter and Brumback. Garcia also had a written escape plan.

Investigators learned that Garcia apparently had another target in mind on the day the Brumbacks were killed. He'd visited the home of Chhanda and Againdra Bewtra, who were not present. He'd tried to break in, possibly to wait for them, but had been unable to do so. Garcia had also looked up their daughter's address, but she had been out of the country.

When Garcia was finally arrested, he had a sledgehammer, a gun, and a crowbar in his car. Police feared he'd been intent on another payback incident, heading toward a place in Louisiana from which he'd recently been fired. Garcia was not just angry. He had the sort of personality that had to keep his enemies from winning, which kept his lethal rage simmering until he could try again (Cooper & Cortez, 2018).

This extended spree presented an opportunity for police. Just 4 days after the killings in the Hunter home, an admissions official at the university had provided authorities with a list of five former medical residents who might hold a grudge. Garcia was on it. Two months later, an email to the Omaha police had also mentioned Garica, along with his motive. Apparently, no one had followed up. Leads were pursued, but not this one. Had police better understood the kind of obsessive unresolved anger that can drive a spree killer, they might have looked more deeply into Garcia's background. They would have discovered that he drove the kind of car seen outside the Hunter home when the double homicide occurred there (Cooper, 2018).

David John Copeland

Age/race-ethnicity: 22/Caucasian

Victims: 3 dead, 140 injured

Place/number of locations: London, England/3, but the dead were all at 1

Date/duration: April 17–30, 1999/2 weeks

Weapon: bombs

Copeland went to enough locations in a short period of time and killed enough victims to be considered a spree killer, except that all three murders occurred at one of the locations. Thus, he committed a triple homicide but does not qualify for the spree category.

The London Nail Bombings occurred over the course of 3 weeks. All were homemade bombs using fireworks explosives and up to 1,500 four-inch nails. In the first location, 48 people were injured; at the second, 13; and at the third, three people were killed and 79 were injured.

On May 2, operating on a tip, police arrested neo-Nazi militant David Copeland and charged him with murder. They learned that he'd aimed for London's gay and minority communities. The reason he had not killed more was because the bags in which he'd placed the bombs had been moved before detonation. Copeland told the evaluating psychiatrists that he'd been dreaming of sadistic acts since he was 12, especially against minorities. They diagnosed him with paranoid schizophrenia. Copeland had followed the predictions of the racist propaganda, *The Turner Diaries*, and had hoped to participate in a race war. Convicted, he received concurrent life sentences.

Russell Lee Smith

Age/race-ethnicity: 30/Black

Victims: 2 dead, 9 wounded, 2 raped

Place/number of locations: Dayton, Ohio/multiple

Date/duration: May 31, 1975/2.5 hours

Weapon: firearm

Ended in suicide

Smith would have been an "Anger – Targeted and Random" spree killer, except that only two victims died.

Smith confronted a man at a motorcycle club who'd been involved with his 16-year-old girlfriend, shooting him. When another man emerged from the club, Smith shot him as well. Then he killed his girlfriend and put her body in the car. Driving, he randomly shot a man on the sidewalk. Then Smith dumped the body at a hospital emergency ramp. Apparently aimless, he shot at people. On foot, he approached a family, shooting all four. He then killed a woman emerging from a car. He took two women hostage and raped them. As he was about to shoot one more person, police surrounded him, so he killed himself (Newson, 1975).

Muharem Kurbegovic

Age/race-ethnicity: 31/Caucasian

Victims: 3 dead, 36 injured, intended more

Place/number of locations: California/2 (with 5 earlier attack locations)

Date/Duration: August 6, 1974/several days

Weapon: fire, bomb

The man who would become the "Alphabet Bomber" immigrated to the United States in 1967, finding work in the aerospace industry. Caught engaging in lewd behavior in a public place, this crime compromised Kurbegovic's ability to open a business. Swearing revenge, he firebombed three officials' houses and set several other fires. Seven months later, he set a bomb in the Greyhound Bus station and another at the airport, where he killed three people and injured 36. He stated that his objective was to "undermine and erode the foundation of Western Civilization, which is the Holy Bible." Kurbegovic's trial was delayed on grounds of mental incompetence. Defending himself, he claimed to be the Messiah. He was convicted of murder, arson, attempted murder, possession of explosives, and exploding a bomb. His three murders were all at the same location.

John Salvi

Age/race-ethnicity: 22/Caucasian

Victims: 2 dead, 5 wounded/more intended

Place/number of locations: Brookline, Massachusetts/2

Date/duration: December 30, 1974/1 day

Weapon: firearm

At mid-morning, John Salvi walked into the Planned Parenthood clinic on Beacon Street with a black duffle bag. In a waiting room full of people, he removed a modified semiautomatic .22 rifle and opened fire. He wounded a clinic assistant in the abdomen, fatally shot a receptionist in the neck, and wounded three clients. Salvi left the building and drove west on Beacon Street to the Preterm Health Services office. There, he shot and killed the receptionist and fired on people in the reception area, wounding a part-time security guard that fired back, hitting him. Salvi dropped his bag and fled. The bag contained receipts from a gun shop, so police were able to identify the gunman. They caught him in Virginia, where he'd fired shots into a closed clinic. Had it been open, and Salvi killed people, he would have qualified as a "Mission" spree killer, because he was trying to use violence to make an antiabortion statement.

Salvi was arrested. He tried a mental illness defense, which failed. His parents claimed to have seen signs of mental illness, but they'd been afraid of a stigma that might hinder his ability to live on his own. In 1996, eight months after he was sentenced to life in prison, Salvi killed himself.

Ben Nathaniel Smith

Age/race-ethnicity: 21/Caucasian

Victims: 2 dead, 10 wounded, 9 more intended

Place/number of locations: Illinois, Indiana/6

Date/duration: July 2–4, 1999/3 days

Weapon: firearms

Ended in suicide

Smith was part of a white supremacist neo-Nazi organization and was devoted to its leader, Matthew Hale. When Hale was denied his license to practice law in Illinois, Smith reacted. He believed he had a mission. He got into his car and went on a 3-day shooting spree, targeting Asians, Jews, and Blacks. He shot and wounded nine people who were Orthodox Jews in a Chicago neighborhood. In Skokie, Smith shot African American Ricky Birdsong, a former Northwestern University basketball coach. The next day, Smith went to Urbana, Springfield, and Decatur, wounding a minister. On July 4, Smith traveled to Bloomington, Indiana, where he killed Won-Joon Yoon, a Korean graduate student. Smith also shot at nine more people but missed. Police chased him, but Smith wounded himself and crashed his car into a pole. He then shot himself in the heart.

Raoul Moat

Age/race-ethnicity: 37/Caucasian

Victims: 1 dead, 2 injured

Place/number of locations: Northumberland, England/2

Date/duration: July 3–4, 2010/2 days

Weapon: firearm

Ended in suicide

A major police operation took place in England, during which police were deployed to apprehend Raoul "Moaty" Moat, who fled after shooting three people he'd targeted. His first victims were ex-girlfriend Samantha Stobbart and her new partner, Chris Brown. Brown died and Stobbart was hospitalized. She would survive. A day later, Moat shot police officer David Rathband. He survived but was permanently blinded. Rathband had once confiscated Moat's van on the suspicion that it was not insured. Moat also made threats that he would kill any officer who attempted to stop him. Afraid he would shoot more officers, a manhunt ensued until police cornered Moat on July 9. Moat shot himself.

Peter John Peters

Age/race-ethnicity: 28/Caucasian

Victims: 2 dead, 1 wounded

Place/number of locations: Toronto, Canada/3

Date/duration: Jan 20–25, 1990/5 days

Weapons: strangulation, suffocation with plastic bag, iron bar, knife

Peters had emigrated from London. In 1990, he went on a crime spree, killing two and intending to kill one more. He strangled and stabbed to death a female friend in her apartment. Two days later, he bludgeoned a man to death in a parking garage. The following day, Peters abducted Sandie Bellows and made her drive him in a car he'd stolen until he forced her into a wooded area to assault. He raped her, kicked her, and stabbed her repeatedly in the back before a police officer interrupted him, saving Bellows. Peters headed to Ontario, where he robbed a bank and tried but failed to abduct a 15-year-old girl before he was arrested.

Robert Poulin

Age/race-ethnicity: 18/Caucasian

Victims: 2 killed, 6 injured

Place/number of locations: Ottowa, Ontario, Canada/2

Date/duration: October 27, 1975/1 hour

Weapons: knife, firearm

Ended in suicide

Poulin abducted a girl he'd stalked, raping her and stabbing her to death. He proceeded to a school two miles away and shot at Father Robert Bedard and the 78 students in his class, wounding seven. One died.

Mark Richard Hilburn

Age/race-ethnicity: 39/Caucasian

Victims: 2 killed, 5 wounded

Place/number of locations: Corona del Mar, Dana Point, California/3+

Date/duration: May 5–6, 1993/2 days

Weapon: knife, firearm

Hilburn had worked at the Dana Point post office for nearly 4 years before he was fired in December, due in part to stalking a female employee. He arrived back on the grounds on May 6 wearing a T-shirt that said "Psycho." He had already fatally stabbed his mother and her dog in her Corona del Mar home. After killing a letter carrier, Hilburn tried to shoot another postal worker and the postmaster. He wounded five people in Dana Point, Newport Beach and Fountain Valley.

REFERENCES

Boone, R. (2009, August 19). Delling sentenced to life in Idaho road-trip murders. *The Spokesman-Review*. Retrieved from http://www.spokesman.com/stories/2009/aug/19/delling-sentenced-to-life-in-idaho-road-trip/

Cooper, T. (2018, November 26). New book reveals Omaha police could have zeroed in on Anthony Garcia before he killed again. *Omaha World-Herald*. Retrieved from https://www.apnews.com/769e7cc90dfc4eada5e139646dca8f13

Cooper, T., & Cortez, J. (2018, September 15). Anthony Garcia sentenced to death for murders of four Omahans. *Omaha World-Herald*, p. 1.

Egginton, J. (1991). *Day of fury: The story of the tragic shootings that forever changed the village of Winnetka*. New York, NY: William Morrow and Company.

Newson, C. (1975, May 31). Jealous 'nut' kills 2, self: shoots 9. *The Afro American*. https://news.google.com/newspapers?nid=2211&dat=19750531&id=ChpKAAAAIBAJ&sjid=QyENAAAAIBAJ&pg=2052,2325667

CHAPTER 11

Unique Circumstances

Some multicides fail to fit the criteria that would include them in one of the three primary categories of serial, spree, or mass but nevertheless resemble sprees. These cases do not count in the totals or analytical calculations, but they seem interesting enough to include in a discussion about spree killing. One perpetrator wasn't even alive when the murders occurred, and another wasn't present. In the remaining case, it's unclear who the actual perpetrators were or if there will ever be a way to decide. If convicted, they might end up as team killers in the Anger-Targeted category, or in Movement in Tight Locations.

Evril LeBaron

Age/race-ethnicity: NA (dead before incidents)/Caucasian

Victims: 4 dead

Place/number of locations: Irving and Houston, Texas/3

Date/duration: June 27, 1988/7 minutes

Weapon: firearms

From the grave, 7 years after his death, LeBaron seemed to have coordinated the simultaneous murder of four people in three different places. This mass slaughter is referred to as the 4 O'clock murders. It caps a long story of religious legacy and sibling rivalry.

After the Church of Jesus Christ of Latter-day Saints banned the practice of polygamy in 1890, a faction that wanted to practice it split off and moved to Mexico. Evril, the son of one of the leaders, grew up on a family commune called Colonia LeBaron. His older brother, Joel, eventually inherited the leadership role, with Evril as second-in-command. Evril acquired 13 wives and had 53 children.

The community attracted other families and established associates in the United States. However, the brothers fought, so in 1972, Evril moved to the United States to form his own church in San Diego. He called himself the true heir of Joseph Smith's legacy and the rightful leader of the Mormon Church. Somewhat maniacal, he sought full control, which meant that Joel had to die. Leadership of Joel's church went to their younger brother, Verlan, whom Evril tried and failed to have murdered.

Mexico tried Evril for Joel's murder, but his conviction was overturned on a technicality (or a bribe). He continued to try to take over the polygamous sects, using his 13th wife to murder a rival leader. He used another wife to kill a traitor and put a death sentence – "blood atonement" – on any who failed to follow his commandments. Many feared him and did what he ordered.

Evril was linked to other murders, and in 1979 he was arrested and sent to trial in Utah. There, Evril was convicted of having ordered an assassination. He received a life sentence. He died in 1981 at the age of 56, and his brother, Verlan, died 2 days later in a "car accident." Yet Evril had a loyal following.

He had written a bible, *The Book of the New Covenants*, that included a hit list and a commandment to kill the disobedient. Twenty copies were distributed. Seven men appointed themselves Evril LeBaron's punishers. They formed a plan to carry out his wishes posthumously.

On June 27, 1988, at 4:00 p.m., these punishers carried out hits in three locations on three men and a child. At the same time, they shot and killed Eddie Marsto in Irving, Texas and Mark Chenowyth in Houston, Texas. Seven minutes later at another Houston location, they fatally shot Duane Chenowith and his 8-year-old daughter.

Five of the seven perpetrators were arrested and found guilty of murder. One was granted immunity for her testimony, and the final participant, another woman, pleaded guilty to conspiracy. Some sources stated that around three-dozen people were eliminated on Evril LeBaron's orders from prison, but the 4 o'clock murders comprise a rather strange type of spree.

Michael Stevens

Age/race-ethnicity: 52/Caucasian

Victims: 5 dead

Place/number of locations: New York/4

Date/duration: December 28, 1993/NA

Weapon: bombs

Stevens plotted for at least 6 months to kill Brenda Chevere's relatives and lay the blame on an alcoholic associate, Earl Figley. He was angry at Chevere's family for excluding him and afraid that Cheveres might vanish with their 2-year-old son. He sent six bombs to locations where several of Chevere's family members lived, killing five. Four bombs exploded, one was intercepted by authorities, and another failed to go off. The offender did not travel to kill but had sent bombs by mail and courier to multiple locations.

Edward Wagner, George Wagner III, Angela Wagner, and George Wagner IV

Age/race-ethnicity: 26, 47, 48, and 27/Caucasian

Victims: 8 dead

Place/number of locations: Peebles, Ohio/4

Date/duration: April 21–22, 2016/unclear

Weapon: firearms

Edward "Jake" Wagner got into a custody dispute with his former girlfriend, Hannah Rhoden, over their 2-year-old daughter. He had tried to convince her to sign over her custody rights, but she'd refused. When the child was in his care, one or more people in his family acted.

In preparation, Edward and his older brother and parents had been spying on Hannah and her family to learn their routines, security systems, and home layouts. During the night of April 21–22, 2016, they visited four locations (three mobile homes and a camper) to eliminate everyone in the family. Some were beaten and all were shot. A coroner report said all but one of the victims was shot more than once, including two people shot five times and one shot nine times. Two of the scenes were within walking distance of each other, another a mile away, and the fourth was eight miles away. The police suspected coordinated attacks by at least two shooters.

Someone in the Wagner family then allegedly forged signatures on child custody documents, and they took the girl and moved to Alaska. In November 2018, four of the Wagners were arrested and charged in the murders. Prosecutors were aware that they had a plan to escape and "seek revenge" by targeting Ohio Attorney General Mike DeWine and Pike County Sheriff Charles Reader. Although a reconstruction supports a hypothesis of at least two shooters, it remains unclear at this writing which suspects will be identified and taken to trial.

* * * * *

There are likely other spree-like cases, but these three show the difficulty of categorizing every possible incident into neatly defined categories. Those that most concern us are the spree cases in which law enforcement can take action and possibly prevent a spree killer from achieving his, her, or their full objectives. We conclude this book with a chapter specifically for law enforcement.

CHAPTER 12

Tips for Law Enforcement

We began this book with the FBI's removal of "spree killer" from the multicide classifications, citing its lack of utility for law enforcement. In cases such as random spree killing, or the categories of Movement in Tight Locations and Robbery/Thrill, the Bureau is correct. Unless there is a way to anticipate where and when a killer might strike via specific locations, business activities, and victim associations, responders cannot plan or gather resources for best effect. In this chapter, we address some of the key issues in responding to a spree, as well as offer some tips gleaned from the cases we've presented and analyzed in prior chapters.

ISSUES TO CONSIDER

We have already identified the Anger/Revenge-Targeted subcategory as the most likely to offer effective information for a plan of action, followed by certain types of cases in the Mission category. Let's look at why the others pose challenges.

Spree killers in the Desperation category are often on the run, often just several steps ahead of law enforcement. They have no set plan and they think only as far ahead as the next location. They have nothing to lose. They just hope to avoid capture. Their movement tends to cover greater distances, going from county to county and state to state, even crossing into other countries. They often steal money or cars, leaving a string of random victims, from carjackings to convenience stores to isolated farmhouses. Most were just in the wrong place at the wrong time. The murders are thus difficult to predict.

In the Mental Illness category, predictive ability is also quite limited. Many of these cases are of short duration, from minutes to hours. In the longer sprees, the randomness of victim selection undermines law enforcement's ability to spot a pattern that assists with a cogent response. Often the delusion-inspired acts make sense only to the offender.

In cases of Movement in Tight Locations, the extremely limited time frame, which is close to that of mass murder, often prevents law enforcement from having the time to adequately organize resources and respond, even when the victims are clearly targeted.

In the Robbery/Thrill category, although the time frame can last long enough for a response, we often see larger and more dispersed geographical distances. The larger area often involves multiple unrelated law enforcement agencies, some even crossing county and state lines. The randomness of target selection in these cases, where the same offender might target a homeowner, gas station, local business, or someone encountered on the road, can also prevent law enforcement from initially linking the killings to the same offender(s) and developing an adequate response plan.

In the Mixed Multicide categories that involve serial and mass murder, law enforcement responds in a primarily reactive role. In serial murder, the killer usually tries to remain under the radar by selecting strangers, hiding bodies, destroying evidence, and then acting normally between killings. In mass murder, most of the murders have already occurred by the time first responders arrive. Many of these offenders commit suicide before police arrive or do so at the point of confrontation.

Should they choose to engage in armed confrontation, the police, with superior training, manpower, and equipment, will probably win. Responders must be prepared for the potential for "suicide by cop," wherein they are used to complete an offender's suicidal act (Mohandie & Meloy, 2000). Data concerning such incidents show that, in the Anger/Revenge category, 40% of those in the Random-Opportunistic subcategory engaged police in armed confrontation. About 27% did so in the Targeted and Random-Opportunistic subcategory. Although no Mission: Psychotic offenders engaged police, 22% of Mission: Nonpsychotic offenders did so, as did more than 14% of those in the Mental Illness category.

Offenders in the Movement in Tight Locations category are often suicidal and thus are likely to engage police in the hope of being shot. On May 31, 2019, Wayne Craddock, a reportedly disgruntled public works employee in Virginia Beach, Virginia, killed 12 people on three floors in the public works building. When police arrived, he engaged them in lengthy gunplay, seriously injuring one before being killed. Since there seemed to be little hope for him of escape, he seemed to have set up a suicide-by-cop. In addition to this kind of danger, some spree killers intentionally ambush and kill police. In 1993, Michael Sonner escaped from jail and stole a car, killing people in various locations during his flight. When a state trooper followed him and pulled him over, Sonner waited until he was close and then shot the officer in the head.

EFFECTIVE RESPONSE

Looking broadly at the spree classification, we identified several categories and their attendant subcategories that gave us a way to identify those cases that do, in fact, have predictive utility for law enforcement. The most useful is Anger/Revenge. Within this category there are three subcategories, two of which offer response opportunities. The first is Targeted. In this subcategory (61%), the offender targets specific victims exclusively. For example, Dakota Theriot had made threats to burn down his parents' house with them inside. They banned him from their home. With a history of mental illness and broken relationships, he moved in with a girlfriend and her family in Livingston Parish, Louisiana. Something happened on January 26, 2019 to set Theriot off. He murdered his host family before driving to the next county to fatally shoot his parents. Police were able to predict where he was likely to go, either to complete his spree with his grandmother or to turn to her for help. Because Theriot had clear targets toward which his anger drove him, police not only got a future potential victim out of harm's way but also arrested Theriot when he arrived.

A red flag about his future dangerousness came from a police report made in December 2015 by Theriot's then-wife. She had left him after 11 days, claiming he had choked, punched, and slapped her throughout the 3 years they'd been involved. While drunk once, he'd thrown her through a window, breaking her wrist. He'd also been court-martialed from the military for unspecified reasons, and he'd been kicked out of both high school and an alternate educational program. Trained authorities who were aware of this report would have understood the kind of person they were dealing with.

We now know that strangulation in domestic violence is a more significant marker that portends homicidal acts more than any other. Gael Strack, chief executive of the Training Institute on Strangulation Prevention in San Diego, says the mere presence of this behavior during domestic abuse increases the chances of a future homicide sevenfold. "Statistically, we know that once the hands are on the neck, the very next step is homicide," Strack said. "They don't go backwards." (Strack & Gwinn, 2011, p. 35). In 2014, the U.S. Sentencing Commission recognized strangulation as a marker of dangerousness and recommended increased prison time for those who were convicted of it.

Yet law enforcement has not been trained to understand this signal. As a result, victim injuries can be minimized in police reports and are commonly noted as mere scratches or redness around the neck, according to a study of 300 nonfatal strangulation cases (Pritchard, Reckdenwald, & Nordham, 2017). Police also failed to recognize that the person who strangles someone is at greater risk not just for domestic homicide but also to act out more broadly, such as in mass shootings. Theriot was a walking time bomb.

On an intuitive level, we recognize that spree killers who are driven by anger or revenge are usually angry at someone they know for real or perceived wrongs perpetrated against them. The nature of such anger and the desire to seek revenge often develop when there is a close relationship between the killer and the targeted victim, and this relationship is very often familial. The risk for violence rises with rigid, paranoid personalities. Additionally, the anger and subsequent acting out for revenge can also be directed to a business, entity, or location that the offender associates with the real or perceived injustices (e.g., getting fired). In such cases the offender usually has a list of people that he or she believes are responsible for a situation.

When examining homicides where the relationship between the victim and the offender is known, 76% occur between people where some relationship exists between them (FBI, 2017). This dynamic, once recognized, can be used to identify the killer, as well as ascertain linkage to potential future victims in order to alert them to the pending threat. The Anger/Revenge – Targeted subcategory provides the best opportunity for law enforcement to link two or more homicides that occur relatively in quick succession and close proximity by identifying clear targets and a motive consistent with each target. If they have an extended time frame in which to seek the public's assistance, they can plan a response and protect future potential targets.

The second most populous subcategory for Anger/Revenge is Targeted and Random-Opportunistic, where the offender initially targets specific victims but then continues the spree by selecting victims at random or in opportunistic places, such as a targeted workplace. Depending on the circumstances and duration, a plan of action might be effective, but the randomness limits its potential for success.

The third subcategory for Anger/Revenge, Random-Opportunistic, has virtually no chance of success, even with extended duration, as the victims and geographic locations cannot be easily predicted. Fortunately, at 9%, this is the smallest of the subcategories.

Some predictability is also possible with cases in the Mission category, especially the Nonpsychotic subcategory where the mission describes clear targets. For example, Richard Baumhammers worshipped Adolf Hitler and wanted to form a political party that would block immigrants. Having twice signed himself into a psychiatric institution for emotional problems, he had shown anti-Semitic sentiment when he slapped a female bartender for being Jewish. He'd also set up a website that called for an end to nonwhite immigration, fearing an imminent threat to the Caucasian race. In 2000, he went on a shooting spree that targeted Jews and minorities. He killed five and wounded one. There were red flags in his messages and personality.

It's also possible to act on sprees if tips are called in early. This happened with the Theriot case described above, and also in the case of Michigan Uber driver Jason Brian Dalton in 2016. He seemed to have been in the mood to create havoc. He picked up a young man who observed such dangerous, erratic behavior that he called 9-1-1 as soon as he could to describe the car and give the license plate number. Officials had the information they needed to check it out, but no one investigated. Although Dalton switched to his wife's car, police could still have gone to his home to speak with his wife. She'd seen her husband's odd behavior, although she did not know just how deranged he was. Dalton went on to damage several vehicles and shoot eight people at random, killing six, before police caught up. His spree had lasted 6 hours, during which time he'd picked up other fares without incident. It could have been cut short much earlier. The psychiatrist who evaluated Dalton found evidence of planning, contradicting his claim to have had a psychotic break. He'd covered his behavior with lies, had known the news would feature him, and had no record of mental illness.

OVERVIEW AND TIPS

In the analysis of many complex homicide cases, law enforcement personnel are often focused on what they see: the activities of the offender in the crime scene and during the crime. In essence, they see what the offender did and how he did it, as well as recognizing the significance of the *absence* of evidence can be equally important.

Motives in homicide cases can vary, but several are regularly observed. Financial gain is one. In the spree categories this dynamic is captured in the Robbery/Thrill category. Thrill killing, although a rare motive for a spree, is represented in this same category, often intertwined with robbery, especially with teams of offenders. Sexually motivated crime often involving sexual assault is another common motivator, but one that's rarely seen during a spree. We describe sexual assaults in some Robbery/Thrill cases, as well as in Desperation. Personal cause homicide (Douglas, Burgess, Burgess & Ressler, 2013) results from an interpersonal conflict between two people in which the conflict can only be resolved by the death of one of the parties involved. With this motive, we usually see an absence of other types of activity. Rarely is there robbery, theft of property, destruction of property, or a sexually motivated component to the crime, unless the offender tries to deflect investigators by staging a scene that suggests a different motive.

As shown above, the most helpful spree categories for law enforcement reflect personal cause homicides, specifically that the killing is the only activity. When faced with two homicides that seem related by personal cause, the potential for a spree killing should be clear enough to consider the offender's likely identity, along with future potential victims. We started this book with the case of Dwight Lamon Jones. Several seemingly unrelated shootings over 2 days were linked by their common association to a contentious divorce case. Although Jones killed again before he was caught, officers knew who they were looking for and where Jones resided. Their approach triggered his suicide and stopped him from pursuing his likely next targets.

For law enforcement to be in this position, the quick collection and analysis of data is essential for informed awareness and training for effective response to a spree killer. From our data, we found that many spree killers in two Anger/Revenge subcategories and the Mission: Nonpsychotic subcategory showed medium-to-high predictability in their movements and targets. If there were sufficient time and distance once the killers started, officers could form an effective plan for locating and stopping them. The fact that the Anger/Revenge category also represents the largest spree category where law enforcement has an opportunity to intercede should be justification enough to become trained in a proactive response to spree killers.

Among the resources we offer in this book is a comprehensive and fully analyzed database, categories for spree killing, a set of cases that illustrate how to respond to a certain type of spree killer, and tips for being proactively prepared. This will assist with a general plan. In addition, cases that involve hate crimes, threats, paranoid types of mental illness, and domestic abuse could be placed in a "high risk" category for easier access in the case of a sudden spree. Although police officers receive little training in the psychological angles of the assessment of risk of future danger, forming plans of action for responding to sprees will inevitably bring them into contact with such information.

Even experienced professionals, while believing that their experience base is sufficient for judgment, can still be wrong. If a database exists for a questioned area, consulting it decreases the chance for bias or error. In spree cases, even a small error can mean the difference between life and death for some victims. Trainings should emphasize the practice of looking at statistically analyzed data, which adds weight to expertise.

When homicides are identified, especially those that appear to be Personal Cause in nature, social media sites used by the victim should be examined for relevant historical information about potential offenders. This includes YouTube channels. Elliot Rodger posted threats against specific groups, with a localized target, which police could have reviewed during their initial welfare check on him 3 weeks before his deadly spree. Quickly identifying relatives and family members for interviews can uncover useful information pertaining to a potential offender. When dealing with two or more murders, utilizing television and radio media to highlight both the victims and locations might enable viewers and listeners to recognize a connection between them that is unknown to investigators, as happened when Dr. Connie Jones and her husband recognized the association among Dwight Lamont Jones' murder victims. They acted quickly to inform police and provide important information. In the approximately 4% of cases that fall into the Mission: Nonpsychotic subcategory, offenders often use social media sites like Facebook, YouTube, and Instagram to post warnings, video diaries, manifestos, blogs, or clearly identified targets. People who know the offender generally know the content of their threats, obsessions, and delusions.

Another successful example of a case of Anger/Revenge-Targeted that reflects the Personal Cause motive involved John M. Goins. It's an old case, but the principles still apply. In March 1926, Goins was angry. A series of family issues and legal difficulties had culminated in a pending divorce. Goins acted out his frustration. He drove to his former home in Stockton, California, where his wife Florence and her sister lived. He fatally shot them both. He then drove downtown to the law offices of Stanley Arndt and George McNoble. He blamed McNoble for the divorce. He learned that McNoble was away on a trip to San Francisco, so Goins drove to McNoble's home and shot his wife. Although news was spreading to identify him as the killer, he drove north over 20 miles to Galt. Since he was punishing people for wrongs he couldn't forgive, he turned his attention to rancher Alex Marengo, who had tried to have Goins prosecuted years earlier for stealing horses. After arriving at the ranch, Goins killed Marengo, Marengo's wife, and their daughter. Ranch hands notified law enforcement, who pursued Goins. He killed himself before they could arrest him, but on his person, they found a list he'd made of other people he'd planned to kill. The ranch hand's tip had foiled the plan.

Unlike serial and mass murder, in which law enforcement are left responding in a reactive manner, spree murder presents an opportunity for law enforcement to respond in a proactive way that can identify the offender, the offender's relationship to the targeted victims, and most importantly, the ability to identify and warn future victims of the pending threat. Understanding how to identify and use the different categories and subcategories and knowing which can yield useful information, if properly applied, is critical for success. Also knowing which categories will yield little or nothing of value enables the police to utilize time-proven methods of investigation. Bringing this type of multicide back to a prominent place of recognition will benefit all those who take the time to understand what we can and cannot do with these types of offenders.

SUMMARY AND TIPS

1. Unlike other types of multicides, spree murder offers law enforcement the potential to respond in a proactive way to identify the offender and warn future victims.
2. Training in the categories of spree murder will assist police in correctly identifying the primary category.
3. The two Anger/Revenge subcategories of Targeted and Targeted and Random-Opportunistic, along with the Mission: Nonpsychotic subcategory, are the most likely to produce success for Law Enforcement.
4. Recognizing crime attributes similar to Personal Cause will assist in an investigation and response in the Anger/Revenge category.
5. Examining victimology to recognize linkage between victims, along with interviews of family and friends, will assist with the Anger/Revenge category investigation and response.
6. Immediate broadcast of the cases to the public seeking linkage assistance through television and radio media outlets can generate connections between victims and locations that police have not made.
7. Review of social media apps like Facebook, YouTube, Instagram, along with video diaries and blogs can alert police to potential victims and target locations.

REFERENCES

Douglas, J., Burgess, A., Burgess, A., & Ressler, R. (2013). *Crime classification manual: A standard system for investigating and classifying violent crimes* (3rd ed.). San Francisco, CA: John Wiley & Sons.

Federal Bureau of Investigation (FBI). (2017, September). Crime in the United States, 2017. Retrieved from https://ucr.fbi.gov/crime-in-the-u.s/2017/crime-in-the-u.s.-2017/topic-pages/expanded-homicide

Mohandie, K., & Meloy, J. R. (2000). Clinical and forensic indicators of "suicide by cop". *Journal of Forensic Sciences*, *45*(2), 384–389.

Pritchard, A. J., Reckdenwald, A., & Nordham, A. (2017). Nonfatal strangulation as part of domestic assault: A review of research. *Trauma, Violence, and Abuse*, *18*(4). doi:10.1177/1524838015622439

Strack, G. B., & Gwinn, C. (2011). On the edge of homicide: Strangulation as a prelude. *Criminal Justice*, *26*(3), 32–36.

Index

For Product Safety Concerns and Information please contact our EU representative GPSR@taylorandfrancis.com Taylor & Francis Verlag GmbH, Kaufingerstraße 24, 80331 München, Germany

Batch number: 10725802

Printed by Printforce, the Netherlands